COOKING LIGHT

way to
bake

ISBN-13: 978-0-8487-4237-9
ISBN-10: 0-8487-4237-0
Library of Congress Control Number: 2013934191
Printed in the United States of America
Second printing 2013

Be sure to check with your health-care provider before making any changes in your diet.

Oxmoor House

VP, Publishing Director: Jim Childs
Editorial Director: Susan Payne Dobbs
Brand Manager: Michelle Turner Aycock
Senior Editor: Heather Averett
Managing Editor: Laurie S. Herr

Cooking Light® Way to Bake

Editor: Rachel Quinlivan West, R.D.
Project Editor: Holly D. Smith
Senior Designer: Emily Albright Parrish
Assistant Designer: Allison L. Sperando
Director, Test Kitchens: Elizabeth Tyler Austin
Assistant Directors,
Test Kitchens: Julie Christopher, Julie Gunter
Test Kitchens Professionals: Wendy Ball, R.D.;
Allison E. Cox; Victoria E. Cox;
Margaret Monroe Dickey;
Alyson Moreland Haynes;
Stefanie Maloney; Callie Nash;
Catherine Crowell Steele;
Leah Van Deren
Photography Director: Jim Bathie
Senior Photo Stylist: Kay E. Clarke
Associate Photo Stylist: Katherine Eckert Coyne
Assistant Photo Stylist: Mary Louise Menendez
Production Manager: Theresa Beste-Farley

Contributors

Designer: Teresa Cole
Copy Editor: Jasmine Hodges
Proofreaders: Jacqueline Giovanelli,
Norma McKittrick
Indexer: Mary Ann Laurens
Interns: Erin Bishop, Sarah H. Doss,
Blair Gillespie, Alison Loughman,
Lindsay A. Rozier, Caitlin Watzke
Test Kitchens Professional: Kathleen Royal Phillips
Photographer: Mary Britton Senseney
Photo Stylist: Missie Neville Crawford
Nutrition Analysis: Caroline Glagola, Kate Grigsby

Time Home Entertainment Inc.

Publisher: Richard Fraiman
Vice President, Strategy &
Business Development: Steven Sandonato
Executive Director,
Marketing Services: Carol Pittard
Executive Director,
Retail & Special Sales: Tom Mifsud
Director, New Product
Development: Peter Harper
Director, Bookazine
Development & Marketing: Laura Adam
Assistant Director,
Brand Marketing: Joy Butts
Associate Counsel: Helen Wan

Cooking Light®

Editor: Scott Mowbray
Creative Director: Carla Frank
Deputy Editor: Phillip Rhodes
Executive Editor, Food: Ann Taylor Pittman
Special Publications Editor: Mary Simpson Creel, MS, RD
Senior Food Editor: Julianna Grimes
Senior Editor: Cindy Hatcher
Associate Food Editor: Timothy Q. Cebula
Assistant Editor, Nutrition: Sidney Fry, MS, RD
Assistant Editors: Kimberly Holland, Phoebe Wu
Test Kitchen Director: Vanessa T. Pruett
Assistant Test Kitchen Director: Tiffany Vickers Davis
Recipe Testers and Developers: Robin Bashinsky,
Adam Hickman, Deb Wise
Art Director: Fernande Bondarenko
Junior Deputy Art Director: Alexander Spacher
Associate Art Director: Rachel Lasserre
Designer: Chase Turberville
Photo Director: Kristen Schaefer
Assistant Photo Editor: Amy Delaune
Senior Photographer: Randy Mayor
Senior Photo Stylist: Cindy Barr
Photo Stylist: Leigh Ann Ross
Chief Food Stylist: Charlotte Autry
Senior Food Stylist: Kellie Gerber Kelley
Copy Chief: Maria Parker Hopkins
Assistant Copy Chief: Susan Roberts
Research Editor: Michelle Gibson Daniels
Editorial Production Director: Liz Rhoades
Production Editor: Hazel R. Eddins
Assistant Production Editor: Josh Rutledge
Administrative Coordinator: Carol D. Johnson
Cookinglight.com Editor: Allison Long Lowery
Nutrition Editor: Holley Johnson Grainger, MS, RD
Production Assistant: Mallory Daugherty

To order additional publications, call 1-800-765-6400 or 1-800-491-0551.

For more books to enrich your life, visit **oxmoorhouse.com**

To search, savor, and share thousands of recipes, visit **myrecipes.com**

Cooking Light
way to bake

Oxmoor House®

Contents

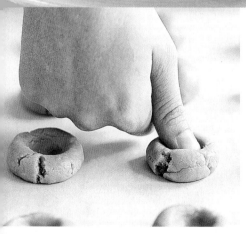

Welcome

It's no wonder many of our most beloved hand-me-down recipes are for baked treats. We treasure the batter-spattered, hand-annotated formulas for Grandma's biscuits and Mom's strawberry layer cake because these are the dishes that sweeten our memories of days with loved ones: birthdays, Thanksgiving, Christmas, Hanukkah, the Fourth of July.

But baking can also be a wonderful part of everyday cooking and eating, just as it was when Grandma and Mom might have had a bit more time in the kitchen. Reliable recipes for quick breads and muffins can fill a Sunday morning kitchen with wonderful aromas—and fill a freezer with weekday treats.

Baking is of course as much science as art; it requires a respect for precision in measurement and the use of the right ingredients in the right order—and a good working knowledge of things like your oven's temperatures and hot spots. As for healthy baking, well, it's no more difficult than "regular" baking, but it does require a new set of recipes, each meticulously designed and tested to turn out superior results as simply as possible. That's where *Cooking Light* comes in. Using our tested recipes, you can prepare cakes, cookies, and pies in a modern, nutrition-aware way while maintaining the distinct pleasures of each dish—from the irresistible sugar-crust on a loaf of banana bread to the moist, dense crumb of a pound cake to the snap of a shortbread cookie.

Technique is important, but flavor always rules our kitchen; our recipes strike an enlightened food-lover's balance between indulgent, delicious, and absolutely necessary ingredients (like butter, chocolate, and cream) and good-for-you ingredients (like oils, nuts, and whole grains).

This book shares new techniques and cooking tips to help you successfully make not just great baked goods, but extraordinary ones—recipes to remember, personalize, and hand down.

Scott Mowbray
Cooking Light *Editor*

Cooking Light
way to bake

way to bake

Although the nuances of baking are numerous, certain techniques and principles always hold true. Your baked goods rely on the right proportion of ingredients, but you can make them shine with a few essential facts and easy-to-learn skills.

1 Results start in the mixing bowl.

What happens in the mixing bowl relies on the chemical reactions of these key ingredients.

Flour

Flour thickens the batter and provides gluten, a protein that gives baked products structure and elasticity. Gluten forms when flour is combined with a liquid and stirred or mixed. The more you mix, the more gluten develops. You'll also notice that some recipes call for sifted flour. Sifting aerates the flour (sifted flour weighs less), thoroughly incorporates ingredients, and removes any lumps in the dry ingredients, which gives baked products a lighter, more delicate texture. Many different flours are available, containing varying percentages of protein—the more protein, the more gluten. For a glossary, as well as information about properly measuring flour, see page 15.

Leaveners

Baking soda and baking powder are common leavening agents that produce carbon dioxide bubbles, which are trapped by the starch in batter and expand during baking to make baked goods rise. Baking powder contains baking soda, cream of tartar, and cornstarch. It begins to rise when it becomes wet and rises again when it's exposed to heat. That's why you see "double-acting" on the label. Baking soda is typically used when the recipe contains an acid, such as buttermilk or yogurt. When the soda and the acid are combined, the bread or cake immediately begins to rise.

In yeast bread, yeast serves as the leavening agent. It converts sugar and starch into carbon dioxide bubbles and alcohol. These bubbles become trapped in the dough, making the bread rise and become light and airy, while the alcohol that is produced burns off during baking. For more information about yeast, see page 355.

Fats

Fats like butter, shortening, and oil provide moisture and act as tenderizers. Some fats can be used to simply add flavor—for example, when you use olive oil in a cake. When a recipe calls for softened butter, the butter should yield slightly to pressure, but it shouldn't lose its shape when touched. It should be pliable but not spreadable. To soften butter, leave it out at room temperature for 30 to 45 minutes, or, if you need it more quickly, cut the butter into 1-tablespoon pieces, and leave it at room temperature for 10 to 15 minutes. Do not microwave it because it's easy to overdo it and soften it too much.

Sugars

Sugar has multiple functions: It tenderizes; absorbs liquid, which keeps the baked goods moist; and caramelizes in baking, enriching the flavors and helping with browning. See page 12 for more information about the different types of sugar.

Eggs

The protein in eggs makes them firm up when cooked, which helps batters set in the oven. Egg yolks contain fat as well as lecithin, which allows fats and water to mix smoothly and ensures even texture.

kitchen how-to:
check the strength of baking powder & baking soda

The effectiveness of baking powder and baking soda can start to weaken after 6 months.

1. To check the strength of baking powder, add 2 teaspoons powder to 1 cup hot water.
2. Stir the powder in. If there's an immediate fizz, the powder is fine. To check baking soda, stir 1 teaspoon into ¼ cup vinegar and check for the fizz.

granulated sugar

powdered sugar

dark brown sugar

light brown sugar

turbinado sugar

Sugar Glossary

Sugar and natural sweeteners take many forms. Some are solid, while others are liquid. What all sugars have in common is sweetness, but different sugars play different roles in cooking, and the success of a recipe often depends on using the right one at the right time.

Granulated Sugar: Granulated, or white, sugar is the most refined. The juices from sugarcane or sugar beets are processed to remove the molasses and then filtered, crystallized, and dried into fine granules. Granulated sugar adds sweetness and moisture to baked goods and also gives them structure and helps them brown. It makes pastries tender and gives crunch to some cookies. Superfine sugar is an ultrafine granulated sugar that's called for when it's important for the sugar to dissolve quickly.

Powdered Sugar: Also called confectioner's sugar, this variety is 10 times finer than granulated sugar. It's used mostly as a garnish dusted over cakes and cookies and to make icings and frostings since it dissolves quickly. Because of its powdery nature, it tends to attract water, so a small amount of absorbent cornstarch is usually added before packaging to keep it dry.

Dark Brown Sugar: A small amount of molasses is added to granulated sugar to create brown sugar, which has a moist, pliable texture. Dark brown sugar has more molasses, giving it a deeper, richer color and flavor.

Light Brown Sugar: Often just called "brown sugar," light brown sugar contains less molasses than the dark variety, which lends it a delicate flavor. Light and dark brown sugar can be used interchangeably in recipes, but the final product will have a more subtle or more assertive flavor depending on which you use.

Turbinado Sugar: This dry, pourable blond sugar (as opposed to many brown sugars, which are moist) has large, coarse crystals with a more subtle molasses flavor than brown sugar. It gets its name from the part of the sugar-making process in which raw cane is spun in a turbine. It's often sprinkled on top of scones, cookies, and other baked goods to add crunch.

Corn Syrup: Available in light and dark varieties, corn syrup is created by combining cornstarch with an enzyme that converts the starch to sugar. Corn syrup adds moisture and smoothness to baked goods. Dark corn syrup is a mixture of light corn syrup and a darker syrup produced during the refining of sugar; it's often used in pecan pie fillings to provide a deeper flavor. Light corn syrup has a more neutral flavor.

Maple Syrup: Boiled-down sap from the sugar maple has been used as a sweetener for hundreds of years. It adds moisture and a unique flavor to cakes, cookies, and frostings. It's available in different grades (see page 101 for more information)—the lighter the color, the milder the flavor. Whichever you buy, be sure the label says "pure maple syrup"; syrups labeled "maple flavored" are usually a mix of corn syrup and artificial maple flavoring.

Honey: Honey has an intense sweetness, but the flavor is determined by the source of the flower nectar. In general, the darker the honey, the stronger the flavor. Like corn syrup, honey adds moisture to cakes and cookies. Unlike corn syrup, which has a fairly neutral flavor, honey adds a distinctive flavor. Be sure to taste the honey before you use

it. Intensely flavored honey may overwhelm more delicate baked goods.

Molasses: Molasses is a by-product of sugar refining. Boiling the juices extracted from sugarcane and sugar beets transforms them into a syrup from which sugar crystals are extracted; the liquid left behind is molasses. Dark molasses is darker, thicker, stronger in flavor, and less sweet than light molasses, which, as its name implies, is light in both color and flavor.

kitchen how-to:
save crystallized honey & syrup

Sometimes honey and syrup crystallize after long storage. To reliquefy honey or syrup, leave it in the jar, and place it in a saucepan of water over low heat until the crystals dissolve. Measure and use what you'll need. Or, microwave the honey at HIGH 15 to 60 seconds.

2 Follow the recipe, period.

Read through the recipe from start to finish. Baking is as much science as art, so to prevent disastrous results, avoid substituting ingredients. Although sugar substitutes are widely available, using them in your baked products can result in a tougher, denser product with little volume. Similarly, we don't recommend using applesauce or fruit puree to replace fat. If you want to experiment (as we do all the time), regard it as an experiment, and expect a few failures along the way.

kitchen how-to:
soften hard brown sugar

If your brown sugar has become as hard as a brick, you can soften it by adding a cut apple to the container, closing it, and waiting a day or so. The moisture from the apple will soften the sugar.

❸ Measure liquid ingredients properly.

Water, oil, milk, and other wet ingredients should be poured into a clear liquid measuring cup on a level counter, then checked at eye level, not from above. For measurements of 1 cup or less, a 1-cup glass measure will give you a more accurate reading than a larger one.

❹ Weigh, don't measure, flour.

A kitchen scale is a great addition to your equipment list, especially if you enjoy baking at home. Weighing is the most accurate way to measure flour. Depending on how tightly you pack a measuring cup, you could end up with much more flour than intended. That's why we give flour measurements in ounces first. But, if you don't have a scale, be sure to measure accurately.

all-purpose flour

whole-wheat flour

cake flour

whole-wheat pastry flour

Flour Glossary

Different flours have varying levels of protein and fiber, which affect the final baked product. Here are the ones *Cooking Light* often uses.

All-Purpose Flour: As its name states, this flour has many uses and is the one most frequently used in baking. It's a middle-of-the-road flour in terms of protein content, and produces tender cakes.

Whole-Wheat Flour: Milled from the complete wheat kernel—both the bran and the germ—this flour retains many nutrients and is higher in fiber than many other flours. It gives baked products a nuttier flavor and denser texture than all-purpose flour, which is why it's often mixed with all-purpose flour.

Cake Flour: Cake flour has the least protein and yields very light baked goods, making it ideal for delicate products such as sponge cakes and some cookie doughs.

Pastry Flour: Containing only a bit more protein than cake flour, pastry flour is made by grinding soft wheat into a fine flour. It's good for making feathery light pastry, pies, and cookies. It's available in a whole-wheat variety, too.

Bread Flour: Bread flour has the most protein and is used to make denser items, including breads and pizza dough, where you want a chewier texture.

1

2

kitchen how-to:
properly measure flour

1. Stir the flour in the canister to aerate it. Lightly spoon the flour into the measuring cup without compacting it.

2. Level off the excess flour with the flat edge of a knife.

⑤ Know your oven.

Get an oven thermometer to prevent under- or overdone baked products. It's the best way to ensure your oven is properly calibrated. You also need to be aware of any hot spots. If your cake emerges from the oven with a wavy rather than flat top, hot spots are the problem. To find your oven's hot spots, arrange bread slices on a pan, and place it on the middle rack of the oven. Bake the bread at 350° for a few minutes and see which slices get singed—their location marks your oven's hot spots. Once you've identified a hot spot, avoid putting pans in that location, or rotate them accordingly.

⑥ Preheat your oven.

Baked goods need an initial blast of heat to activate the leavening. Although it's tempting, don't put your pan in before that preheat light goes off. If the oven isn't up to the correct temperature, your recipe will take longer to bake, and you'll run the risk of the end product having a dry texture and low volume.

7 The cooldown is important.

Baked items such as muffins and quick breads should be removed from their pans soon after baking, or they will sweat on the bottom. Cakes, however, need to cool before they are removed from the pan or frosted. Let cookies sit a few minutes on the baking sheet to set; they will fall apart if you scoop them up while they're still hot.

8 Choose the proper pan.

Did you know that baking pans and baking dishes are not the same? If you're using a glass or ceramic baking dish when the recipe calls for a metal baking pan, don't fret. Simply decrease the oven temperature by 25°.

9 Stock essential equipment.

Having the right equipment is the first step in creating delicious baked goods. This list will get you started.

Stand Mixer and Handheld Mixer: A stand mixer with its multiple attachments and large bowl capacity is ideal for making doughs and mixing thick batters. A handheld mixer is great for small mixing jobs and allows you to control the mixer's movement in a freestanding bowl.

Food Processor: Available in various sizes, a food processor will easily chop, grate, or shred a variety of ingredients. However, the bowls of food processors can leak at the base if overloaded with liquid. A mini food processor is ideal for smaller jobs and chopping ingredients in batches.

Baking Sheets and Jelly-Roll Pans: A large, sturdy baking sheet is a useful baking tool. This flat metal pan, also called a cookie sheet, has at least one flat side that allows baked products to easily slide off the end. A jelly-roll pan, also called a sheet pan, is similar to a baking sheet but has a rim around all sides.

Baking Pans and Dishes: Pans are metal; dishes are glass. You'll often use 8- and 9-inch square metal baking pans and glass or ceramic baking dishes, a 13 x 9–inch metal baking pan and glass or ceramic baking dish, and an 11 x 7–inch glass or ceramic baking dish.

Cake Pan: Invest in 8- and 9-inch round cake pans. If you regularly make layer cakes, you may want to purchase multiple ones of both sizes. Also consider buying a tube pan for angel food cake, a Bundt pan for pound cakes, and a springform pan for cheesecakes.

Muffin Pan: Purchase a muffin pan that holds 12 muffins, which is a standard yield for muffin recipes. Most muffin cups measure 2½ inches across the top, but mini muffin pans and Texas muffin pans are also available for smaller and larger muffins, respectively.

Loaf Pan: The standard measures for these metal pans are 9 x 5–inch and 8 x 4–inch.

Pie Plate: For pie plates, use glass, ceramic, or dull metal. The standard size is 9 inches. Deep-dish pie plates are 10 inches.

Wire Cooling Rack: Invest in a large wire oven rack (or more than one) for all-purpose use cooling everything from cookies to cake layers. You can also purchase small round or square ones if you have less room in your kitchen or if you make cakes regularly.

Cutting Board: A wooden or plastic cutting board is a standard baking need. Make sure you wash and sanitize your board regularly.

Whisks: A medium-sized stainless steel wire whisk is a good all-purpose whisk to have on hand. Use a balloon whisk for whipping egg whites.

Dry Measuring Cups: Select a set of metal or plastic measuring cups for dry ingredients. They come in graduated sizes of 1 cup, ½ cup, ⅓ cup, and ¼ cup.

Liquid Measuring Cup: You'll need a glass or clear plastic measuring cup for liquid ingredients. They come in 1-cup, 2-cup, and 4-cup sizes.

Measuring Spoons: Purchase a set of measuring spoons that includes measures for ⅛ teaspoon up to 1 tablespoon.

Spatulas and Wooden Spoons: Consider investing in a few of these. They're versatile and hardworking baking utensils.

Pastry Blender: This tool makes easy work of cutting fat (usually butter) into the dry ingredients. You can use two knives, but it does take significantly longer to cut in the butter to the proper size.

Rolling Pin: A large wooden rolling pin easily rolls out dough and pastry, but you could also choose a tapered rolling pin, which is lighter.

Sifter: Use this to sift flour and powdered sugar. Never wash a sifter; just shake out the excess powder.

Handheld Grater: Handheld graters, also called Microplanes®, come in a variety of sizes. Use them to grate citrus rind, hard cheese, and chocolate.

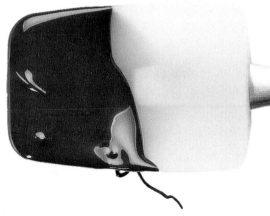

way to bake

muffins & quick bread loaves

muffins & quick bread loaves

Quick breads, like muffins and loaves, are easy to make, requiring only that you measure precisely and mix lightly. The procedure for making them is basically the same—it's the shape of the pan that makes the difference.

Muffins & Loaves

When making muffins and quick bread loaves, the method is straightforward: Simply combine the dry ingredients, add the wet, mix them together, and scrape the batter into a loaf pan or divide the batter among muffin cups, and bake. Both loaves and muffins are done when a wooden pick inserted in the center comes out clean. Muffins bake in less time than a loaf. You may need to use muffin cup liners, but the recipe will specify if you do.

Overmixing

As in all light baking, precise measurements are key, but you'll also need to pay attention to how you mix the ingredients. When combining the dry ingredients with the liquid ingredients, mix the batter in a few swift strokes—just until the mixture is combined and the dry ingredients have been incorporated. (A few lumps are OK.) If you overmix the batter, the bread will be dense and chewy; if you undermix, patches of flour will speckle the bread.

Freezing

It's easy to make multiple loaves or muffins and freeze them to enjoy later. To get the best results, wrap a loaf in heavy-duty foil, and freeze for up to a month. To freeze slices or muffins, place them in heavy-duty zip-top plastic bags, remove excess air from each bag, and seal. Or, you can wrap the slices or muffins in foil and freeze for up to a month. To thaw, let stand at room temperature.

1

kitchen how-to:
make muffins & quick bread loaves

Whether you're making muffins or loaves, most quick breads follow the same four-step process. The result is a coarse, yet tender, crumb.

1. Weigh or lightly spoon flour into dry measuring cups; level with a knife.
2. Combine dry ingredients in a large bowl, and make a well in the center for the wet ingredients. The well allows you to smoothly stir the ingredients with no more mixing than necessary to blend the batter, which is the best way to maintain tenderness.
3. Add the wet ingredients to the dry ingredients.
4. Stir the batter just until moist.

2 **3**

4

muffins

Muffins are deliciously versatile. Whether you prefer savory or sweet varieties, endless combinations will keep your taste buds entertained.

Apple Fritter Muffins

Cooking spray
- 6 ounces cake flour (about 1½ cups)
- 2.38 ounces whole-wheat flour (about ½ cup)
- ½ cup packed light brown sugar
- 1 tablespoon baking powder
- ½ teaspoon ground Saigon cinnamon
- ¼ teaspoon salt
- 4½ tablespoons vanilla-flavored soy milk, divided
- 3 tablespoons canola oil
- 1 (6-ounce) carton plain fat-free yogurt
- 1 large egg
- 1 cup finely diced unpeeled Granny Smith apple
- ¼ cup powdered sugar

1. Preheat oven to 350°.
2. Place 12 paper muffin cup liners in muffin cups; coat liners with cooking spray.
3. Weigh or lightly spoon flours into dry measuring cups; level with a knife. Combine flours and next 4 ingredients in a large bowl; stir with a whisk. Make a well in center of mixture. Combine ¼ cup soy milk, oil, yogurt, and egg in a bowl, stirring well with a whisk. Add to flour mixture; stir just until moist. Fold in apple. Spoon about 2 tablespoons batter into each prepared muffin liner.
4. Bake at 350° for 18 minutes or until muffins spring back when touched lightly in center. Remove muffins from pans immediately; place on a wire rack.
5. Combine powdered sugar and 1½ teaspoons soy milk, stirring with a whisk until smooth. Drizzle ½ teaspoon glaze over each muffin. Serve warm. **Yield: 12 servings (serving size: 1 muffin).**

CALORIES 178; FAT 4.3g (sat 0.4g, mono 2.4g, poly 1.2g); PROTEIN 3.7g; CARB 31.7g; FIBER 1.2g; CHOL 18mg; IRON 1.6mg; SODIUM 175mg; CALC 109mg

Cake Flour
What it adds: This fine-textured flour contains little protein—protein promotes the production of gluten, which can make baked goods tough. The result: a lighter, fluffier muffin with a tender crumb.

Saigon Cinnamon
What it adds: This Vietnamese cinnamon has a more intensely sweet flavor and aroma and consequently costs a bit more. You can use ground cinnamon in place of it, if you'd like.

Vanilla Soy Milk
What it adds: Using a flavored soy milk is an easy way to add extra vanilla flavor.

Blueberry-Oatmeal Muffins

1⅔ cups quick-cooking oats
3 ounces all-purpose flour (about ⅔ cup)
2.33 ounces whole-wheat flour (about ½ cup)
¾ cup packed light brown sugar
2 teaspoons ground cinnamon
1 teaspoon baking powder
1 teaspoon baking soda
¾ teaspoon salt
1½ cups low-fat buttermilk
¼ cup canola oil
2 teaspoons grated lemon rind
2 large eggs
2 cups frozen blueberries
2 tablespoons all-purpose flour
Cooking spray
2 tablespoons granulated sugar

1. Preheat oven to 400°.
2. Place oats in a food processor; pulse 5 to 6 times or until oats resemble coarse meal. Place in a large bowl.
3. Weigh or lightly spoon flours into dry measuring cups; level with a knife. Add flours and next 5 ingredients to oats; stir well. Make a well in center of mixture.
4. Combine buttermilk and next 3 ingredients. Add to flour mixture; stir just until moist.
5. Toss berries with 2 tablespoons all-purpose flour, and gently fold into batter. Spoon batter into 16 muffin cups coated with cooking spray; sprinkle 2 tablespoons granulated sugar evenly over batter. Bake at 400° for 20 minutes or until muffins spring back when touched lightly in center. Remove muffins from pans immediately; place on a wire rack. **Yield: 16 servings (serving size: 1 muffin).**

CALORIES 190; FAT 5g (sat 0.6g, mono 2.4g, poly 1.2g); PROTEIN 4.2g; CARB 33.3g; FIBER 2.4g; CHOL 23mg; IRON 1.6mg; SODIUM 248mg; CALC 74mg

kitchen how-to: make perfect blueberry muffins

Tossing frozen blueberries with flour before adding them to the batter keeps the blueberries from sinking to the bottom while the muffins bake. It also prevents the batter from turning purple. If you use fresh blueberries, skip this step.

1. Toss the frozen berries with 2 tablespoons flour.
2. Gently fold coated berries into the batter.

Lemon-Orange Muffins

Cooking spray
4.5 ounces all-purpose flour (about 1 cup)
½ cup granulated sugar
1 teaspoon baking soda
¼ teaspoon salt
¾ cup low-fat buttermilk
2 tablespoons butter, melted
2 tablespoons canola oil
1 tablespoon grated orange rind
2 teaspoons grated lemon rind
1 large egg
1 tablespoon turbinado or granulated sugar
Candied zest (optional)

1. Preheat oven to 375°.
2. Place 12 paper muffin cup liners in muffin cups; coat liners with cooking spray.

3. Weigh or lightly spoon flour into a dry measuring cup; level with a knife. Combine flour and next 3 ingredients in a large bowl; stir with a whisk. Make a well in center of mixture. Combine buttermilk and next 5 ingredients. Add buttermilk mixture to flour mixture, stirring just until moist. Spoon batter evenly into prepared muffin cups. Sprinkle batter evenly with turbinado sugar.
4. Bake at 375° for 15 minutes or until muffins spring back when touched lightly in center. Remove muffins from pans immediately; place on a wire rack. Top with candied zest, if desired. Serve warm or at room temperature. **Yield: 12 servings (serving size: 1 muffin).**

CALORIES 187; FAT 7.5g (sat 2.4g, mono 3.3g, poly 1.3g); PROTEIN 3.2g; CARB 27.3g; FIBER 0.6g; CHOL 35mg; IRON 0.9mg; SODIUM 284mg; CALC 35mg

kitchen how-to: make candied zest

Candied citrus peel is a gorgeous garnish you'll find easy to master. You can use any citrus peel you like to create a sweet-tart garnish to serve on ice cream or pair with chocolate for an elegant after-dinner treat. Store candied peel layered in wax paper in an airtight container for up to a month. Sprinkle each layer with the excess sugar left over from the final coating to prevent the pieces from clumping together.

1. Use a sharp vegetable peeler to remove the peel from 2 medium-sized lemons, limes, or oranges or 1 grapefruit. Reserve the fruit for another use.

2. Scrape the bitter white pith from the back of the peel with a small paring knife; discard pith.

3. Cut peel into ¼-inch-thick strips 3 inches in length. You'll get about 40 strips per fruit.

4. Combine ¼ cup sugar and 2 tablespoons water in a saucepan to make a simple syrup.

5. Bring mixture to a boil over medium heat, stirring constantly until sugar dissolves.

6. Add peel, cover, reduce heat, and simmer 3 minutes. Remove from heat; cool completely.

7. Strain through a sieve, shaking off excess moisture to prevent clumping. Discard liquid.

8. Separate pieces of rind, and allow the pieces to air-dry on a sheet of wax paper.

9. Place ¼ cup sugar and citrus pieces in a bowl; toss well to coat.

Honey-Gingerbread Muffins

4.5 ounces all-purpose flour (about 1 cup)
4.5 ounces whole-wheat pastry flour
     (about 1 cup)
 ¾   cup packed dark brown sugar
1½   teaspoons baking powder
 ½   teaspoon baking soda
 ½   teaspoon salt
 ½   teaspoon ground cinnamon
 ¼   teaspoon ground allspice
 ½   cup golden raisins
 2   large egg whites
 1   large egg yolk
 1   cup low-fat buttermilk
 ¼   cup butter, melted
 1   teaspoon grated peeled fresh ginger
 2   tablespoons honey

1. Preheat oven to 375°.
2. Place 12 paper muffin cup liners in muffin cups.
3. Weigh or lightly spoon flours into dry measuring cups; level with a knife. Combine flours and next 6 ingredients; stir well with a whisk. Stir in raisins. Make a well in center of mixture. Place egg whites in a medium bowl; beat with a mixer at high speed until stiff peaks form. Combine egg yolk, buttermilk, butter, and ginger in a bowl, stirring well with a whisk; add to flour mixture, stirring just until moist. Fold egg whites into batter. Spoon batter evenly into prepared muffin cups.
4. Bake at 375° for 20 minutes or until muffins spring back when touched lightly in center. Remove muffins from pans; cool slightly. Drizzle muffins evenly with honey. Serve immediately. **Yield: 12 servings (serving size: 1 muffin).**

CALORIES 209; FAT 4.7g (sat 2.7g, mono 1.2g, poly 0.3g); PROTEIN 3.9g; CARB 38.7g; FIBER 2g; CHOL 29mg; IRON 1.3mg; SODIUM 263mg; CALC 82mg

all about dark vs. light brown sugar

Brown sugar owes its moist, pliable texture and caramel-like flavor to molasses, a small amount of which is added to granulated sugar to create brown sugar. Dark brown sugar has more molasses and therefore a richer, deeper, more assertive taste than light brown sugar. For a more delicate flavor, use light brown sugar in recipes.

Monkey Bread Muffins

While these aren't technically muffins, they're muffin-like versions of a familiar favorite. The sweet, buttery mixture poured over the muffins can get hot, so let them cool before biting into them.

½ (25-ounce) package frozen Parker House–style roll dough (12 rolls)
¼ cup sugar
¼ cup granulated honey
2 teaspoons ground cinnamon
¼ cup butter, melted
Cooking spray

1. Thaw roll dough in refrigerator overnight.
2. Combine sugar, granulated honey, and cinnamon in a shallow dish; stir with a whisk. Cut each piece of roll dough into quarters with kitchen shears. Dip dough quarters, 1 at a time, into melted butter, and roll in sugar mixture. Arrange 4 quarters in each of 12 muffin cups coated with cooking spray. Drizzle any remaining butter evenly over top of dough. Cover and let rise in a warm place (85°), free from drafts, 1 hour or until doubled in size.
3. Preheat oven to 350°.
4. Uncover and bake at 350° for 13 to 15 minutes or until lightly browned. Loosen edges with a knife immediately. Cool 10 minutes before serving. Serve warm. **Yield: 12 servings (serving size: 1 muffin).**

CALORIES 115; FAT 4.1g (sat 2.4g, mono 0.8g, poly 0.1g); PROTEIN 1.6g; CARB 18.1g; FIBER 0.6g; CHOL 8mg; IRON 0mg; SODIUM 130mg; CALC 4mg

kitchen how-to: make monkey bread muffins

The muffins are easy to prepare. You can use a knife to cut the dough into quarters, but kitchen shears will speed up the preparation process.

1. Combine sugar, granulated honey, and cinnamon in a shallow dish. Granulated honey adds the sweetness and richness of honey without the stickiness.

2. Cut each piece of roll dough into quarters.

3. Dip each dough quarter into the melted butter.

4. Roll the quarters in the sugar mixture.

5. Place 4 quarters in each of 12 muffin cups coated with cooking spray.

6. Drizzle any remaining butter evenly over the top of the dough.

Herbed Goat Cheese Muffins

6.75 ounces all-purpose flour (about 1½ cups)
  1 tablespoon baking powder
  1 teaspoon sugar
  ¼ teaspoon salt
  ½ cup (4 ounces) goat cheese, crumbled
  1 cup 1% low-fat milk, divided
  2 tablespoons unsalted butter, melted
  2 tablespoons canola oil
  ½ cup chopped green onions
  ¼ cup chopped fresh chives
  ¼ cup chopped fresh parsley
  1 large egg
  Cooking spray

1. Preheat oven to 400°.
2. Weigh or lightly spoon flour into dry measuring cups; level with a knife. Combine flour and next 3 ingredients in a large bowl, stirring with a whisk. Make a well in center of mixture.
3. Combine goat cheese and 2 tablespoons milk in a small bowl, stirring with a spoon until blended. Combine remaining milk, butter, and next 5 ingredients in a medium bowl, stirring with a whisk. Add butter mixture to flour mixture, stirring just until moist.
4. Spoon half of batter evenly into 12 muffin cups coated with cooking spray. Top each with about 2 teaspoons goat cheese filling. Spoon remaining batter evenly over filling.
5. Bake at 400° for 20 minutes or until muffins spring back when touched lightly in center. Cool in pans 2 minutes. Remove muffins from pans; place on a wire rack. **Yield: 12 servings (serving size: 1 muffin).**

CALORIES 149; FAT 7.9g (sat 3.6g, mono 2.9g, poly 0.9g); PROTEIN 5.1g; CARB 14.2g; FIBER 0.6g; CHOL 31mg; IRON 1.1mg; SODIUM 214mg; CALC 123mg

kitchen how-to: make stuffed muffins

The procedure for making stuffed muffins is simple. Follow these steps for the best results.

1. Spoon half of batter evenly into muffin cups coated with cooking spray.
2. Top each with goat cheese or whatever filling you'd like, such as chocolate, jelly, or fruit.
3. Spoon remaining batter evenly over filling, and bake until golden brown.

Center-Cut Bacon
What it adds: This cut of bacon has the same satisfying flavor of regular bacon, but because it's cut closer to the bone, it contains fewer calories and about 20% less saturated fat than regular bacon.

Extrasharp Cheddar Cheese
What it adds: Extrasharp cheddar cheese provides the most intense cheddar flavor.

Yellow Cornmeal
What it adds: Cornmeal adds a pleasingly crunchy texture to the muffins.

Bacon-Cheddar Corn Muffins

These muffins are great for breakfast, served with soup or salad for lunch, or as a change of pace for dinner. Split and toast leftovers.

Cooking spray
6.75 ounces all-purpose flour (about 1½ cups)
½ cup yellow cornmeal
1 teaspoon baking powder
1 teaspoon baking soda
1 teaspoon sugar
¼ teaspoon salt
1 cup fat-free milk
2 tablespoons lemon juice
2 tablespoons butter, melted
1 large egg
½ cup (2 ounces) shredded extrasharp cheddar cheese
4 center-cut bacon slices, cooked and crumbled

1. Preheat oven to 400°.
2. Place 12 paper muffin cup liners in muffin cups; coat liners with cooking spray.
3. Weigh or lightly spoon flour into dry measuring cups; level with a knife. Combine flour and next 5 ingredients in a large bowl; make a well in center of mixture.
4. Combine milk and juice in a medium bowl; let stand 2 minutes (milk will curdle). Add butter and egg; stir well to combine. Add to flour mixture, stirring just until moist. Stir in cheese and bacon. Spoon batter evenly into prepared muffin cups. Bake at 400° for 17 minutes or until muffins spring back when touched lightly in center. Remove muffins from pans immediately; place on a wire rack. **Yield: 12 servings (serving size: 1 muffin).**

CALORIES 142; FAT 4.8g (sat 2.6g, mono 1.5g, poly 0.3g); PROTEIN 5.2g; CARB 19.1g; FIBER 0.6g; CHOL 30mg; IRON 1.1mg; SODIUM 295mg; CALC 88mg

Cheesy Tamale Muffins

2 ears shucked corn
Cooking spray
4.5 ounces all-purpose flour (about 1 cup)
1.9 ounces masa harina (about ½ cup)
2 tablespoons sugar
2 teaspoons baking powder
½ teaspoon salt
½ teaspoon roasted ground cumin
½ teaspoon chili powder
¼ teaspoon baking soda
½ cup (2 ounces) shredded Monterey Jack
   cheese with jalapeño peppers
1¼ cups low-fat buttermilk
1 (4.5-ounce) can chopped green chiles, drained
1 large egg

1. Preheat grill to medium-high heat.
2. Coat corn with cooking spray. Place corn on grill rack coated with cooking spray. Grill corn 10 minutes or until slightly charred, turning occasionally. Cool corn slightly; cut kernels from cobs.
3. Preheat oven to 400°.
4. Weigh or lightly spoon all-purpose flour and masa harina into dry measuring cups; level with a knife. Combine flours and next 6 ingredients in a large bowl; stir with a whisk. Stir in cheese. Make a well in center of mixture. Combine corn, buttermilk, green chiles, and egg, stirring well with a whisk. Add buttermilk mixture to flour mixture, stirring just until moist. Spoon batter evenly into 12 muffin cups coated with cooking spray.
5. Bake at 400° for 20 minutes or until muffins spring back when touched lightly in center. Remove muffins from pans immediately; place on a wire rack. Serve warm. **Yield: 12 servings (serving size: 1 muffin).**

CALORIES 114; FAT 2.7g (sat 1.2g, mono 0.3g, poly 0.3g); PROTEIN 4.5g; CARB 18.4g; FIBER 1.3g; CHOL 24mg; IRON 1.1mg; SODIUM 290mg; CALC 109mg

kitchen how-to: grill corn

Grilling intensifies the natural sweetness of corn. You can store fresh corn for 3 to 5 days in the refrigerator, but be sure to keep the husks on. If the silks turn dull or dark, the corn is past its prime. See page 54 for information about how to shuck fresh corn.

1. Place the corn on a grill rack coated with cooking spray.
2. Grill the corn 10 minutes or until slightly charred. Make sure you turn it occasionally to prevent one side from overcooking.

all about masa harina

This flour is made from soaking sun-dried corn kernels in lime water, which loosens the hulls from the kernels and softens the corn. The corn is then washed and ground, dried, and powdered to become masa harina. It's traditionally used to make tortillas, tamales, and other Mexican dishes.

quick bread loaves

Quick bread loaves are indeed quick and easy to prepare. Just follow the simple method outlined on page 23 to get perfect loaves every time.

Mummy's Brown Soda Bread

Because the bread uses baking soda as leavening instead of yeast, it requires minimal kneading and no rising, so you can bake it just before dinner and serve it warm.

  9   ounces all-purpose flour (about 2 cups)
9.5   ounces whole-wheat flour (about 2 cups)
1½   teaspoons baking soda
  ½   teaspoon salt
  2   cups buttermilk
      Cooking spray

1. Preheat oven to 450°.
2. Weigh or lightly spoon flours into dry measuring cups; level with a knife. Combine flours, baking soda, and salt in a large bowl; stir with a whisk. Make a well in center of mixture. Add buttermilk to flour mixture; stir until blended (dough will be sticky). Turn dough out onto a generously floured surface; knead lightly 4 to 5 times. Shape dough into an 8-inch round loaf; place on a baking sheet coated with cooking spray. Cut a ¼-inch-deep X in top of dough.
3. Bake at 450° for 15 minutes. Reduce oven temperature to 400° (do not remove bread from oven); bake 15 minutes or until loaf sounds hollow when tapped. Cool on a wire rack. **Yield: 12 servings (serving size: 1 slice).**

CALORIES 169; FAT 1.9g (sat 0.9g, mono 0.1g, poly 0.2g); PROTEIN 6.2g; CARB 32.4g; FIBER 3g; CHOL 6mg; IRON 1.7mg; SODIUM 308mg; CALC 10mg

kitchen how-to: shape brown soda bread

This traditional Irish bread uses only a handful of ingredients.

1. The dough will be sticky, so be sure to generously flour your work surface. Turn the dough out, and knead it lightly 4 or 5 times. Shape the dough into an 8-inch round loaf.

2. Place it on a baking sheet coated with cooking spray, and use a knife to cut a ¼-inch-deep X in the top of the dough. This procedure, known as scoring, is called "blessing the bread." It's decorative but also helps the top get crusty.

Basic Banana Bread

Look for flaxseed meal (sometimes labeled "ground flaxseed") on the baking aisle.

1½ cups mashed ripe banana
⅓ cup plain fat-free yogurt
5 tablespoons butter, melted
2 large eggs
½ cup granulated sugar
½ cup packed brown sugar
6.75 ounces all-purpose flour (about 1½ cups)
¼ cup flaxseed meal
¾ teaspoon baking soda
½ teaspoon salt
½ teaspoon ground cinnamon
⅛ teaspoon ground allspice
Cooking spray
⅓ cup powdered sugar
1½ teaspoons 1% low-fat milk

1. Preheat oven to 350°.
2. Combine first 4 ingredients in a large bowl; beat with a mixer at medium speed. Add granulated and brown sugars; beat until combined.
3. Weigh or lightly spoon flour into dry measuring cups; level with a knife. Combine flour and next 5 ingredients. Add flour mixture to banana mixture; beat just until blended. Pour batter into a 9 x 5–inch loaf pan coated with cooking spray. Bake at 350° for 55 minutes or until a wooden pick inserted in center comes out clean. Cool 10 minutes in pan on a wire rack; remove from pan. Cool completely on wire rack. Combine powdered sugar and milk, stirring until smooth; drizzle over bread.
Yield: 16 servings (serving size: 1 slice).

CALORIES 167; FAT 5.1g (sat 2.5g, mono 1.3g, poly 0.9g); PROTEIN 2.9g; CARB 28.3g; FIBER 1.5g; CHOL 32mg; IRON 1mg; SODIUM 173mg; CALC 24mg

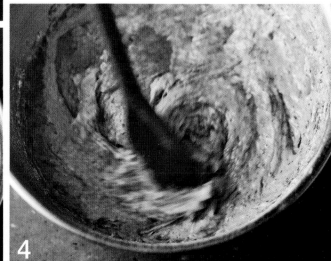

kitchen how-to:
make banana bread

Our banana bread recipes don't use a cup of oil or butter like many traditional banana breads—we use less than half, without sacrificing the moist texture that makes this bread such a treat. But baking lighter loaves does require some attention. Follow these guidelines for perfect results.

1. Combine the wet ingredients. This is a hybrid between a muffin method (combining wet and dry ingredients separately by hand) and a cake method (whipping butter and sugar with a mixer).

2. Add the sugars and beat to incorporate air into the batter. We used a mix of granulated and brown sugars to add sweetness and a hint of caramel.

3. Add the dry ingredients. Weighing flour is the most accurate way to measure. If you don't have a scale, lightly spoon flour into dry measuring cups and level with a knife. Then add the remaining dry ingredients; stir into the sugar mixture.

4. Stir in your flavoring additions. Besides the requisite bananas, you can add lots of tasty ingredients to the batter—chopped nuts, chocolate chips, spices, dried fruit, and alcohol, to name a few.

Carrot Bread

¾ **cup sliced carrot (about 4 ounces)**
7 **ounces whole-wheat flour (about 1½ cups)**
1 **teaspoon ground cinnamon**
¾ **teaspoon salt**
½ **teaspoon baking soda**
½ **teaspoon baking powder**
¼ **teaspoon ground ginger**
¼ **teaspoon ground cloves**
⅔ **cup sugar**
¼ **cup canola oil**
¼ **cup plain fat-free yogurt**
1 **large egg**
1 **large egg white**
Cooking spray

1. Preheat oven to 350°.
2. Cook carrot in boiling water 15 minutes or until tender; drain. Place carrot in a food processor; process until smooth.
3. Weigh or lightly spoon flour into dry measuring cups; level with a knife. Combine flour and next 6 ingredients in a large bowl. Combine carrot, sugar, and next 4 ingredients in a small bowl, stirring with a whisk. Add carrot mixture to flour mixture, stirring just until combined.
4. Pour batter into an 8 x 4–inch loaf pan coated with cooking spray. Bake at 350° for 50 minutes or until a wooden pick inserted in center comes out clean. Cool 10 minutes in pan on a wire rack; remove from pan. Cool completely on wire rack. Cut bread into 12 slices.
Yield: 12 servings (serving size: 1 slice).

CALORIES 151; FAT 5.3g (sat 0.5g, mono 3g, poly 1.6g); PROTEIN 3.2g; CARB 24g; FIBER 2.1g; CHOL 15mg; IRON 0.9mg; SODIUM 240mg; CALC 34mg

kitchen how-to:
prepare carrots for carrot bread

Adding pureed carrots to the batter disperses the carrot flavor throughout the bread and helps keep this loaf moist.

1. Cook carrot in boiling water for 15 minutes or until tender; drain.
2. Place carrot in a food processor.
3. Process carrot until smooth.

Orange-Pecan Tea Bread

A small amount of salt in a quick bread or cake batter balances its sweetness.

7.9   ounces all-purpose flour (about 1¾ cups)
1   teaspoon baking powder
½   teaspoon baking soda
¼   teaspoon salt
¼   teaspoon ground nutmeg
¼   teaspoon ground allspice
½   cup granulated sugar
½   cup low-fat buttermilk
¼   cup chopped pecans, toasted
3   tablespoons 1% low-fat milk
3   tablespoons orange marmalade
3   tablespoons canola oil
2   teaspoons grated orange rind
2   large eggs
    Cooking spray
½   cup powdered sugar
1   tablespoon fresh orange juice
1½   teaspoons chopped pecans, toasted

1. Preheat oven to 350°.
2. Weigh or lightly spoon flour into dry measuring cups; level with a knife. Combine flour and next 5 ingredients in a large bowl, stirring with a whisk; make a well in center of mixture. Combine granulated sugar and next 7 ingredients, stirring with a whisk; add to flour mixture, stirring just until moist.
3. Spoon batter into an 8 x 4-inch loaf pan coated with cooking spray. Bake at 350° for 45 minutes or until a wooden pick inserted in center comes out clean. Cool 10 minutes in pan on a wire rack; remove from pan. Cool completely on wire rack.
4. Combine powdered sugar and juice, stirring until smooth. Drizzle glaze evenly over bread; sprinkle with 1½ teaspoons pecans. **Yield: 14 servings (serving size: 1 slice).**

CALORIES 164; FAT 5.4g (sat 0.6g, mono 3.1g, poly 1.5g); PROTEIN 3g; CARB 26.6g; FIBER 0.6g; CHOL 26mg; IRON 1mg; SODIUM 136mg; CALC 46mg

all about orange marmalade

Orange marmalade is made by boiling orange peel with sugar and water. Depending on the type of oranges used, the marmalade can have a slightly bitter flavor (such as when Seville oranges are used), which is traditional, or a sweet flavor.

Orange Juice

What it adds: Mixing orange juice in with the powdered sugar creates an easy-to-drizzle glaze that adds another burst of orange flavor to this loaf.

Allspice

What it adds: As the name suggests, allspice is a mixture of cinnamon, nutmeg, and a touch of clove. It adds a deep, warm flavor to this bread.

Loaf Pan

What it adds: By using the pan size specified, you'll get a peaked top and the traditional crack in the center of the loaf. Using a larger pan will produce a flat top.

Sweet Persimmon and Toasted Walnut Bread

This simple quick bread uses sweet and spicy persimmon puree. We liked the slightly tart flavor from the golden raisins, but you may omit them, if you prefer.

13.5 ounces all-purpose flour (about 3 cups)
  2 teaspoons baking soda
  ½ teaspoon salt
  1 cup sugar
  1 cup ripe Hachiya persimmon puree
    (about 2 fruits)
  ½ cup 1% low-fat milk
  ⅓ cup butter, melted
  1 teaspoon vanilla extract
  2 large eggs
  ⅓ cup chopped walnuts, toasted
  ⅓ cup golden raisins
  Cooking spray

1. Preheat oven to 350°.
2. Weigh or lightly spoon flour into dry measuring cups; level with a knife. Combine flour, baking soda, and salt in a large bowl; stir with a whisk.
3. Combine sugar and next 5 ingredients in a medium bowl; beat with a mixer at medium speed until blended. Add persimmon mixture to flour mixture, stirring just until blended. Stir in walnuts and golden raisins. Spoon batter into 2 (8 x 4–inch) loaf pans coated with cooking spray. Bake at 350° for 45 minutes or until a wooden pick inserted in center comes out clean. Cool 10 minutes in pans on a wire rack; remove from pans. Cool completely on wire rack.
Yield: 24 servings (serving size: 1 slice).

CALORIES 146; FAT 4.1g (sat 1.9g, mono 1g, poly 0.9g); PROTEIN 2.7g; CARB 25.1g; FIBER 1.1g; CHOL 25mg; IRON 0.9mg; SODIUM 181mg; CALC 15mg

all about persimmons

This winter fruit is sometimes compared to apricots or plums in flavor and texture and, when fully ripe, has sweet hints of cinnamon and clove. To puree persimmons for this recipe, follow these tips: To speed the ripening process, freeze the fruit overnight or until solid. Thaw the persimmon; when soft, it will be sweeter and less astringent. Cut the ripe fruit in half. Scoop out the pulp with a spoon. To achieve an even consistency, place the flesh in a mini-chopper and process until smooth. This ensures the persimmon puree will incorporate evenly into batters.

Pumpkin–Honey Beer Quick Bread

Give the second loaf away, or wrap in plastic wrap and freeze for up to 2 months. Flaxseed meal and water add moisture to the batter for a smooth-textured bread.

14.6 ounces all-purpose flour (about 3¼ cups)
  2 teaspoons salt
  2 teaspoons baking soda
  1 teaspoon baking powder
  1 teaspoon ground cinnamon
  1 teaspoon pumpkin pie spice
  ½ cup water
  ⅓ cup flaxseed meal
 2½ cups sugar
  ⅔ cup canola oil
  ⅔ cup honey beer (at room temperature)
  4 large egg whites
  2 large eggs
  1 (15-ounce) can pumpkin
Cooking spray

1. Preheat oven to 350°.
2. Weigh or lightly spoon flour into dry measuring cups; level with a knife. Combine flour, salt, and next 4 ingredients in a medium bowl; stir with a whisk.
3. Combine ½ cup water and flaxseed.
4. Place sugar and next 4 ingredients in a large bowl; beat with a mixer at medium-high speed until well blended. Add flaxseed mixture and pumpkin; beat at low speed just until blended. Add flour mixture; beat just until combined. Divide batter between 2 (9 x 5–inch) loaf pans coated with cooking spray. Bake at 350° for 1 hour and 10 minutes or until a wooden pick inserted in center comes out clean. Cool 10 minutes in pans on a wire rack; remove from pans. Cool completely on wire rack. **Yield: 28 servings (serving size: 1 slice).**

CALORIES 194; FAT 6.5g (sat 0.6g, mono 3.4g, poly 2.1g); PROTEIN 2.9g; CARB 31.3g; FIBER 1.3g; CHOL 15mg; IRON 1.2mg; SODIUM 287mg; CALC 27mg

all about using beer in bread

When using beer in quick breads, keep in mind that beer varieties with a more intense flavor yield more intensely flavored bread. You'll want to bring the beer to room temperature before stirring it into the batter because cold liquids can delay the formation of gluten, which helps give bread structure.

Maple and Walnut Quick Bread

5.8 ounces all-purpose flour (about 1¼ cups)
3.3 ounces whole-wheat flour (about ¾ cup)
  ½ cup sugar
  2 teaspoons baking powder
  ½ teaspoon baking soda
  ½ teaspoon salt
  1 cup low-fat buttermilk
  ⅓ cup maple syrup
  ¼ cup walnut oil
  1 large egg
  ½ teaspoon vanilla extract
Cooking spray
  ⅓ cup finely chopped walnuts, toasted

1. Preheat oven to 350°.
2. Weigh or lightly spoon flours into dry measuring cups; level with a knife. Combine flours and next 4 ingredients in a large bowl; make a well in center of mixture. Combine buttermilk and next 3 ingredients in a bowl; add to flour mixture, stirring just until moist. Stir in vanilla. Spoon batter into an 8 x 4–inch loaf pan coated with cooking spray. Sprinkle with walnuts. Bake at 350° for 50 minutes or until a wooden pick inserted in center comes out clean. Cool 10 minutes in pan on a wire rack; remove from pan. Cool completely on wire rack. **Yield: 14 servings (serving size: 1 slice).**

CALORIES 178; FAT 6.5g (sat 0.8g, mono 1.4g, poly 3.9g); PROTEIN 3.6g;
CARB 27.5g; FIBER 1.3g; CHOL 16mg; IRON 1.1mg; SODIUM 224mg; CALC 73mg

Walnut Oil
What it adds: Walnut oil in the batter underscores the nutty flavor in this walnut-topped loaf. It also adds heart-healthy omega-3 fatty acids.

Walnuts
What they add: Walnuts are a good source of polyunsaturated fats, and they add great texture to this recipe.

Pure Maple Syrup
What it adds: Pure maple syrup adds a rich flavor to this bread. The darker the syrup, the more intense the maple flavor.

kitchen how-to: shuck fresh corn & remove kernels

Always buy fresh ears of corn in their husks. The husk is essential because it helps retain the corn's natural moisture, making it taste fresher. Look for green husks that don't appear dry. Then pull back an edge of the husk to check that the kernels are plump and a vivid color.

1. To shuck the corn, hold each ear with the tip facing down, and pull the husks and silks up toward your body. This helps remove more silks.

2. Twist a damp paper towel back and forth over the corn to remove any remaining silks.

3. Cut about ½ inch from the tip of each ear to create a flat base on which to stand the cob while removing the kernels.

4. Stand the cob upright in a pie plate or bowl to catch the kernels, and use a sharp knife to slice away the kernels in a slow, sawing motion.

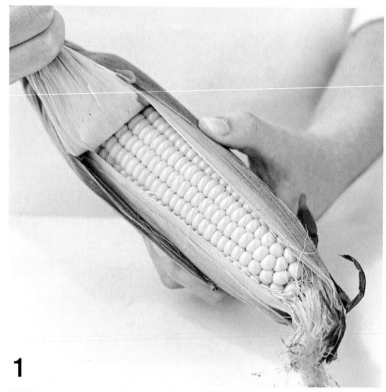

1

2

3

4

Thyme Corn Bread

Familiar bread recipes taste brand new with the addition of even a small spoonful of herbs. Stir them in right before baking.

4.5 ounces all-purpose flour (about 1 cup)
¾ cup yellow cornmeal
1 tablespoon sugar
1 teaspoon baking soda
½ teaspoon salt
¾ cup low-fat buttermilk
2 tablespoons canola oil
1 large egg
½ cup fresh corn kernels (about 1 ear)
1½ tablespoons fresh thyme leaves
   Cooking spray

1. Preheat oven to 350°.

2. Weigh or lightly spoon flour into a dry measuring cup; level with a knife. Combine flour, cornmeal, sugar, baking soda, and salt in a bowl. Make a well in center of mixture. Combine buttermilk, oil, and egg in a bowl; stir in corn and thyme. Add buttermilk mixture to flour mixture; stir just until moist.

3. Spoon batter into an 8-inch square metal baking pan lightly coated with cooking spray. Bake at 350° for 25 minutes or until corn bread is lightly browned and begins to pull away from sides of pan. Cool 5 minutes in pan on a wire rack. **Yield: 9 servings (serving size: 1 piece).**

CALORIES 161; FAT 4.4g (sat 0.7g, mono 2.3g, poly 1.1g); PROTEIN 4.2g; CARB 25.5g; FIBER 0.9g; CHOL 25mg; IRON 1.1mg; SODIUM 300mg; CALC 39mg

way to bake

biscuits & scones

biscuits & scones

Biscuits and scones have a divine texture created by bits of butter that melt during baking. We'll show you how to create lighter versions that are simply delicious.

Cutting In

When making biscuits and scones, the cutting-in procedure—cutting the butter into the dry ingredients—is key to creating those signature flaky layers. Make sure the butter is chilled so it doesn't melt, and it's best to use a pastry blender to cut the butter into the dry ingredients. Push the pastry blender into the butter-flour mixture until it resembles coarse meal. The "cutting" action distributes little lumps of butter through the flour. This flour-coated butter melts during baking and gives biscuits and scones their lovely texture. You can use 2 knives to cut in the butter if you don't have a pastry blender, but it will take you a bit longer.

Avoid Overworking

The secret to getting tender, flaky biscuits and scones is handling the dough as little as possible. When adding the liquid ingredients, stir just until the dry ingredients are moistened. Too much mixing increases the development of gluten, which makes them heavy and tough.

Rising

These quick breads generally use baking powder and baking soda instead of yeast as leavening—one

exception in this chapter is the Cinnamon-Raisin Angel Biscuits with Cream Cheese Icing on page 68. If you notice that your biscuits and scones (or any baked product, for that matter) are not rising properly, you might want to check the expiration dates on your baking powder and baking soda. See page 11 for more information about testing the strength of these leavening agents.

biscuits

Biscuits get their characteristic flavor and texture from butter. We'll show you how to get those same delicious results in a healthier package.

kitchen how-to: make drop biscuits

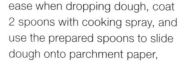

Drop biscuits have a higher proportion of liquid to dry ingredients than rolled biscuits, so you'll have a thick batter rather than a soft dough. Follow these steps for the best results.

1. Combine the dry ingredients in a large bowl, stirring well with a whisk.
2. Cut in butter using a pastry blender or 2 knives until mixture resembles coarse meal.
3. Add wet ingredients.
4. Stir ingredients together just until moist.
5. Drop dough onto baking sheets lined with parchment paper or coated with cooking spray. For

ease when dropping dough, coat 2 spoons with cooking spray, and use the prepared spoons to slide dough onto parchment paper,

recoating with cooking spray as needed. Place the mounds of dough about 2 inches apart to ensure they have room to spread.

Fig-Maple Drop Biscuits

You can use any fig variety in this recipe, but we prefer Calimyrna because they are incredibly sweet.

⅓ cup low-fat buttermilk
5 tablespoons 1% low-fat milk, divided
3 tablespoons maple syrup
6.75 ounces all-purpose flour (about 1½ cups)
1.1 ounces whole-wheat pastry flour (about ¼ cup)
¼ cup granulated sugar
¼ cup maple sugar, divided
½ teaspoon salt
½ teaspoon baking powder
¼ teaspoon baking soda
6 tablespoons unsalted butter, cut into ½-inch cubes
¾ cup dried Calimyrna figs (about 4 ounces), chopped
1 large egg white

1. Preheat oven to 400°.
2. Combine buttermilk, ¼ cup milk, and syrup in a small bowl. Weigh or lightly spoon flours into dry measuring cups; level with a knife. Combine flours, granulated sugar, 2 tablespoons maple sugar, and next 3 ingredients in a large bowl, stirring well with a whisk. Cut in butter with a pastry blender or 2 knives until mixture resembles coarse meal. Stir in figs. Add buttermilk mixture; stir just until moist.
3. Drop dough by 2 tablespoons 2 inches apart onto baking sheets lined with parchment paper. Combine remaining 1 tablespoon milk and egg white, stirring with a whisk; brush over tops of biscuits. Sprinkle biscuits with remaining 2 tablespoons maple sugar.
4. Bake at 400° for 15 minutes or until golden. **Yield: 20 servings (serving size: 1 biscuit).**

CALORIES 113; FAT 3.7g (sat 2.3g, mono 0.9g, poly 0.2g); PROTEIN 1.8g; CARB 18.7g; FIBER 1g; CHOL 10mg; IRON 0.7mg; SODIUM 94mg; CALC 32mg

Cheddar-Garlic Drop Biscuits

9   ounces all-purpose flour (about 2 cups)
1   tablespoon baking powder
¾   teaspoon salt
½   teaspoon onion powder
½   teaspoon garlic powder
1   cup (4 ounces) shredded reduced-fat sharp
    cheddar cheese
1½ tablespoons finely chopped fresh
    parsley, divided
1   cup 1% low-fat milk
3   tablespoons canola oil
  Cooking spray
1½ tablespoons tub-style garlic butter, melted

1. Preheat oven to 450°.
2. Weigh or lightly spoon flour into dry measuring cups;
level with a knife. Combine flour and next 4 ingredients;
stir with a whisk. Stir in cheese and 1 tablespoon
parsley. Combine milk and oil; add to flour mixture,
stirring just until moist.
3. Drop dough by 2 heaping tablespoons 2 inches apart
onto a baking sheet coated with cooking spray. Combine
butter and remaining 1½ teaspoons parsley. Brush
butter mixture evenly over dough.
4. Bake at 450° for 11 to 12 minutes or until lightly
browned. **Yield: 15 servings (serving size: 1 biscuit).**

CALORIES 129; FAT 5.9g (sat 1.9g, mono 1.8g, poly 0.9g); PROTEIN 4.2g; CARB 14g;
FIBER 0.5g; CHOL 8mg; IRON 0.8mg; SODIUM 280mg; CALC 125mg

kitchen how-to:
make flavored butter

Using flavored butter is an easy way to amp up
the flavor of light biscuits. You can start with a flavored
butter or add to plain regular butter whatever herbs
and spices you like.

1. Finely chop fresh herbs.
2. Combine melted butter and flavorings, such
as fresh or dried herbs and spices.
3. Brush butter mixture evenly over dough.

Caramelized Pear, Sage, and Orange Biscuit Bites

- 1 tablespoon butter
- 1 cup diced peeled Bartlett pear (about 1 pear)
- 1 tablespoon chopped fresh sage
- 1 tablespoon brown sugar
- 6.75 ounces all-purpose flour (about 1½ cups)
- 2½ teaspoons baking powder
- ½ teaspoon salt
- 5 tablespoons chilled butter, cut into small pieces
- ¾ cup nonfat buttermilk
- 2 teaspoons grated orange rind
- Cooking spray

1. Preheat oven to 450°.

2. Melt butter in a medium nonstick skillet over medium-high heat. Sauté pear and sage in butter 8 minutes or until pear is tender and begins to brown. Add brown sugar; sauté 1 minute or until sugar melts. Remove from heat.

3. Weigh or lightly spoon flour into dry measuring cups; level with a knife. Combine flour, baking powder, and salt in a large bowl; cut in butter with a pastry blender or 2 knives until mixture resembles coarse meal.

4. Combine buttermilk and orange rind, stirring with a whisk; add to flour mixture, stirring just until moist. Fold in pear mixture. Coat 21 miniature muffin cups with cooking spray. Drop dough evenly into prepared muffin cups. Coat dough with cooking spray.

5. Bake at 450° for 10 minutes or until lightly browned.

Yield: 21 servings (serving size: 1 biscuit).

CALORIES 73; FAT 3.4g (sat 2.1g, mono 0.9g, poly 0.2g); PROTEIN 1.3g; CARB 9.4g; FIBER 0.5g; CHOL 9mg; IRON 0.4mg; SODIUM 135mg; CALC 44mg

kitchen how-to: caramelize pear

Cooking pears deepens their color and intensifies their sweetness.

1. Melt butter in a skillet over medium-high heat. Add pear and herbs.
2. Sauté pear and herbs 8 minutes or until pear is tender and begins to brown.
3. Add brown sugar, and sauté 1 minute or until sugar melts.

rolled biscuits

Rolled biscuits take a bit more practice than drop biscuits, since this variety requires kneading. We'll show you how.

Strawberry Biscuits

4.5 ounces all-purpose flour (about 1 cup)
3 tablespoons sugar, divided
1½ teaspoons baking powder
¼ teaspoon salt
⅛ teaspoon baking soda
3 tablespoons chilled butter, cut into small pieces
½ cup finely diced strawberries
2 teaspoons all-purpose flour
⅓ cup evaporated fat-free milk
½ teaspoon vanilla extract
Butter-flavored cooking spray

1. Preheat oven to 425°.
2. Weigh or lightly spoon 4.5 ounces flour (about 1 cup) into a dry measuring cup; level with a knife. Combine flour, 2 tablespoons sugar, and next 3 ingredients in a bowl, stirring well with a whisk; cut in butter with a pastry blender or 2 knives until mixture resembles coarse meal.
3. Press strawberries between several layers of paper towels to remove excess moisture. Combine strawberries and 2 teaspoons flour in a small bowl, stirring gently with a fork. Add strawberry mixture to flour mixture, stirring gently with a fork. Combine milk and vanilla; add to flour mixture, stirring with a fork just until moist.
4. Turn dough out onto a lightly floured surface; knead dough lightly 3 to 4 times with floured hands. Roll dough to a 1-inch thickness. Cut with a 1½-inch biscuit cutter into 9 biscuits. Gather remaining dough. Roll to a 1-inch thickness, and cut with a 1½-inch biscuit cutter into 3 biscuits. Place biscuits 1 inch apart on a baking sheet lined with parchment paper. Coat biscuits with cooking spray, and sprinkle with remaining 1 tablespoon sugar.
5. Bake at 425° for 10 to 12 minutes or until golden. Remove from pan; cool 2 minutes on wire racks. Serve warm. **Yield: 12 servings (serving size: 1 biscuit).**

CALORIES 87; FAT 3.1g (sat 1.9g, mono 0.8g, poly 0.2g); PROTEIN 1.8g; CARB 13g; FIBER 0.4g; CHOL 8mg; IRON 0.6mg; SODIUM 140mg; CALC 54mg

kitchen how-to: make rolled biscuits

A good rolled biscuit dough will be slightly sticky to the touch and should be kneaded lightly just a few times.

1. Combine dry ingredients; cut in butter with a pastry blender or 2 knives until mixture resembles coarse meal. Combine wet ingredients; add to dry ingredients, stirring just until moist.
2. Lightly flour your work surface to prevent the dough from sticking. Turn dough out onto surface, and knead dough lightly 3 to 4 times with floured hands. Roll dough to a 1-inch thickness (or whatever thickness your recipe calls for).
3. Cut dough with a biscuit cutter.
4. Place biscuits on a baking sheet lined with parchment paper or coated with cooking spray.

Cinnamon-Raisin Angel Biscuits with Cream Cheese Icing

These tender biscuits are full of plump raisins and drizzled with a generous amount of cream cheese icing. You can omit the icing, if you'd like; the biscuits are delicious on their own.

Biscuits:
- 1 package dry yeast (about 2¼ teaspoons)
- 3 tablespoons warm water (100° to 110°)
- 11.7 ounces low-fat baking mix (about 3 cups)
- ¼ cup packed light brown sugar
- 1½ teaspoons ground cinnamon
- 1 cup raisins
- ¾ cup low-fat buttermilk
- 2 teaspoons vanilla extract
- Butter-flavored cooking spray

Icing:
- ¼ cup (2 ounces) ⅓-less-fat cream cheese, softened
- ½ teaspoon vanilla extract
- 1 cup powdered sugar
- 1 tablespoon 2% reduced-fat milk

1. To prepare biscuits, combine yeast and 3 tablespoons warm water (100° to 110°) in a small bowl; let stand 5 minutes.

2. Weigh or lightly spoon baking mix into dry measuring cups; level with a knife. Combine baking mix, brown sugar, and cinnamon in a large bowl; stir with a whisk. Stir in raisins. Add yeast mixture, buttermilk, and 2 teaspoons vanilla; stir just until moist. Cover and chill at least 8 hours.

3. Preheat oven to 350°.

4. Turn dough out onto a lightly floured surface; knead dough lightly 3 times with floured hands. Roll dough to a ¾-inch thickness; cut with a 2¼-inch biscuit cutter into 12 biscuits. Gather remaining dough. Roll to a ¾-inch thickness, and cut with a 2¼-inch biscuit cutter into 3 biscuits. Place biscuits 1 inch apart on a baking sheet coated with cooking spray. Coat tops of biscuits with cooking spray.

5. Bake at 350° for 15 minutes or until golden. Remove biscuits from pan, and cool slightly on wire racks.

6. To prepare icing, place cream cheese and ½ teaspoon vanilla in a bowl. Beat with a mixer at medium speed for 30 seconds. Reduce speed to low. Gradually add powdered sugar, beating until blended. Add milk, beating until drizzling consistency. Drizzle icing evenly over tops of biscuits. **Yield: 15 servings (serving size: 1 biscuit).**

CALORIES 179; FAT 2.6g (sat 0.6g, mono 1g, poly 0.3g); PROTEIN 3.1g; CARB 37g; FIBER 1.2g; CHOL 3mg; IRON 1.2mg; SODIUM 291mg; CALC 150mg

kitchen how-to: make angel biscuits

Using yeast instead of baking powder as their leavening, angel biscuits are a cross between a biscuit and a yeast roll.

1. Dissolve yeast in warm water; let stand 5 minutes.

2. Combine dry ingredients. Add wet ingredients, and stir just until moist.

3. Cover and chill at least 8 hours and up to 24 hours.

4. Turn dough out onto a lightly floured surface, and knead dough lightly 3 times with floured hands.

5. Roll dough to a ¾-inch thickness (or whatever thickness your recipe calls for); cut with a biscuit cutter.

6. Place biscuits on a baking sheet coated with cooking spray. Coat tops with cooking spray, which will enhance browning. Bake until biscuits are golden.

Cornmeal Buttermilk Biscuits

Cornmeal lends texture to these tall biscuits. Split and toast the biscuits, and drizzle with honey.

  5.6   ounces all-purpose flour (about 1¼ cups)
  2.38 ounces whole-wheat flour (about ½ cup)
  ¾   cup yellow cornmeal
  2   tablespoons sugar
  1½   teaspoons baking powder
  ½   teaspoon baking soda
  ½   teaspoon salt
  ¼   cup chilled butter, cut into small pieces
  1   cup nonfat buttermilk
  Butter-flavored cooking spray

1. Preheat oven to 450°.
2. Weigh or lightly spoon flours into dry measuring cups; level with a knife. Combine flours and next 5 ingredients in a large bowl; stir with a whisk. Cut in butter with a pastry blender or 2 knives until mixture resembles coarse meal. Add buttermilk; stir just until moist.
3. Turn dough out onto a lightly floured surface; knead dough lightly 3 to 4 times with floured hands. Roll dough to a 1-inch thickness; cut with a 2-inch biscuit cutter into 12 biscuits. Gather remaining dough. Roll to a 1-inch thickness, and cut with a 2-inch biscuit cutter into 2 biscuits. Place biscuits with sides barely touching on a baking sheet lined with parchment paper. Coat tops with cooking spray.
4. Bake at 450° for 15 minutes or until golden. **Yield: 14 servings (serving size: 1 biscuit).**

CALORIES 132; FAT 3.6g (sat 2.1g, mono 0.9g, poly 0.2g); PROTEIN 3.1g; CARB 21.8g; FIBER 1.1g; CHOL 9mg; IRON 0.9mg; SODIUM 212mg; CALC 52mg

kitchen how-to:
get more biscuits by rerolling dough

Rerolling the biscuit dough is an easy way to maximize the number of biscuits you get. However, don't reroll the dough more than once. Reworking the dough too much will yield tough biscuits.

1. After the dough is rolled to the proper thickness, cut it with a biscuit cutter, and place biscuits on a baking sheet lined with parchment paper or coated with cooking spray.
2. After cutting the dough with biscuit cutter, gather the remaining dough.
3. Pat or roll to a 1-inch thickness (or whatever thickness your recipe calls for).
4. Cut the rerolled dough with biscuit cutter. Place biscuits on baking sheet, and bake until golden.

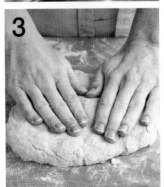

Potato–Sour Cream Biscuits

These savory treats are delicious alongside roast beef, chicken, or ham. They are great for sandwiches, too.

  8 ounces cubed peeled Yukon gold potato
  ½ cup low-fat buttermilk
  ¼ cup reduced-fat sour cream
  2 tablespoons butter, cut into small pieces
7.9 ounces all-purpose flour (about 1¾ cups)
  1 tablespoon baking powder
  1 teaspoon salt
  ½ teaspoon baking soda
     Cooking spray

1. Preheat oven to 450°.
2. Place potato in a medium saucepan; cover with water. Bring to a boil. Reduce heat, and simmer 15 minutes or until tender; drain. Return potato to pan. Add buttermilk, sour cream, and butter to pan; mash with a potato masher until smooth.
3. Weigh or lightly spoon flour into dry measuring cups; level with a knife. Combine flour and next 3 ingredients in a large bowl. Add potato mixture; stir just until moist.
4. Turn dough out onto a lightly floured surface; knead dough lightly 5 times with floured hands. Roll dough to a ¾-inch thickness. Cut with a 2-inch biscuit cutter into 15 biscuits. Place biscuits 2 inches apart on a baking sheet coated with cooking spray.
5. Bake at 450° for 15 minutes or until lightly browned. Serve warm. **Yield: 15 biscuits (serving size: 1 biscuit).**

CALORIES 87; FAT 2.2g (sat 1.3g, mono 0.6g, poly 0.1g); PROTEIN 2.2g; CARB 14.5g; FIBER 0.6g; CHOL 6mg; IRON 0.9mg; SODIUM 298mg; CALC 70mg

kitchen how-to:
peel potatoes

Peeling potatoes yields a softer texture, which is preferable when they're being added to a biscuit dough. You can easily remove the skin from a potato using a vegetable peeler.

Feta-Dill Wheat Biscuits

¾ cup fat-free milk
¼ cup plain fat-free Greek yogurt
6.75 ounces all-purpose flour (about 1½ cups)
2.25 ounces whole-wheat pastry flour (about ½ cup)
  2 teaspoons baking powder
½ teaspoon salt
¼ teaspoon sugar
¼ cup chilled butter, cut into small cubes
  3 tablespoons chopped fresh dill
½ cup (2 ounces) crumbled feta cheese
Cooking spray

1. Preheat oven to 425°.
2. Combine milk and yogurt in a small bowl. Weigh or lightly spoon flours into dry measuring cups; level with a knife. Combine flours and next 3 ingredients in a large bowl, stirring with a whisk. Cut in butter with a pastry blender or 2 knives until mixture resembles coarse meal. Stir in dill and cheese. Add milk mixture, stirring just until moist.
3. Turn dough out onto a lightly floured surface; knead dough lightly 5 times with floured hands. Roll dough to a ½-inch thickness. Cut with a 2-inch biscuit cutter into 12 biscuits. Gather remaining dough. Roll to a ½-inch thickness, and cut with a 2-inch biscuit cutter into 4 biscuits. Place biscuits on a baking sheet coated with cooking spray.
4. Bake at 425° for 12 minutes or until golden. **Yield: 16 servings (serving size: 1 biscuit).**

CALORIES 98; FAT 3.9g (sat 2.4g, mono 0.9g, poly 0.2g); PROTEIN 2.8g; CARB 12.8g; FIBER 0.8g; CHOL 11mg; IRON 0.8mg; SODIUM 189mg; CALC 70mg

Whole-Wheat Pastry Flour
What it adds: This very finely ground flour keeps these biscuits from becoming too dense, and it adds healthy whole grains.

Feta Cheese
What it adds: This classic Greek cheese adds a tangy burst of flavor to these biscuits.

Fresh Dill
What it adds: Fresh dill adds a crisp, clean flavor. Use fresh dill rather than dried to get the most flavor.

Cordon Bleu Biscuits

9 ounces all-purpose flour (about 2 cups)
1 tablespoon sugar
4 teaspoons baking powder
¼ teaspoon salt
¼ cup chilled butter, cut into small pieces
½ cup chopped lower-sodium Virginia ham
    (3 ounces)
½ cup (2 ounces) shredded reduced-fat
    Jarlsberg cheese
⅔ cup fat-free milk
1 large egg
Cooking spray

1. Preheat oven to 450°.
2. Weigh or lightly spoon flour into dry measuring
cups; level with a knife. Combine flour and next
3 ingredients in a medium bowl, stirring with a whisk.
Cut in butter with a pastry blender or 2 knives until
mixture resembles coarse meal. Stir in ham and
cheese. Combine milk and egg in a small bowl,
stirring well with a whisk. Add milk mixture to flour
mixture; stir just until moist.
3. Turn dough out onto a lightly floured surface;
knead dough lightly 3 to 4 times with floured hands.
Roll dough to a ¾-inch thickness; cut with a 2½-inch
biscuit cutter into 8 biscuits. Gather remaining dough.
Roll to a ¾-inch thickness, and cut with a 2½-inch
biscuit cutter into 2 biscuits. Place biscuits on a baking
sheet coated with cooking spray.
4. Bake at 450° for 10 minutes. Serve warm. **Yield:**
10 servings (serving size: 1 biscuit).

CALORIES 177; FAT 6.7g (sat 3.7g, mono 1.9g, poly 0.4g); PROTEIN 7.3g; CARB 22.2g;
FIBER 0.7g; CHOL 40mg; IRON 1.3mg; SODIUM 343mg; CALC 178mg

kitchen how-to:
brown light biscuits

Sometimes biscuits are brushed with an
egg wash or melted butter to ensure their tops
brown nicely. You can get similar results by
coating the top of the dough with cooking spray
before placing the baking sheet in the oven.

scones

The biscuit-like texture of scones makes them a hearty option for breakfast, brunch, or a snack. They're also a good choice to make for company because they bake quickly.

Chocolate-Cherry-Almond Scones

9 ounces all-purpose flour (about 2 cups)
⅓ cup sugar, divided
1½ teaspoons baking powder
¼ teaspoon salt
5 tablespoons chilled butter, cut into small pieces
¼ cup dried tart cherries, chopped
1.5 ounces bittersweet chocolate, chopped (¼ cup)
1 large egg
¾ cup fat-free milk, divided
½ teaspoon almond extract
2 teaspoons sliced almonds

1. Preheat oven to 450°.
2. Weigh or lightly spoon flour into dry measuring cups; level with a knife. Combine flour, 5 tablespoons sugar, baking powder, and salt in a bowl; stir with a whisk. Cut in butter using a pastry blender or 2 knives until mixture resembles coarse meal. Stir in cherries and chocolate.
3. Combine egg, ½ cup plus 3 tablespoons milk, and almond extract, stirring well with a whisk. Add milk mixture to flour mixture, stirring just until moist. (Dough will be sticky.)

4. Pat dough into an 8-inch circle with floured hands on a baking sheet lined with parchment paper. Cut dough into 12 equal wedges, cutting into but not through dough. Brush top of dough with remaining 1 tablespoon milk, and sprinkle with remaining 1 teaspoon sugar and almonds.
5. Bake at 450° for 15 minutes or until golden brown. **Yield: 12 servings (serving size: 1 scone).**

CALORIES 186; FAT 6.9g (sat 3.9g, mono 1.5g, poly 0.4g); PROTEIN 3.7g; CARB 27.3g; FIBER 1.3g; CHOL 31mg; IRON 1.3mg; SODIUM 146mg; CALC 60mg

kitchen how-to: make scones

The secret to making tender scones is handling the dough as little as possible.

1. Combine dry ingredients, stirring well with a whisk. Cut in butter using a pastry blender or 2 knives until the mixture resembles coarse meal.
2. Combine wet ingredients. Add to dry ingredients, and stir just until moist.
3. Pat dough into a circle on a baking sheet lined with parchment paper or coated with cooking spray.
4. Dip the knife in flour before cutting the scones to prevent the dough from sticking to the knife. Cut dough into equal wedges, cutting into but not through the dough. This allows the wedges to bake as one large scone; they'll be much moister than scones baked separately.
5. Sprinkle the top of the dough with sugar before baking to add a delicious sweet crunch to your scones. You can use turbinado sugar instead of granulated, if you'd like. Turbinado's larger crystals make a pretty topping. Bake until golden.

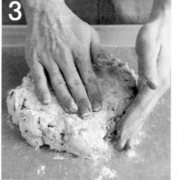

Bittersweet Chocolate
What it adds: Bittersweet chocolate adds intense chocolate flavor to these scones. Finely chopping it helps disperse it throughout the scones.

Fat-Free Half-and-Half
What it adds: Fat-free half-and-half adds richness while helping keep calories and saturated fat in check.

Bittersweet Chocolate Scones

Big bittersweet flavor shines through in these indulgent scones. They're at their best right out of the oven.

> 9 ounces all-purpose flour (about 2 cups)
> ⅓ cup sugar
> 2½ teaspoons baking powder
> ¼ teaspoon salt
> 5 tablespoons chilled butter, cut into small pieces
> 1 (4-ounce) bar bittersweet chocolate, very finely chopped
> ½ cup fat-free half-and-half
> 1 large egg
> 2 teaspoons vanilla extract
> 1 large egg white, beaten
> 2 teaspoons sugar

1. Preheat oven to 400°.
2. Weigh or lightly spoon flour into dry measuring cups; level with a knife. Combine flour, ⅓ cup sugar, baking powder, and salt in a large bowl; cut in butter with a pastry blender or 2 knives until mixture resembles coarse meal. Stir in chocolate.
3. Combine half-and-half, egg, and vanilla, stirring with a whisk until blended. Add egg mixture to flour mixture; stir with a fork just until moist.
4. Turn dough out onto a lightly floured surface. Divide dough in half. Pat each portion into 2 (5-inch) circles on a baking sheet lined with parchment paper. Cut each circle into 6 wedges, cutting into but not through dough. Brush egg white over dough; sprinkle evenly with 2 teaspoons sugar.
5. Bake at 400° for 18 minutes or until golden brown. Remove from pan; cool 2 minutes on a wire rack. Serve warm. **Yield: 12 servings (serving size: 1 scone).**

CALORIES 207; FAT 9.5g (sat 5.2g, mono 1.4g, poly 0.3g); PROTEIN 3.8g; CARB 28.3g; FIBER 1.3g; CHOL 30mg; IRON 1.3mg; SODIUM 187mg; CALC 64mg

Hazelnut Scones

4.5 ounces all-purpose flour (about 1 cup)
4.5 ounces whole-wheat pastry flour (about 1 cup)
 ¼ cup packed brown sugar
 2 teaspoons baking powder
 ½ teaspoon baking soda
 ½ teaspoon salt
 5 tablespoons chilled butter, cut into small pieces
 1 cup fat-free sour cream
 ¼ cup fat-free milk
 1 teaspoon vanilla extract
 ½ cup chopped hazelnuts, toasted and skinned
Cooking spray
 ¼ cup chocolate-hazelnut spread

1. Preheat oven to 400°.
2. Weigh or lightly spoon flours into dry measuring cups; level with a knife. Combine flours and next 4 ingredients in a large bowl. Cut in butter with a pastry blender or 2 knives until mixture resembles coarse meal. Combine sour cream, milk, and vanilla, stirring with a whisk. Add sour cream mixture and nuts to flour mixture, stirring just until moist.
3. Turn dough out onto a lightly floured surface; knead lightly 3 times with floured hands. (Dough will be sticky.) Roll dough to a ¾-inch thickness. Cut with a 2½-inch biscuit cutter into 12 rounds. Place rounds 1 inch apart on a baking sheet coated with cooking spray. Bake at 400° for 12 minutes or until golden brown. Remove scones from pan; cool on a wire rack.
4. Spoon chocolate-hazelnut spread into a small microwave-safe bowl. Microwave at HIGH 30 seconds or until warm, stirring after 15 seconds. Drizzle spread evenly over scones. **Yield: 12 servings (serving size: 1 scone).**

CALORIES 215; FAT 9.9g (sat 3.9g, mono 3.4g, poly 0.6g); PROTEIN 4.2g; CARB 28.2g; FIBER 2.3g; CHOL 15mg; IRON 1.4mg; SODIUM 286mg; CALC 99mg

kitchen how-to:
skin hazelnuts

Toasting enhances the flavor of hazelnuts, making them smoky and crunchy. After toasting, it's important to remove the bitter brown skin for a better flavor.

1. Spread shelled hazelnuts in a single layer on a baking sheet. Bake at 350° for 15 minutes or until the skins begin to split, turning once.
2. Transfer the toasted hazelnuts to a colander or dish, and rub briskly with a towel to remove the skins.

Broccoli, Pancetta, and White Cheddar Scones

A small amount of pancetta makes a big statement in these savory scones, which can be enjoyed as part of any meal.

Cooking spray
¼ cup diced pancetta (1.5 ounces)
8 ounces cake flour (about 2 cups)
1 tablespoon baking powder
¼ teaspoon roasted ground cumin
¼ teaspoon freshly ground mixed peppercorns
⅛ teaspoon salt
3 tablespoons chilled unsalted butter, cut into small pieces
1 cup finely chopped broccoli florets
½ cup (2 ounces) shredded reduced-fat sharp white cheddar cheese
¾ cup nonfat buttermilk
1 large egg

1. Preheat oven to 400°.
2. Heat a small skillet over medium-high heat. Coat pan with cooking spray. Add pancetta; sauté 3 minutes or until lightly browned. Drain.
3. Weigh or lightly spoon flour into dry measuring cups; level with a knife. Combine flour and next 4 ingredients in a large bowl; cut in butter with a pastry blender or 2 knives until mixture resembles coarse meal. Stir in pancetta, broccoli, and cheese. Combine buttermilk and egg, stirring with a whisk; add to flour mixture, stirring just until moist.
4. Turn dough out onto a lightly floured surface; knead lightly 4 to 5 times with floured hands. (Dough will feel sticky.) Pat dough into an 8-inch circle on a baking sheet coated with cooking spray. Cut dough into 8 wedges, cutting into but not through dough. Coat dough with cooking spray.
5. Bake at 400° for 16 minutes or until lightly browned. Serve warm. **Yield: 8 servings (serving size: 1 scone).**

CALORIES 204; FAT 8.6g (sat 4.7g, mono 2.5g, poly 0.5g); PROTEIN 6.8g; CARB 24.3g; FIBER 0.8g; CHOL 47mg; IRON 2.3mg; SODIUM 355mg; CALC 182mg

kitchen how-to:
easily chop broccoli

You can use a knife to finely chop broccoli, but using a box grater instead can be a real time-saver. Simply grate the head of broccoli using the larger holes of the box.

Acorn Squash Scones

Any extra squash puree can be saved for your next batch of scones. If you don't have time to bake and puree your own squash, substitute canned pumpkin.

> 1 small acorn squash (about 5 ounces)
> 10.13 ounces all-purpose flour (about 2¼ cups)
> ¼ cup granulated sugar
> 1½ teaspoons baking powder
> ½ teaspoon ground cinnamon
> ¼ teaspoon salt
> ⅛ teaspoon ground allspice
> ¼ cup unsalted butter, cut into small pieces
> ½ cup low-fat buttermilk
> 2 tablespoons turbinado sugar

1. Preheat oven to 400°.
2. Cut squash in half lengthwise. Discard seeds and membrane. Place squash, cut sides up, on a foil-lined baking sheet. Bake at 400° for 45 minutes or until tender; cool.

3. Preheat oven to 425°.
4. Scoop out squash with a spoon; discard skin. Place squash in a food processor; process until pureed, scraping sides of bowl. Measure ¾ cup squash; reserve remaining squash for another use.
5. Weigh or lightly spoon flour into dry measuring cups; level with a knife. Combine flour and next 5 ingredients in a large bowl; stir well with a whisk. Cut in butter with a pastry blender or 2 knives until mixture resembles coarse crumbs.
6. Combine buttermilk and ¾ cup pureed squash, stirring with a whisk. Add squash mixture to flour mixture; stir just until moist (dough will be very soft).
7. Place dough on a baking sheet lined with parchment paper. Pat dough into an 8-inch circle using floured hands. Cut dough into 10 wedges, cutting into but not through dough. Sprinkle dough with turbinado sugar.
8. Bake at 425° for 25 minutes or until golden brown. Serve warm. **Yield: 10 servings (serving size: 1 scone).**

CALORIES 180; FAT 5g (sat 3g, mono 1.3g, poly 0.3g); PROTEIN 3.5g; CARB 30.5g; FIBER 1.1g; CHOL 13mg; IRON 1.4mg; SODIUM 133mg; CALC 62mg

kitchen how-to:
roast & puree acorn squash

Acorn squash is at its best from early fall through winter. When selecting, look for those that are solid and heavy with stems that are full, firm, and have a corky feel. Avoid those that have cracks, soft spots, or moldy areas.

1. Cut squash in half lengthwise.
2. Scoop out membranes and seeds with a spoon, and discard.
3. Place squash, cut sides up, on a foil-lined baking sheet. Lining the pan with foil will make for easy cleanup. Bake until squash is tender. Cool until it's cool enough to handle.
4. Scoop out cooked squash with a spoon, and discard skin.
5. Place squash in a food processor; process until pureed, scraping sides of bowl. You can also use a food mill to puree it, if you'd like.

1

2

3

4

5

Butternut Squash and Sage Scones

- 9 ounces all-purpose flour (about 2 cups)
- 1 tablespoon chopped fresh sage
- 2 teaspoons baking powder
- ½ teaspoon baking soda
- ½ teaspoon salt
- ½ teaspoon freshly ground black pepper
- ¼ cup chilled butter, cut into small pieces
- 1 (12-ounce) container frozen butternut squash
- ½ cup vanilla low-fat yogurt
- 2 large egg whites
- Butter-flavored cooking spray
- 2 tablespoons grated fresh Parmesan cheese

1. Preheat oven to 425°.

2. Weigh or lightly spoon flour into dry measuring cups; level with a knife. Combine flour and next 5 ingredients in a large bowl; stir with a whisk. Cut in butter with a pastry blender or 2 knives until mixture resembles coarse meal.

3. Microwave squash according to package directions, just until thawed. Remove ½ cup squash from container, reserving remaining squash for another use. Combine ½ cup squash, yogurt, and egg whites, stirring with a whisk. Add to flour mixture; stir just until moist.

4. Knead dough lightly in bowl 3 to 4 times with floured hands. Pat dough into an 8-inch circle on a baking sheet lined with parchment paper. Cut dough into 12 wedges, cutting into but not through dough. Coat top of dough heavily with cooking spray. Sprinkle with cheese, pressing lightly to adhere.

5. Bake at 425° for 18 minutes or until golden. Serve warm. **Yield: 12 servings (serving size: 1 scone).**

CALORIES 136; FAT 4.9g (sat 2.8g, mono 1.1g, poly 0.3g); PROTEIN 3.6g; CARB 19.2g; FIBER 0.7g; CHOL 12mg; IRON 1.2mg; SODIUM 295mg; CALC 72mg

Fresh Sage
What it adds: The savory and slightly bitter flavor of sage pairs well with sweet butternut squash in these scones. We used it lightly, since its flavor can overpower a dish.

Low-Fat Yogurt
What it adds: Low-fat yogurt keeps calories in check by replacing higher-fat ingredients like shortening, oil, and butter, but it still yields a wonderfully tender texture.

Butternut Squash
What it adds: The winter squash adds a golden hue and sweet robust flavor to these scones.

Pizza Scones

Dip these bite-sized drop scones in marinara sauce for an extra punch of flavor.

6.75 ounces all-purpose flour (about 1½ cups)
1½ teaspoons baking powder
 1 teaspoon dried Italian seasoning
 ½ teaspoon salt
 ¼ cup chilled unsalted butter, cut into small pieces
 ½ cup (2 ounces) shredded reduced-fat extrasharp cheddar cheese
 ⅓ cup turkey pepperoni, finely chopped
 ¾ cup 1% low-fat milk
Olive oil–flavored cooking spray

1. Preheat oven to 425°.
2. Weigh or lightly spoon flour into dry measuring cups; level with a knife. Combine flour and next 3 ingredients in a bowl; cut in butter with a pastry blender or 2 knives until mixture resembles coarse meal. Stir in cheese and pepperoni. Add milk, stirring with a fork just until moist. (Dough will be slightly sticky.)
3. Drop dough by slightly rounded tablespoons onto a baking sheet coated with cooking spray. Coat tops of scones with cooking spray.
4. Bake at 425° for 13 minutes or until browned. Remove scones from pan; cool slightly on a wire rack. Serve warm. **Yield: 18 servings (serving size: 1 scone).**

CALORIES 80; FAT 3.7g (sat 2.2g, mono 0.8g, poly 0.2g); PROTEIN 2.8g; CARB 8.8g; FIBER 0.3g; CHOL 12mg; IRON 0.5mg; SODIUM 161mg; CALC 57mg

Turkey Pepperoni
What it adds: Turkey pepperoni still adds a kick of spicy pepperoni flavor but with fewer calories than regular pepperoni.

Italian Seasoning
What it adds: This herb blend made up of rosemary, oregano, basil, and thyme is an easy way to add intense flavor.

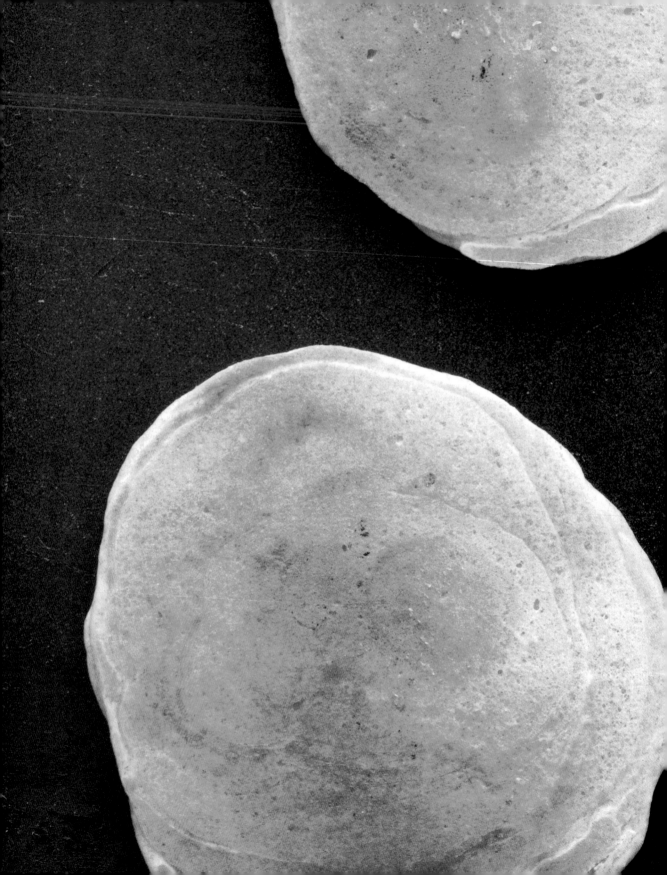

way to bake

waffles, pancakes & crepes

waffles, pancakes & crepes

Rather than the oven, these quick breads rely on the stovetop and a skillet or a waffle maker to create their characteristic flavors—favorites for the weekend or weeknight table.

Mix It

Waffles and pancakes fall into the category of quick breads because they are leavened with baking powder, baking soda, or both, as compared to yeast breads that require long rising times before baking. They are mixed together much the way muffins are, but have a higher liquid-to-dry ingredient ratio and are usually beaten with a whisk to make the batter more pourable.

Don't Rush

When making these types of quick breads, the hardest part can be not rushing the cooking process. So don't amp up the heat in order to cook your pancakes or crepes a little faster—you'll just end up with an exterior that burns before the interior is done. Cook at the heat recommended for each recipe, and wait for the exterior of the waffle, pancakes, French toast, or crepe to turn a golden brown. The results and the wait will be worth it.

Keep It Warm

Since waffles, pancakes, and crepes are made one or a few at a time, you'll want to keep the cooked ones warm while you finish preparing the rest. Preheat the oven to 200°, and place the prepared food on a baking pan or oven-safe platter.

waffles

Waffles are the ideal breakfast (or weeknight dinner). Not only are they delicious, but they are also easy to make and cook quickly.

kitchen how-to: make waffles

A basic waffle batter is usually a simple mix of flour, baking powder, salt, milk, oil, and eggs, plus any spices and seasonings you like to make it sweet or savory.

1. Preheat the waffle iron, and then coat the iron with cooking spray.
2. For a 4-inch waffle iron, pour about ⅓ cup batter onto the hot waffle iron. Belgian waffle makers require more batter to fill them out.
3. Spread batter to edges, and close lid.
4. The general rule is to cook the waffle until the iron stops steaming, but cooking times can vary, so check your manufacturer's instructions. In general, each waffle will cook 5 to 6 minutes. Cook them a little bit longer if you like a crisper waffle.

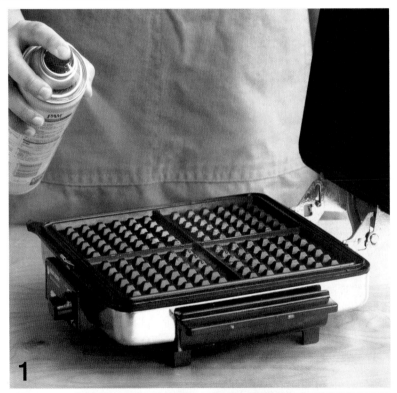

1

2

3

4

Weekend Waffles

6.75 ounces all-purpose flour (about 1½ cups)
2.38 ounces whole-wheat flour (about ½ cup)
 1½ tablespoons ground cinnamon
 2½ teaspoons baking powder
  ½ teaspoon salt
  2 cups 1% low-fat milk
  ¼ cup canola oil
  2 large egg yolks
  2 large egg whites
Dash of sugar
Cooking spray
  1 cup maple syrup
Whole or sliced strawberries (optional)

1. Weigh or lightly spoon flours into dry measuring cups; level with a knife. Combine flours and next 3 ingredients in a large bowl; stir with a whisk. Combine milk, oil, and egg yolks; add to flour mixture, stirring until smooth.

2. Place egg whites in a large bowl, and beat with a mixer at high speed until foamy. Add sugar, beating until soft peaks form. Fold egg white mixture into batter.

3. Preheat waffle iron. Coat iron with cooking spray. Spoon about ⅓ cup batter per 4-inch waffle onto hot waffle iron, spreading batter to edges. Cook 5 to 6 minutes or until steaming stops; repeat procedure with remaining batter. Serve with syrup; garnish with strawberries, if desired. **Yield: 8 servings (serving size: 2 waffles and 2 tablespoons syrup).**

CALORIES 328; FAT 9.3g (sat 1.9g, mono 2.2g, poly 4.9g); PROTEIN 7.3g; CARB 55.7g; FIBER 2.5g; CHOL 55mg; IRON 2.2mg; SODIUM 320mg; CALC 202mg

Apple Pie Waffles

As their name implies, Honeycrisp apples have a crisp texture and juicy flesh that holds up well during cooking. Try Granny Smith for a tart substitute.

6.75 ounces all-purpose flour (about 1½ cups)
  2 teaspoons baking powder
1½ teaspoons apple pie spice
  ¼ teaspoon salt
  1 cup 1% low-fat milk
  ¼ cup packed dark brown sugar
  1 tablespoon canola oil
  5 large egg whites, divided
  ½ cup grated peeled Honeycrisp apple
Cooking spray
  ⅔ cup maple syrup
Apple slices (optional)

1. Weigh or lightly spoon flour into dry measuring cups; level with a knife. Combine flour and next 3 ingredients in a large bowl, stirring with a whisk. Combine milk, brown sugar, oil, and 4 egg whites in a bowl; add to flour mixture, stirring just until moist. Stir in grated apple.
2. Beat remaining 1 egg white with a mixer until stiff peaks form; fold into batter.
3. Preheat waffle iron. Coat iron with cooking spray. Spoon about ¼ cup batter per 4-inch waffle onto hot waffle iron, spreading batter to edges. Cook 6 to 7 minutes or until steaming stops; repeat procedure with remaining batter. Serve immediately with syrup and, if desired, apple slices. **Yield: 6 servings (serving size: 2 waffles and about 1½ tablespoons syrup).**

CALORIES 299; FAT 3.7g (sat 0.7g, mono 1.3g, poly 1.4g); PROTEIN 6.6g; CARB 60.7g; FIBER 1.3g; CHOL 2mg; IRON 2.3mg; SODIUM 283mg; CALC 176mg

kitchen how-to: select a waffle iron

It's best to select a waffle iron with a nonstick surface so there's no need to add oil or butter to prevent sticking. This variety is also easy to clean. Let the iron cool completely; then just wipe it with a damp cloth or paper towel to pick up any remaining crumbs—no soap required. Choose one with a range of temperature settings so you can adjust doneness to suit your taste. A Belgian waffle maker produces larger waffles with deeper indentations. It requires more batter per waffle, though, so take that into account when you're making them. Generally, if you use ⅓ cup batter per waffle in a regular waffle iron, you'll need about ½ cup in a Belgian waffle iron.

Bacon-Maple Waffles

Bacon and maple are a natural match—maybe that's why many people dip bacon into their pancake syrup. In this recipe, crumbled bacon is cooked into maple-sweetened waffles, so every bite contains that classic pairing.

    9   ounces all-purpose flour (about 2 cups)
    1   tablespoon baking powder
    ¼   teaspoon salt
    1¼ cups 2% reduced-fat milk
    3   tablespoons maple syrup
    2   tablespoons butter, melted
    4   center-cut bacon slices, cooked and
        crumbled
    3   large eggs, lightly beaten
        Cooking spray
    ⅓   cup maple syrup (optional)

1. Weigh or lightly spoon flour into dry measuring cups; level with a knife. Combine flour, baking powder, and salt in a bowl, stirring with a whisk. Make a well in center of mixture. Combine milk and next 4 ingredients, stirring with a whisk. Add milk mixture to flour mixture; stir just until moist.

2. Preheat waffle iron. Coat iron with cooking spray. Spoon about ⅓ cup batter per 4-inch waffle onto hot waffle iron, spreading batter to edges. Cook 4 to 5 minutes or until steaming stops; repeat procedure with remaining batter. Serve waffles with maple syrup, if desired. **Yield: 5 servings (serving size: 2 waffles).**

CALORIES 341; FAT 10.5g (sat 5.1g, mono 2.7g, poly 0.8g); PROTEIN 12.7g; CARB 48g; FIBER 1.4g; CHOL 148mg; IRON 2.9mg; SODIUM 526mg; CALC 240mg

all about
maple syrup grades

The U.S. Department of Agriculture has set the standard by which maple syrup is graded. Grading is based on the color of the syrup, not the flavor—though color is a general indication of flavor (the lighter the color, the more delicate the taste). Each bottle of syrup is labeled with one of four grades.

• U.S. Grade A Light Amber is the lightest in color—transparent gold—and flavor. Although it can be used at the table for pancakes and waffles, it's often poured over ice cream or used to make maple candy.

• U.S. Grade A Medium Amber is darker than Grade A Light and has a slightly more intense maple flavor. It is the most popular grade of table syrup.

• U.S. Grade A Dark Amber has an even stronger flavor, is somewhat thicker, and is often used in cooking. The darker syrup (including Grade B syrup) is preferred for cooking because the assertive taste is apparent even when the syrup is combined and cooked with other ingredients.

• U.S. Grade B is sometimes called "cooking syrup" and is preferred by many chefs for baking and cooking because of its deep maple flavor and caramel undertones.

pancakes

Easy and delicious, pancakes are crowd-pleasers and are open to endless variations.

Whole-Wheat Buttermilk Pancakes

3.6   ounces whole-wheat flour (about ¾ cup)

3.4   ounces all-purpose flour (about ¾ cup)

  3   tablespoons sugar

1½   teaspoons baking powder

  ½   teaspoon baking soda

  ½   teaspoon salt

1½   cups low-fat buttermilk

  1   tablespoon canola oil

  1   large egg

  1   large egg white

  ¾   cup maple syrup

  3   tablespoons butter

1. Weigh or lightly spoon flours into dry measuring cups; level with a knife. Combine flours and next 4 ingredients in a large bowl, stirring with a whisk.

Combine buttermilk and next 3 ingredients, stirring with a whisk. Add buttermilk mixture to flour mixture, stirring just until moist.

2. Pour about ¼ cup batter per pancake onto a hot nonstick griddle or nonstick skillet. Cook over medium heat 2 minutes or until tops are covered with bubbles and edges look cooked. Carefully turn pancakes over; cook 2 minutes or until bottoms are lightly browned. Serve with syrup and butter. **Yield: 6 servings (serving size: 2 pancakes, 2 tablespoons syrup, and 1½ teaspoons butter).**

CALORIES 351; FAT 10g (sat 4.6g, mono 2.8g, poly 1.9g); PROTEIN 7.6g; CARB 59.7g; FIBER 2.3g; CHOL 55mg; IRON 2.1mg; SODIUM 570mg; CALC 176mg

kitchen how-to:
make perfect pancakes

Always pour the wet ingredients into the dry ones to avoid clumps. Stir until the batter is smooth, and use it immediately. If you wait too long, it will thicken.

1. Preheat a large nonstick griddle or nonstick skillet over medium heat. Medium heat is key since a higher heat will burn the pancakes. For precision, use a measuring cup to spoon ¼ cup of batter per pancake into the pan. Pour the batter and let it spread, rather than pouring it in a circle.

2. Cook 1 to 2 minutes or until bubbles begin to cover the surface and the edges look cooked, and then slide a spatula beneath the pancake. Quickly flip it over, and cook 2 more minutes or until the bottoms are lightly browned.

Oatmeal Pancakes

- **1.1** ounces all-purpose flour (about ¼ cup)
- **1** cup quick-cooking oats
- **1** tablespoon sugar
- **½** teaspoon baking powder
- **½** teaspoon baking soda
- **¼** teaspoon ground cinnamon
- **⅛** teaspoon salt
- **1** cup nonfat buttermilk
- **2** tablespoons butter, melted
- **1** large egg

1. Weigh or lightly spoon flour into a dry measuring cup; level with a knife. Combine flour and next 6 ingredients in a medium bowl, stirring with a whisk.
2. Combine buttermilk, butter, and egg in a small bowl. Add to flour mixture, stirring just until moist.
3. Pour about 2½ tablespoons batter per pancake onto a hot nonstick griddle or nonstick skillet. Cook over medium heat 1 to 2 minutes or until tops are covered with bubbles and edges look cooked. Carefully turn pancakes over; cook 1 to 2 minutes or until bottoms are lightly browned. **Yield: 3 servings (serving size: 4 pancakes).**

CALORIES 273; FAT 11.2g (sat 5.7g, mono 3.3g, poly 1.3g); PROTEIN 10g; CARB 34.7g; FIBER 2.8g; CHOL 91mg; IRON 2.1mg; SODIUM 526mg; CALC 184mg

kitchen how-to:
make silver dollar pancakes

These small pancakes are 2 to 3 inches in diameter. Preheat a nonstick griddle or nonstick skillet over medium heat. Using a measuring spoon, pour 2½ tablespoons batter per pancake onto the pan. You can adjust the measurements slightly up or down, depending on how small you'd like to make them.

Lemon–Poppy Seed Pancakes

Drizzle these pancakes with maple syrup, or top with a dusting of powdered sugar and serve with fresh berries.

7.9 ounces all-purpose flour (about 1¾ cups)
  3 tablespoons sugar
  2 tablespoons poppy seeds
  1 tablespoon baking powder
  ½ teaspoon salt
  ¼ teaspoon baking soda
1¼ cups fat-free half-and-half
  ½ cup light sour cream
  3 tablespoons butter, melted
  2 tablespoons grated lemon rind
  1 teaspoon vanilla extract
  1 large egg yolk
  2 large egg whites

1. Weigh or lightly spoon flour into dry measuring cups; level with a knife. Combine flour and next 5 ingredients in a large bowl; stir with a whisk. Combine half-and-half and next 5 ingredients in a small bowl, stirring with a whisk until blended; add to flour mixture, stirring until smooth.
2. Beat egg whites with a mixer at high speed until stiff peaks form; gently fold into batter. (Batter will be thick.)
3. Pour about ¼ cup batter per pancake onto a hot nonstick griddle or nonstick skillet. Cook over medium heat 2 minutes or until tops are covered with bubbles and edges look cooked. Carefully turn pancakes over; cook 2 minutes or until bottoms are lightly browned.
Yield: 9 servings (serving size: 2 pancakes).

CALORIES 208; FAT 7.2g (sat 3.7g, mono 1.8g, poly 1.1g); PROTEIN 5.1g; CARB 28.3g; FIBER 1g; CHOL 39mg; IRON 1.5mg; SODIUM 388mg; CALC 162mg

kitchen how-to: make fluffy pancakes

Folding stiffly beaten egg whites into pancake batter gives pancakes structure while keeping them light and airy. Be sure to beat egg whites with clean beaters in a clean bowl, and be careful when separating the eggs. Even a small bit of food, grease, or egg yolk will prevent the whites from achieving full volume.

1. Beat egg whites with a mixer at high speed until stiff peaks form.
2. Gently fold the beaten egg whites into the batter, being careful not to overmix. Too much stirring can deflate the whites.

Blueberry Pancakes

These pancakes reheat well in the toaster oven, so you can make a big batch to enjoy all week.

2.38 ounces whole-wheat flour (about ½ cup)
2.25 ounces all-purpose flour (about ½ cup)
   1 tablespoon sugar
   1 teaspoon baking powder
   ½ teaspoon baking soda
   ⅛ teaspoon salt
   ⅛ teaspoon ground nutmeg
   ¾ cup vanilla fat-free yogurt
   2 tablespoons butter, melted
   2 teaspoons fresh lemon juice
   ½ teaspoon vanilla extract
   2 large eggs, lightly beaten
   1 cup fresh blueberries

1. Weigh or lightly spoon flours into dry measuring cups; level with a knife. Combine flours and next 5 ingredients in a large bowl, stirring well with a whisk. Combine yogurt and next 4 ingredients in a small bowl; add to flour mixture, stirring until smooth.

2. Pour about ¼ cup batter per pancake onto a hot nonstick griddle or nonstick skillet. Top each pancake with 2 tablespoons blueberries. Cook over medium heat 2 minutes or until tops are covered with bubbles and edges look cooked. Carefully turn pancakes over; cook 2 minutes or until bottoms are lightly browned. **Yield: 4 servings (serving size: 2 pancakes).**

CALORIES 272; FAT 8.8g (sat 4.5g, mono 2.5g, poly 0.8g); PROTEIN 9.5g; CARB 40.1g; FIBER 3.2g; CHOL 122mg; IRON 2mg; SODIUM 403mg; CALC 192mg

kitchen how-to: make perfect blueberry pancakes

Blueberries have a striking deep-blue color that means they're loaded with good-for-you antioxidants. Look for plump berries with a white bloom on them—the white dusty coating. If there's no bloom, it means they're probably past their prime. Wash the berries just before you use them.

1. Pour about ¼ cup batter per pancake onto a hot nonstick griddle or skillet.

2. Top each pancake with 2 tablespoons blueberries, and cook over medium heat until done.

Pancakes with Peanut Butter–Banana Compote

You can drizzle these pancakes with maple syrup, too, if you'd like.

Pancakes:
- 4.5 ounces all-purpose flour (about 1 cup)
- 1.85 ounces almond flour (about ½ cup)
- 3 tablespoons sugar
- 2 teaspoons baking powder
- ½ teaspoon baking soda
- ½ teaspoon salt
- 1½ cups low-fat buttermilk
- 1 tablespoon canola oil
- 2 large eggs

Compote:
- ½ cup banana nectar
- 1 tablespoon creamy peanut butter
- 1 cup chopped banana (2 bananas)

1. To prepare pancakes, weigh or lightly spoon flours into dry measuring cups; level with a knife. Combine flours and next 4 ingredients in a large bowl, stirring with a whisk. Combine buttermilk, oil, and eggs in a small bowl, stirring well with a whisk. Add buttermilk mixture to flour mixture, stirring until smooth.

2. Pour about ¼ cup batter per pancake onto a hot nonstick griddle or nonstick skillet. Cook over medium heat 2 minutes or until tops are covered with bubbles and edges look cooked. Carefully turn pancakes over; cook 2 minutes or until bottoms are lightly browned.

3. To prepare banana compote, bring banana nectar to a simmer in a small saucepan. Add peanut butter, stirring until blended; remove from heat. Add banana, and toss to coat. Serve pancakes with compote.

Yield: 6 servings (serving size: 2 pancakes and 3 tablespoons compote).

CALORIES 273; FAT 10.6g (sat 1.7g, mono 2.9g, poly 1.4g); PROTEIN 9.2g; CARB 37.5g; FIBER 2.5g; CHOL 73mg; IRON 1.8mg; SODIUM 533mg; CALC 185mg

kitchen how-to:
make banana compote

You can use this sweet topping on any flavor of pancake and skip the maple syrup.

1. Bring banana nectar to a simmer in a small saucepan. Add peanut butter, and stir until blended.
2. Remove pan from heat. Add chopped banana.
3. Toss to coat.

S'mores Pancakes

- 3.4 ounces all-purpose flour (about ¾ cup)
- ⅔ cup graham cracker crumbs
- 2 tablespoons toasted wheat germ
- 1 tablespoon baking powder
- ¼ teaspoon salt
- 1¼ cups fat-free milk
- 1 large egg
- 2 tablespoons butter, melted
- 10 teaspoons marshmallow creme
- 5 tablespoons fat-free chocolate syrup
- ¼ cup semisweet chocolate minichips

1. Weigh or lightly spoon flour into a dry measuring cup; level with a knife. Combine flour and next 4 ingredients in a medium bowl, stirring well with a whisk. Combine milk, egg, and butter in a bowl, stirring with a whisk. Add milk mixture to flour mixture, stirring just until smooth. Let batter stand 3 minutes.

2. Pour about ¼ cup batter per pancake onto a hot nonstick griddle or nonstick skillet. Cook over medium heat 3 minutes or until tops are covered with bubbles and edges look cooked. Carefully turn pancakes over; cook 1 to 2 minutes or until bottoms are lightly browned. Top each serving with 2 teaspoons marshmallow creme, 1 tablespoon chocolate syrup, and about 1 tablespoon chocolate chips. **Yield: 5 servings (serving size: 2 pancakes).**

CALORIES 314; FAT 10g (sat 5g, mono 2.9g, poly 1.1g); PROTEIN 7.8g; CARB 49.5g; FIBER 2.3g; CHOL 56mg; IRON 2mg; SODIUM 511mg; CALC 237mg

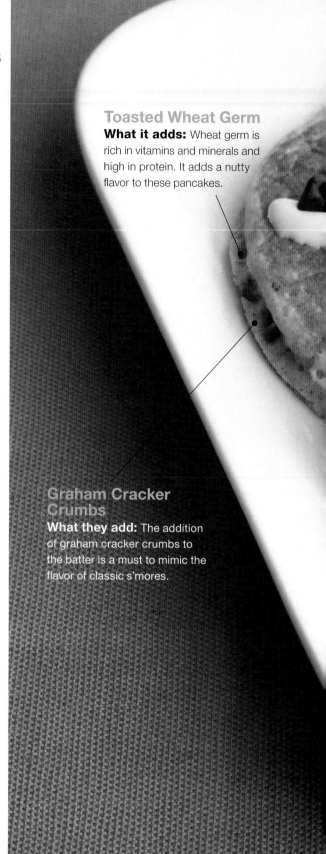

Toasted Wheat Germ
What it adds: Wheat germ is rich in vitamins and minerals and high in protein. It adds a nutty flavor to these pancakes.

Graham Cracker Crumbs
What they add: The addition of graham cracker crumbs to the batter is a must to mimic the flavor of classic s'mores.

Chocolate Minichips

What they add: Minichips sprinkled over the top
of these pancakes provide a sweet burst of chocolaty
flavor. You can stir them into the batter, if you like, or
leave them out altogether to simplify the dish.

Raspberry Dutch Baby

  2   large eggs
  2   tablespoons sugar
  ½   teaspoon grated lemon rind
  ¼   teaspoon salt
2.25 ounces all-purpose flour (about ½ cup)
  ¾   cup 2% reduced-fat milk
  1   tablespoon butter
  1   cup fresh raspberries
  2   tablespoons powdered sugar

1. Place a 9-inch cast-iron skillet in oven; preheat oven to 450°.

2. While pan heats, combine first 4 ingredients in a medium bowl; stir with a whisk. Weigh or lightly spoon flour into a dry measuring cup; level with a knife. Add flour and milk to egg mixture, stirring with a whisk until smooth.

3. Melt butter in preheated pan, swirling to coat pan. Add batter; sprinkle with raspberries. Bake at 450° for 12 minutes or until puffed and browned.

4. Dust pancake with powdered sugar, and cut into 6 wedges. Serve immediately. **Yield: 6 servings (serving size: 1 wedge).**

CALORIES 131; FAT 4.4g (sat 2.1g, mono 1.3g, poly 0.4g); PROTEIN 4.5g; CARB 18.8g; FIBER 1.6g; CHOL 78mg; IRON 1mg; SODIUM 147mg; CALC 52mg

kitchen how-to: make an oven-puffed pancake

An oven-puffed pancake, also known as a Dutch baby or German pancake, is essentially a large popover leavened with steam. It falls quickly after removal from the oven, so have everyone seated at the table to enjoy the dramatic presentation of this striking pancake.

1. Prepare batter. Generally the batter is made with eggs, flour, and milk; vanilla, cinnamon, and sometimes sugar are added for sweetness. Place a cast-iron skillet in the oven while the oven preheats. Remove the hot pan from the oven, and add butter, swirling to allow it to melt and coat the pan.

2. Add batter.

3. You can top the batter with berries or leave it plain, if you like. Bake until puffed and browned. Dust with powdered sugar.

German Apple Pancake

Batter:

2.25	ounces all-purpose flour (about ½ cup)
1	tablespoon granulated sugar
½	teaspoon baking powder
⅛	teaspoon salt
⅛	teaspoon grated whole nutmeg
8	large egg whites
1	cup fat-free milk
2	tablespoons butter, melted
1	teaspoon vanilla extract

Apple Mixture:

	Cooking spray
½	cup granulated sugar, divided
½	teaspoon ground cinnamon
½	teaspoon grated whole nutmeg
1	cup thinly sliced Granny Smith apple

Remaining Ingredient:

1	tablespoon powdered sugar

1. To prepare batter, weigh or lightly spoon flour into a dry measuring cup; level with a knife. Combine flour, 1 tablespoon granulated sugar, baking powder, salt, and ⅛ teaspoon nutmeg in a medium bowl, stirring with a whisk. Combine egg whites and next 3 ingredients in a small bowl, stirring with a whisk. Add egg white mixture to flour mixture, stirring with a whisk. Let stand 30 minutes.

2. Preheat oven to 425°.

3. To prepare apple mixture, coat bottom and sides of a 10-inch ovenproof skillet with cooking spray. Combine ¼ cup granulated sugar, cinnamon, and ½ teaspoon nutmeg; sprinkle evenly over bottom and sides of pan. Arrange apple in an even spokelike layer in pan. Sprinkle apple with remaining ¼ cup granulated sugar. Cook over medium heat 8 minutes or until mixture bubbles. Slowly pour batter over apple mixture.

4. Bake at 425° for 15 minutes. Reduce oven temperature to 375° (do not remove pancake from oven); bake an additional 13 minutes or until center is set. Carefully loosen pancake with a spatula. Gently slide pancake onto a serving platter. Sift powdered sugar over top. Cut into 6 wedges; serve immediately. **Yield: 6 servings (serving size: 1 wedge).**

CALORIES 173; FAT 5.4g (sat 2.8g, mono 1.4g, poly 0.9g); PROTEIN 7.7g; CARB 23.2g; FIBER 0.9g; CHOL 11mg; IRON 1.5mg; SODIUM 213mg; CALC 101mg

Egg Whites & Milk
What they add: This mixture of egg whites and fat-free milk creates a wonderful custardlike texture beneath the sweet apple topping.

Granny Smith Apple
What it adds: This apple variety adds a tart flavor to this pancake. You could substitute Pippin, Northern Spy, or Sierra Beauty, if you'd like.

french toast

This classic breakfast of bread soaked in a mixture of beaten eggs, milk, and cinnamon and then toasted in a pan is a memorable way to begin your day.

Ciabatta French Toast with Orange Marmalade Drizzle

Sturdy ciabatta bread makes for great French toast; you can use the remaining bread for lunch.

⅓ **cup fresh orange juice**
½ **cup orange marmalade**
½ **cup 2% reduced-fat milk**
½ **teaspoon ground cinnamon**
2 **large eggs**
8 **(1-ounce) slices ciabatta bread**
2 **tablespoons butter**

1. Place orange juice and marmalade in a small saucepan over medium heat; bring to a simmer. Remove from heat; keep warm.

2. Combine milk, cinnamon, and eggs in a shallow dish; stir with a whisk. Dip bread slices in egg mixture; let slices stand in egg mixture 20 seconds on each side.
3. Melt 1 tablespoon butter in a large nonstick skillet over medium-high heat. Place 4 bread slices in pan; cook 2 minutes on each side or until lightly browned. Remove from pan. Repeat procedure with remaining 1 tablespoon butter and bread slices. Drizzle with marmalade syrup. **Yield: 4 servings (serving size: 2 bread slices and about 3 tablespoons syrup).**

CALORIES 360; FAT 11.3g (sat 5g, mono 4.5g, poly 0.8g); PROTEIN 9.4g; CARB 56.9g; FIBER 1.2g; CHOL 123mg; IRON 2.4mg; SODIUM 479mg; CALC 58mg

kitchen how-to: make French toast

A sturdy bread is essential when making French toast. Bread sliced too thinly tends to get mushy and fall apart after soaking in the egg-milk mixture.

1. A basic dipping mixture for French toast usually includes milk, eggs, and cinnamon, but feel free to add any additional spices you like.

Combine them in a shallow dish, stirring with a whisk.

2. Dip bread slices in the egg mixture, and let them stand 20 seconds per side. Don't let the bread stand for too much longer since it could result in mushy toast.

3. You can coat the pan with cooking spray, if you like, or use butter to add rich flavor. Use about

1 tablespoon per batch, and melt it in a large skillet over medium-high heat.

4. Place bread slices in pan. Unless you're cooking for a small number, you'll need to cook the toast in batches.

5. Cook 2 minutes on each side or until bread is lightly browned. Remove from pan, and drizzle with syrup.

French Toast with Maple-Apple Compote

Compote:
Cooking spray
1 tablespoon butter
3 cups sliced peeled Pink Lady apple (about 1½ pounds)
¼ cup maple syrup
½ teaspoon ground cinnamon

French Toast:
2 tablespoons granulated sugar
1 teaspoon ground cinnamon
1 cup 2% reduced-fat milk
2 teaspoons vanilla extract
⅛ teaspoon salt
4 large eggs, lightly beaten
12 (1-ounce) slices challah bread
4 teaspoons butter
Powdered sugar (optional)

1. Preheat oven to 250°. Place wire rack on a baking sheet, and place in oven.
2. To prepare compote, heat a large nonstick skillet over medium-high heat. Coat pan with cooking spray; melt 1 tablespoon butter in pan. Add apple to pan; sauté 8 minutes or until tender. Stir in maple syrup and ½ teaspoon cinnamon. Keep warm.
3. To prepare French toast, combine granulated sugar and 1 teaspoon cinnamon in a medium bowl, stirring with a whisk. Add milk and next 3 ingredients; stir with a whisk until well blended. Working with 1 bread slice at a time, dip bread slices in milk mixture, turning gently to coat both sides.
4. Heat a large nonstick skillet over medium-high heat. Melt 1 teaspoon butter in pan. Add 3 coated bread slices; cook 2 minutes on each side or until lightly browned. Place on rack in oven to keep warm. Repeat procedure 3 times with remaining 3 teaspoons butter and remaining 9 coated bread slices. Serve French toast with compote. Sprinkle with powdered sugar, if desired. **Yield: 6 servings (serving size: 2 pieces toast and about ⅓ cup compote).**

CALORIES 370; FAT 12.1g (sat 5.3g, mono 4g, poly 1.3g); PROTEIN 11.3g; CARB 55.3g; FIBER 2.9g; CHOL 185mg; IRON 2.7mg; SODIUM 427mg; CALC 146mg

Apple Compote
What it adds: This topping is a sweet replacement for traditional syrup. Pink Lady apples hold up well to being sautéed, but Liberty, Fuji, or Jonagold apples would also work.

Challah

What it adds: This sweet egg bread is a sturdy option for French toast. Substitute Hawaiian bread if challah isn't available.

crepes

Versatile crepes can be made ahead or made to order and paired with a variety of sweet and savory fillings.

Basic Crepes

Although you'll only need about 3 tablespoons batter to make each crepe, we found a ¼-cup dry measuring cup is the best tool to scoop and pour the batter into the pan so the crepes cook evenly. The small amount of sugar gives the crepes a golden appearance and crisp edges without adding noticeable sweetness, so this recipe works in both savory and sweet applications. Fill crepes with sausage and cheese for breakfast; chicken, pork, or vegetables for lunch; or a spinach and mushroom mixture for a side dish at dinner.

4.5 ounces all-purpose flour (about 1 cup)
  2 teaspoons sugar
  ¼ teaspoon salt
  1 cup 1% low-fat milk
  ½ cup water
  2 teaspoons butter, melted
  2 large eggs

1. Weigh or lightly spoon flour into a dry measuring cup; level with a knife. Combine flour, sugar, and salt in a small bowl. Combine milk and next 3 ingredients in a blender. Add flour mixture to milk mixture in blender, and process until smooth. Cover batter; chill for 1 hour.
2. Heat an 8-inch nonstick skillet or crepe pan over medium heat. Pour a scant ¼ cup batter (about 3 tablespoons) into pan; quickly tilt pan in all directions so batter covers pan with a thin film. Cook about 1 minute. Carefully lift edge of crepe with a spatula to test for doneness. Turn crepe over when it can be shaken loose from pan and underside is lightly browned; cook 30 seconds or until center is set.
3. Place crepe on a towel; cool completely. Repeat procedure with remaining batter, stirring batter between crepes. Stack crepes between single layers of wax paper to prevent sticking. **Yield: 13 servings (serving size: 1 crepe).**

CALORIES 62; FAT 1.6g (sat 0.8g, mono 0.5g, poly 0.2g); PROTEIN 2.6g; CARB 8.9g; FIBER 0.3g; CHOL 35mg; IRON 0.6mg; SODIUM 70mg; CALC 29mg

kitchen how-to:
make crepes

The consistency of the crepe batter is key—it should be similar to that of heavy whipping cream. This produces a thin, even crepe with enough structure to hold it together. The trickiest part of the process is swirling just the right amount of batter in the pan. It's not difficult; it just takes a little practice. Crepes will keep 5 days if stacked between layers of wax paper and chilled. Or, freeze them for up to 2 months.

1. An 8-inch nonstick skillet or crepe pan, a ¼-cup dry measuring cup, and a rubber spatula are the only tools needed to cook beautiful crepes. But a blender and whisk ensure a smooth batter.

2. Simply combine all the ingredients in a blender, and process to make the batter.

3. The consistency of the batter after it rests should be about that of unwhipped heavy whipping cream.

4. Add the batter to the center of the pan, and gently tilt the pan in a circular motion, allowing the batter to reach the sides of the pan.

5. After 1 minute, the edges of the crepe should be crisp, the underside brown, and the center will come loose if you gently shake the pan. Carefully flip the crepe.

6. Spoon filling evenly down the center of each crepe. Fold the ends and sides over to completely cover the filling. You can stack, roll, or fold the crepes any way you wish.

Savory Buckwheat Crepes with Ham and Mornay Sauce

Crepes:
- 3 ounces all-purpose flour (about ⅔ cup)
- 1 cup fat-free milk
- 2 tablespoons buckwheat flour
- ¼ teaspoon salt
- 1 large egg, lightly beaten

Cooking spray

Filling:
- 1 cup chopped 33%-less-sodium smoked ham (about 3 ounces)
- 1 garlic clove, thinly sliced
- 4 cups sliced shiitake mushroom caps (about 10 ounces)
- ½ cup fat-free, lower-sodium chicken broth
- 1 tablespoon minced fresh flat-leaf parsley
- ¼ teaspoon freshly ground black pepper
- 4 tablespoons (1 ounce) shredded Gruyère cheese

Sauce:
- 2 tablespoons butter
- 3 tablespoons minced shallots
- 1 tablespoon all-purpose flour
- 1½ cups fat-free milk
- ½ cup (2 ounces) shredded Gruyère cheese
- ¼ teaspoon salt
- ¼ teaspoon freshly ground black pepper

Dash of grated whole nutmeg

1. To prepare crepes, weigh or lightly spoon 3 ounces all-purpose flour (about ⅔ cup) into dry measuring cups; level with a knife. Combine all-purpose flour and next 4 ingredients in a bowl, stirring with a whisk until smooth. Cover and let stand at room temperature 30 minutes.

2. Heat a 9-inch nonstick skillet or crepe pan over medium heat. Coat pan with cooking spray. Pour about ¼ cup batter into center of pan; quickly tilt pan in all directions so batter covers pan with a thin film. Cook about 1 minute. Carefully lift edge of crepe with a spatula to test for doneness. Turn crepe over when it can be shaken loose from pan and underside is lightly browned; cook 30 seconds. Place crepe on a towel; cool. Repeat procedure 5 times with remaining batter. Stack crepes between single layers of wax paper or paper towels to prevent sticking.

3. Preheat oven to 300°.

4. To prepare filling, heat a large nonstick skillet over medium heat. Coat pan with cooking spray. Add ham and garlic to pan; cook 3 minutes or until garlic is tender and ham is lightly browned, stirring frequently. Add mushrooms; reduce heat to medium-low. Cover and cook 10 minutes or until mushrooms start to soften, stirring occasionally. Add broth, parsley, and pepper; cook, uncovered, 10 minutes or until liquid evaporates and mushrooms are tender. Remove from heat.

5. Spoon ⅓ cup ham mixture into center of each crepe. Top each serving with about 1 tablespoon cheese; fold sides over. Place filled crepes in an 11 x 7–inch glass or ceramic baking dish. Cover with foil; bake at 300° for 20 minutes or until thoroughly heated.

6. To prepare sauce, melt butter in a medium saucepan over medium-low heat. Add shallots; cook 5 minutes or until tender, stirring frequently. Sprinkle 1 tablespoon all-purpose flour into pan; cook 2 minutes, stirring constantly. Slowly add 1½ cups milk, stirring constantly with a whisk until smooth; bring to a simmer over medium heat. Reduce heat, and simmer 10 minutes or until sauce thickens, stirring frequently. Remove from heat. Strain sauce through a fine sieve into a bowl; discard solids. Rinse and dry pan; place over low heat, and return strained sauce to pan. Stir in ½ cup cheese and remaining ingredients; stir until cheese melts. Serve sauce with crepes. **Yield: 6 servings (serving size: 1 filled crepe and about 2½ tablespoons sauce).**

CALORIES 239; FAT 10.5g (sat 5.7g, mono 3.3g, poly 0.7g); PROTEIN 14.4g; CARB 22g; FIBER 1.5g; CHOL 71mg; IRON 1.8mg; SODIUM 507mg; CALC 284mg

buckwheat flour

Buckwheat flour has a rich, nutty flavor. Buckwheat is a whole grain, which means it carries many health benefits. Not only does it help reduce blood cholesterol levels, it is also high in fiber and protein.

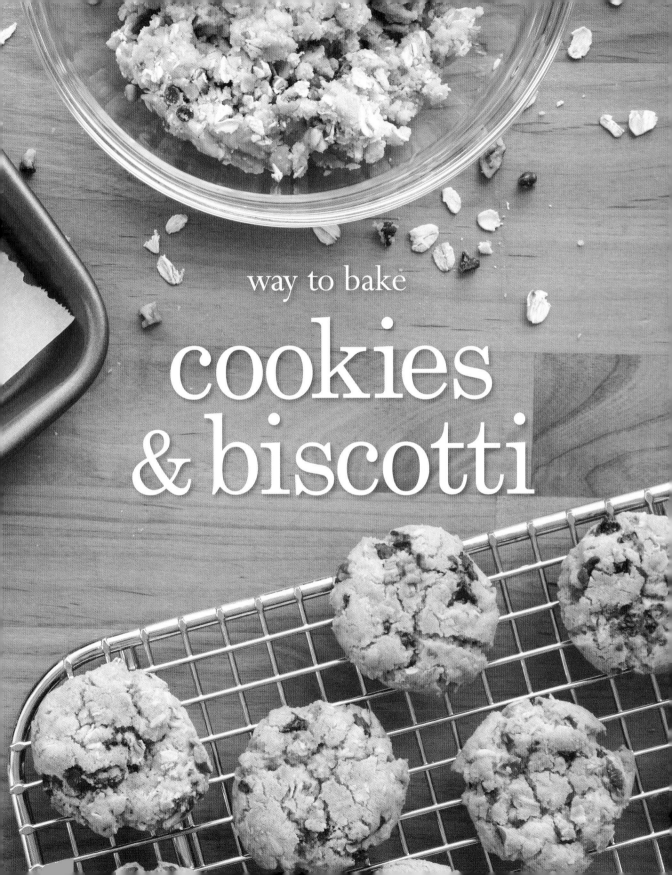

way to bake

cookies
& biscotti

cookies & biscotti

Our cookies and biscotti use less fat than traditional versions, and these healthier trade-offs mean there's a narrower margin for error. We'll fill you in on all the types of cookies and share what you need to know to achieve delicious results.

The Right Fat

When making cookies and biscotti with less fat and fewer calories, knowing a few tricks will help ensure success every time. One important element is the type of fat you use. Our recipes call for oil, butter, or sometimes a blend of the two. Oil disperses better than butter and keeps the cookies moist and tender, while butter keeps the cookies from spreading too much. Don't replace butter with diet margarine, whipped butter, or tub-style spread. These have too much water or air whipped in and too little fat, which will negatively affect the texture of the cookie.

Dough Preparation

As with all baked goods, measure cookie ingredients with precision and use the exact ingredients specified. Many of our recipes first cream together butter and sugar, and then add the dry ingredients. For these recipes, start with softened butter—butter that yields slightly to pressure but doesn't lose its shape when touched. (For more information about softened butter, see page 11.) It's important not to overmix the dough once the dry ingredients are added, as the cookies and biscotti can become tough or fail to rise well. Mix just until the ingredients are combined. Some doughs are chilled before baking; this solidifies the fat and helps prevent overspreading as they bake.

Baking in Batches

If you're baking cookies or biscotti in batches using the same baking sheet, let the sheet cool completely between batches. Placing dough on a hot baking sheet will cause the dough to spread too quickly, and the results will be flat cookies and biscotti. You can quickly cool a baking sheet by placing it under cold running water. Dry it thoroughly before arranging the dough on the pan. If you bake two pans at once, rotate them halfway through the cooking time so you'll get even results.

Storage

Always store baked cookies and biscotti only after they've cooled completely. If you store them while they're still warm, condensation will make them soggy. And be sure to store them in airtight containers to prevent humidity from affecting their texture; most store well for 3 to 5 days. But different cookies sometimes call for different storage methods. When storing rolled cookies, place decorated cookies between layers of wax paper. Because biscotti are crisp and dry, they store well at room temperature for an extended period of time—up to 2 weeks. You can also freeze baked cookies for up to 3 months; thaw at room temperature for 10 to 15 minutes.

drop cookies

These cookies are some of the simplest to make. Spoon mounds of dough onto baking sheets, and bake.

kitchen how-to:
make drop cookies

Ensure even baking by dropping the same amount of dough for each cookie. Use a measuring spoon to scoop the dough, then push it onto the baking sheet with your finger or another spoon. Coat whatever you use to scoop the dough with cooking spray first, which keeps the dough from sticking. There's no need to flatten the cookies; they'll spread and flatten as they bake.

Oatmeal, Chocolate Chip, and Pecan Cookies

These easy drop cookies are crisp on the out-side and slightly chewy on the inside. Chocolate minichips disperse better in the batter, but you can use regular chips.

5.6 ounces all-purpose flour (about 1¼ cups)
1 cup old-fashioned rolled oats
¾ teaspoon baking powder
½ teaspoon baking soda
½ teaspoon salt
¾ cup granulated sugar
½ cup packed brown sugar
⅓ cup butter, softened
1½ teaspoons vanilla extract
1 large egg
¼ cup chopped pecans, toasted
¼ cup semisweet chocolate minichips

1. Preheat oven to 350°.
2. Weigh or lightly spoon flour into dry measuring cups; level with a knife. Combine flour and next 4 ingredients, stirring with a whisk.
3. Place sugars and butter in a large bowl; beat with a mixer at medium speed until well blended. Add vanilla and egg; beat until blended. Gradually add flour mixture, beating at low speed just until combined. Stir in pecans and minichips. Drop dough by tablespoons 2 inches apart onto baking sheets lined with parchment paper. Bake at 350° for 12 minutes or until edges of cookies are lightly browned. Cool on pans 2 minutes. Remove cookies from pans; cool on wire racks. **Yield: 36 cookies (serving size: 1 cookie).**

CALORIES 81; FAT 3g (sat 1.4g, mono 1g, poly 0.3g); PROTEIN 1.1g; CARB 12.9g; FIBER 0.5g; CHOL 10mg; IRON 0.5mg; SODIUM 76mg; CALC 12mg

Almond Butter Snickerdoodles

    1   cup packed brown sugar
    ⅓   cup (about 3 ounces) ⅓-less-fat cream
        cheese, softened
    ¼   cup unsalted butter, softened
    2   tablespoons creamy almond butter
    1   teaspoon grated lemon rind
    1   teaspoon vanilla extract
    2   large egg yolks, lightly beaten
 4.75 ounces white whole-wheat flour (about 1 cup)
  1.5 ounces whole-wheat flour (about ⅓ cup)
    1   teaspoon baking soda
  1½ teaspoons ground cinnamon, divided
    ½   teaspoon salt
    2   tablespoons granulated sugar

1. Preheat oven to 350°.
2. Line a large baking sheet with parchment paper.
3. Place first 4 ingredients in a medium bowl, and beat with a mixer at high speed until well combined (about 2 minutes). Add lemon rind, vanilla, and egg yolks; beat until well blended.
4. Weigh or lightly spoon flours into dry measuring cups; level with a knife. Combine flours, baking soda, ½ teaspoon cinnamon, and salt; stir with a whisk. Add flour mixture to butter mixture; beat at low speed until well combined. Drop half of dough by rounded table-spoons onto prepared baking sheet. Combine remaining 1 teaspoon cinnamon and granulated sugar in a small bowl; sprinkle half of cinnamon-sugar mixture evenly over cookies. Bake at 350° for 6 minutes; flatten cookies with back of a spatula. Bake an additional 6 minutes. Cool on pan 1 minute. Remove from pan, and cool on a wire rack. Repeat procedure with remaining dough and sugar mixture. **Yield: 24 cookies (serving size: 1 cookie).**

CALORIES 104; FAT 3.8g (sat 1.9g, mono 1.2g, poly 0.3g); PROTEIN 1.6g; CARB 16.2g; FIBER 0.5g; CHOL 25mg; IRON 0.7mg; SODIUM 127mg; CALC 19mg

kitchen how-to:
easily scoop drop cookies

For an easy one-handed option when making drop cookies, use a cookie scoop, which looks like a small ice-cream scoop. These gadgets come in a variety of sizes, from a teaspoon up to several tablespoons.

all about almond butter

Like other nut butters, almond butter retains the nutrients of the nuts it's made from, which means it is rich in protein, fiber, and healthy fats. This spread comes in two varieties: raw and roasted. Use raw for a subtle, sweet taste and roasted for a more intense almond flavor.

Amaretti

Look for almond paste in tubes or in cans on your supermarket's baking aisle. For the best results, don't substitute marzipan, which is sweeter and more finely textured, in place of the paste.

1 cup granulated sugar
1 (7-ounce) package almond paste
1 teaspoon amaretto (almond-flavored liqueur)
2 large egg whites
¼ cup turbinado sugar

1. Preheat oven to 350°.
2. Place granulated sugar and almond paste in a large bowl; beat with a mixer at medium speed until almond paste is broken into small pieces. Add amaretto and egg whites; beat at high speed 4 minutes or until smooth. Chill batter 20 minutes.
3. Drop batter by teaspoons 1 inch apart onto parchment paper–lined baking sheets. Sprinkle evenly with turbinado sugar. Bake at 350° for 10 minutes or until edges of cookies are golden brown. Cool completely on pans. Carefully remove cookies from parchment paper; cool on wire racks. **Yield: 40 cookies (serving size: 1 cookie).**

CALORIES 48; FAT 1.4g (sat 0.1g, mono 0.9g, poly 0.3g); PROTEIN 0.6g; CARB 8.6g; FIBER 0.2g; CHOL 0mg; IRON 0.1mg; SODIUM 3mg; CALC 9mg

kitchen how-to: make amaretti

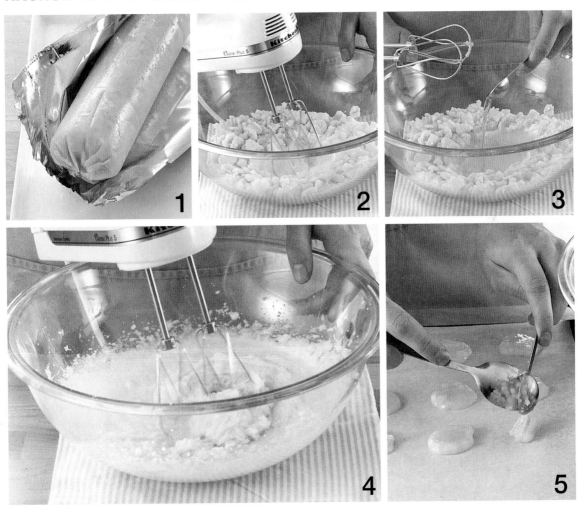

When first baked, these classic Italian cookies are crispy on the outside and chewy on the inside. As they sit, they get crunchier.

1. This cookie is simple to make and uses only a handful of ingredients, most notably almond paste, which is made from ground almonds and sugar. It's similar to marzipan, but marzipan contains more sugar and is more pliable. Don't substitute marzipan in this recipe.

2. Place granulated sugar and almond paste in a large bowl; beat with a mixer at medium speed until almond paste is broken into small pieces.

3. Add amaretto and egg whites.

4. Beat at high speed 4 minutes or until smooth. Chill batter 20 minutes.

5. Drop batter by teaspoons 1 inch apart onto parchment paper–lined baking sheets. Sprinkle evenly with turbinado sugar. Bake until cookies are golden brown.

rolled cookies

Rolled cookies are made by rolling stiff dough into a thin layer and then cutting the dough with cookie cutters or slicing it into various shapes.

kitchen how-to:
make rolled cookies

For the dough to hold its shape once cut, it needs to be firmer than drop cookie dough. Chill the dough thoroughly before cutting it into shapes. Divide the dough in half and chill separately so you can work with one portion while the other stays cold. Roll the dough between sheets of heavy-duty plastic wrap to prevent tearing. When rolling dough, place the rolling pin in the center of the dough and roll outward using gentle strokes. If the dough becomes soft after rolling, place it in the refrigerator for 10 to 15 minutes or in the freezer for 5 minutes until it firms up. Dip cookie cutters in flour or powdered sugar to prevent the dough from sticking to them. When cutting, start at an outside edge and work your way across. After cutting the dough, gather the scraps, knead gently, and reroll. Cut out one more batch of shapes, but don't reroll those scraps—the dough will be overworked, resulting in tough cookies.

Swedish Almond-Cardamom Stars

9 ounces all-purpose flour (about 2 cups)
3 cups powdered sugar, divided
½ teaspoon baking soda
½ teaspoon ground cardamom
¼ teaspoon salt
¼ cup almond paste, crumbled
1 tablespoon chilled butter, cut into small pieces
⅓ cup fresh orange juice
3 tablespoons canola oil
3 tablespoons 2% reduced-fat milk

1. Weigh or lightly spoon flour into dry measuring cups; level with a knife. Place flour, 1 cup sugar, baking soda, cardamom, and salt in a food processor; process until blended. Add almond paste and butter; process until blended. Combine juice and oil. With processor on, slowly pour juice mixture through food chute; process until dough forms a ball.

2. Divide dough in half. Working with 1 portion at a time, gently press dough into a 4-inch square on heavy-duty plastic wrap. Cover with additional plastic wrap. Roll each half of dough, still covered, to a ¼-inch thickness. Chill 1 hour.

3. Preheat oven to 375°.

4. Working with 1 portion of dough at a time, remove top sheet of plastic wrap; turn dough over. Remove remaining plastic wrap. Cut with a 2½-inch star-shaped cookie cutter into 24 stars; place stars 2 inches apart on 2 baking sheets lined with parchment paper. Bake at 375° for 8 minutes or until lightly browned. Cool on pans 5 minutes. Remove from pans; cool on wire racks. Repeat procedure with remaining half of dough.

5. Combine remaining 2 cups sugar and milk, stirring with a whisk until smooth. Spread about 1 teaspoon icing over each warm cookie; chill 1 hour. **Yield: 48 cookies (serving size: 2 cookies).**

CALORIES 124; FAT 2.9g (sat 0.5g, mono 1.6g, poly 0.7g); PROTEIN 1.3g; CARB 23.5g; FIBER 0.4g; CHOL 1.4mg; IRON 0.5mg; SODIUM 55mg; CALC 6mg

make windowpane cookies

These beautiful cookies are easy to prepare.
You can reroll the dough scraps, but chill them first.

1. Roll dough to a ⅛-inch thickness on a floured surface; cut dough with a 2-inch rectangular cookie cutter with fluted edges. (We like fluted rectangular cutters, but round or star-shaped cutters work just as well.) Use a 1-inch rectangular cutter to remove centers of half of cookie cutouts. Arrange cookies 1 inch apart on baking sheets lined with parchment paper; bake until edges are lightly browned. Cool on pans, and then cool cookies on a wire rack.

2. Top the whole cookies with preserves. We used raspberry to add color, but you can use any flavor you like.

3. Sprinkle cutout cookies with powdered sugar, which gives the cutout cookies a snowy holiday glow. Place 1 cutout cookie on top of each whole cookie.

Raspberry Linzer Cookies

Ground almonds give these cookies a hearty taste and extra crunch. We love the look and texture of raspberry preserves with seeds, but use seedless fruit spread, if you like.

7.5 **ounces all-purpose flour (about 1½ cups plus 2 tablespoons), divided**
1 **cup blanched whole almonds**
½ **teaspoon baking powder**
½ **teaspoon ground cinnamon**
¼ **teaspoon salt**
⅔ **cup granulated sugar**
½ **cup unsalted butter, softened**
½ **teaspoon grated lemon rind**
4 **large egg yolks**
6 **tablespoons raspberry preserves with seeds**
2 **teaspoons powdered sugar**

1. Weigh or lightly spoon 2.25 ounces flour (about ½ cup) into a dry measuring cup; level with a knife. Place 2.25 ounces flour and almonds in a food processor; process until finely ground. Weigh or lightly spoon remaining 5.25 ounces flour (about 1 cup plus 2 tablespoons) into a dry measuring cup. Combine almond mixture, remaining 5.25 ounces flour, baking powder, cinnamon, and salt, stirring well with a whisk.
2. Place granulated sugar, butter, and rind in a large bowl; beat with a mixer at medium speed until light and fluffy (about 3 minutes). Add egg yolks; beat until well blended. Beating at low speed, gradually add flour mixture; beat just until a soft dough

forms. Turn dough out onto a sheet of plastic wrap; knead lightly 3 times or until smooth. Divide dough into 2 equal portions; wrap each portion in plastic wrap. Chill 1 hour.
3. Preheat oven to 350°.
4. Roll each dough portion to a ⅛-inch thickness on a floured surface; cut with a 2-inch rectangular cookie cutter with fluted edges into 36 cookies. Repeat procedure with remaining dough portion; use a 1-inch rectangular fluted cutter to remove centers of 36 rectangles. Arrange 1 inch apart on baking

sheets lined with parchment paper. Bake, 1 batch at a time, at 350° for 10 minutes or until edges are lightly browned. Cool on pans 5 minutes. Remove from pans; cool on wire racks.
5. Spread center of each whole cookie with about ½ teaspoon preserves. Sprinkle cutout cookies with powdered sugar. Place 1 cutout cookie on top of each whole cookie.
Yield: 36 cookies (serving size: 1 cookie).

CALORIES 96; FAT 5.1g (sat 1.9g, mono 2.2g, poly 0.7g); PROTEIN 1.8g; CARB 11.4g; FIBER 0.6g; CHOL 29mg; IRON 0.5mg; SODIUM 25mg; CALC 18mg

Iced Browned Butter Sugar Cookies

You can roll out the dough right after combining all the ingredients—no chilling required.

> 9 tablespoons unsalted butter
> 1 cup granulated sugar
> ¾ teaspoon vanilla extract, divided
> 3 large egg yolks
> 8 ounces all-purpose flour (about 1¾ cups)
> ½ teaspoon salt
> ¼ teaspoon baking powder
> 1 cup powdered sugar
> 1½ tablespoons half-and-half
> ⅓ cup pearlized sugar or turbinado sugar

1. Preheat oven to 350°.

2. Melt butter in a large skillet over medium-low heat; cook 6 minutes or until dark brown. Pour butter into a large bowl; let stand 5 minutes. Add granulated sugar and ½ teaspoon vanilla; beat with a mixer at medium speed until well blended (about 2 minutes). Add egg yolks, and beat at medium speed until well blended (about 1 minute).

3. Weigh or lightly spoon flour into dry measuring cups; level with a knife. Combine flour, salt, and baking powder; stir with a whisk. Add flour mixture to butter mixture; beat at low speed just until combined. Turn dough out onto a sheet of wax paper; knead gently 7 times. Roll dough to a ¼-inch thickness. Cut with a 2½-inch star-shaped cookie cutter into 32 cookies; reroll scraps as necessary. Arrange cookies 1 inch apart on baking sheets lined with parchment paper. Bake, 1 batch at a time, at 350° for 10 minutes or until edges are lightly browned. Cool cookies completely on wire racks.

4. Combine powdered sugar, half-and-half, and remaining ¼ teaspoon vanilla, stirring with a whisk until icing is smooth. Spoon about ¾ teaspoon icing onto each cookie; spread to edges. While icing is wet, sprinkle each cookie with ½ teaspoon pearlized sugar. Dry on wire racks. **Yield: 32 cookies (serving size: 1 cookie).**

CALORIES 104; FAT 3.8g (sat 2.2g, mono 1g, poly 0.2g); PROTEIN 1g; CARB 17g; FIBER 0.2g; CHOL 28mg; IRON 0.4mg; SODIUM 42mg; CALC 7mg

kitchen how-to: create cookies with flavor & sparkle

With nutty, caramel notes from browned butter and a fair bit of salt to balance the flavors, these cookies will become an instant favorite. Look for pearlized sugar in gourmet markets or craft stores; the coarse crystals reflect light to give the cookies a sparkly, jewel-like appearance.

1. Brown the butter to add an extra depth of flavor. Melt butter in a large skillet over medium-low heat; cook 6 minutes or until dark brown.

2. Make the cookies shine with coarse sugar for a festive touch. Hold the cookies over a bowl as you sprinkle, so you don't lose any crystals that fall off.

Autumn Maple Cutout Cookies

- ¼ cup butter
- 10.1 ounces all-purpose flour (about 2¼ cups)
- ½ teaspoon baking powder
- ½ teaspoon ground cinnamon
- ¼ teaspoon baking soda
- ¼ teaspoon salt
- ⅛ teaspoon ground nutmeg
- 6 tablespoons granulated sugar
- ½ cup maple syrup
- 1 teaspoon maple flavoring
- 2 large egg whites, divided
- ⅓ cup chopped walnuts
- 2 tablespoons turbinado sugar or granulated sugar
- Cooking spray

1. Melt butter in a small saucepan over low heat. Cook until milk solids stop crackling and turn amber (about 5 minutes), stirring occasionally. Transfer butter mixture to a small bowl, scraping pan to include milk solids. Cover and chill butter mixture in the refrigerator 20 minutes or until soft and congealed but not firm.
2. Weigh or lightly spoon flour into dry measuring cups, and level with a knife. Combine flour and next 5 ingredients in a bowl, stirring with a whisk.

3. Combine chilled butter mixture and granulated sugar in a large bowl; beat with a mixer at medium speed until well blended (about 3 minutes). Add syrup, flavoring, and 1 egg white to butter mixture; beat at low speed 2 minutes or until well blended. Add flour mixture to butter mixture; beat at low speed until blended. Divide dough in half. Shape each portion into a ball; wrap in plastic wrap. Chill 1 hour or until firm.
4. Preheat oven to 350°.
5. Place walnuts and turbinado sugar in a food processor; pulse 15 times or until mixture is coarsely ground. Place remaining 1 egg white in a small bowl; stir with a whisk.
6. Working with 1 portion of dough at a time (keep remaining dough chilled until ready to use), roll dough to a ⅛-inch thickness on a floured surface, and cut with a 2½-inch round or decorative cutter. Place 24 cookies, evenly spaced, on a baking sheet coated with cooking spray. Gently brush tops of cookies with egg white; sprinkle evenly with half of walnut mixture. Bake at 350° for 12 minutes or until pale brown. Remove cookies from pan; cool completely on wire racks. Repeat procedure with remaining dough, egg white, and walnut mixture.
Yield: 48 cookies (serving size: 2 cookies).

CALORIES 104; FAT 3.1g (sat 1.3g, mono 0.7g, poly 0.9g); PROTEIN 1.8g; CARB 17.7g; FIBER 0.5g; CHOL 5mg; IRON 0.7mg; SODIUM 66mg; CALC 15mg

all about choosing & storing maple syrup

Maple syrup, like honey, is available in different strengths. Light syrups are great for adding moisture and an enhanced flavor to your cookies and cakes. For an intense maple flavor, use darker syrups. Make sure to check the syrup's label before buying it. For the best flavor, buy only brands labeled "pure maple syrup," and refrigerate maple syrup once it's opened to protect its flavor. Refrigerated, it will last indefinitely. Those syrups that are labeled "maple flavored" are actually corn syrups that have been artificially flavored.

Black and White Striped Cookies

Vanilla Dough:

- 5.6 ounces all-purpose flour (about 1¼ cups)
- ⅛ teaspoon salt
- ½ cup powdered sugar
- ¼ cup butter, softened
- 1 large egg yolk
- 1½ teaspoons vanilla extract
- 2 tablespoons ice water

Chocolate Dough:

- 3.4 ounces all-purpose flour (about ¾ cup)
- ⅓ cup unsweetened cocoa
- ⅛ teaspoon salt
- 1 cup powdered sugar
- ¼ cup butter, softened
- 1 large egg yolk
- ½ teaspoon vanilla extract
- 2 tablespoons ice water

1. To prepare vanilla dough, weigh or lightly spoon 5.6 ounces flour (about 1¼ cups) into dry measuring cups; level with a knife. Combine 5.6 ounces flour and ⅛ teaspoon salt, stirring well with a whisk. Place ½ cup sugar, ¼ cup butter, and 1 egg yolk in a medium bowl; beat with a mixer at medium speed until smooth. Beat in 1½ teaspoons vanilla. Gradually add flour mixture to butter mixture, beating at low speed just until combined. Sprinkle 2 table-spoons ice water over surface of dough; beat just until moist. (Dough will be slightly crumbly.) Press dough into a 4-inch circle on plastic wrap; cover and chill 1 hour or until firm.

2. To prepare chocolate dough, weigh or lightly spoon 3.4 ounces flour (about ¾ cup) into dry measur-ing cups; level with a knife. Combine 3.4 ounces flour, cocoa, and ⅛ teaspoon salt, stirring well with a whisk. Place 1 cup sugar, ¼ cup butter, and 1 egg yolk in a medium bowl; beat with a mixer at medium speed until smooth. Beat in ½ teaspoon vanilla. Gradually add cocoa mixture to butter mixture, beating at low speed just until combined. Sprinkle 2 tablespoons ice water over surface of dough; beat just until moist. Press dough into a 4-inch circle on plastic wrap; cover and chill 1 hour or until firm.

3. Slightly overlap 2 sheets of plastic wrap on a slightly damp surface. Unwrap and place chilled vanilla

dough on plastic wrap. Cover dough with 2 additional sheets of overlapping plastic wrap. Roll dough, still covered, into a 12 x 8–inch rectangle. Place dough in freezer 5 minutes or until plastic wrap can be easily removed. Remove top sheets of plastic wrap.

4. Slightly overlap 2 sheets of plastic wrap on a slightly damp surface. Unwrap and place chilled chocolate dough on plastic wrap. Cover dough with 2 additional sheets of overlapping plastic wrap. Roll dough, still covered, into a 12 x 8–inch rectangle. Place dough in freezer 5 minutes or until plastic wrap can be easily removed. Remove top sheets of plastic wrap.

5. Place vanilla dough on top of chocolate dough, plastic wrap side up. Remove plastic wrap from vanilla dough; turn dough over onto a lightly floured surface. Remove plastic wrap from chocolate dough. Cut dough stack in half crosswise to form 2 (8 x 6–inch) rectangles. Stack 1 rectangle on top of the other, alternating vanilla and chocolate doughs; wrap in plastic wrap. Freeze 10 minutes or until firm and plastic wrap can be easily removed.

6. Cut dough crosswise into 6 (6 x 1⅓–inch) strips. Place 1 strip on top of another strip to form a stack, alternating vanilla and chocolate to form a striped pattern; wrap in plastic wrap, pressing

gently. Repeat procedure with remaining 4 strips to form 2 stacks (there will be 3 stacks total). Chill 30 minutes or until very firm.

7. Preheat oven to 375°.

8. Working with 1 stack at a time, unwrap dough. Carefully slice each stack into 12 slices. Place dough slices 2 inches apart on baking sheets lined with parchment paper. Bake at 375° for 12 minutes. Cool on pans 5 minutes. Remove cookies from pans; cool completely on wire racks. **Yield: 36 cookies (serving size: 1 cookie).**

CALORIES 73; FAT 3g (sat 1.8g, mono 0.8g, poly 0.2g); PROTEIN 1.1g; CARB 10.8g; FIBER 0.5g; CHOL 18mg; IRON 0.5mg; SODIUM 35mg; CALC 4mg

kitchen how-to: make striped cookies

These unique treats, which use rolled dough that is stacked and sliced, are actually a hybrid— a cross between rolled and sliced or icebox cookies.

1. Prepare doughs. Once chilled, remove top sheets of plastic wrap from chocolate and vanilla doughs. Place vanilla dough on top of chocolate dough, plastic wrap side up. Remove plastic wrap from

vanilla dough; turn dough over onto a lightly floured surface. Remove plastic wrap from chocolate dough. Cut stack in half crosswise to form 2 (8 x 6–inch) rectangles. Stack 1 rectangle on top of the other, alternating vanilla and chocolate doughs; wrap in plastic wrap. Freeze 10 minutes or until firm and plastic wrap can be easily removed.

2. Cut the dough crosswise into 6 (6 x 1⅓–inch) strips. Place 1 strip

on top of another strip to form a stack, alternating vanilla and chocolate to form a striped pattern; wrap in plastic wrap, pressing gently. Repeat procedure to form 2 more stacks. (There will be 3 stacks total.) Chill 30 minutes or until very firm.

3. Working with 1 stack at a time, unwrap dough. Carefully slice each stack into 12 slices. Place dough slices 2 inches apart on baking sheets lined with parchment paper. Bake.

slice-and-bake cookies

Also called refrigerator or icebox cookies, these are formed by shaping dough into a cylinder, and then slicing it into thin disks before baking.

kitchen how-to:
make slice-and-bake cookies

To shape the dough into a log, roll it back and forth across a lightly floured cutting board or work surface, and then chill the dough before slicing. Use a thin, serrated knife to make clean slices. After every 2 or 3 cuts, roll the dough log a quarter turn to make sure it keeps its round shape and doesn't flatten out.

Basic Icebox Sugar Cookies

Rich, tender, and buttery, this basic sugar cookie is guaranteed to please. It's delicious unadorned, but it's also an ideal base for frosting, sprinkles, or other decorations.

4.5   ounces all-purpose flour (about 1 cup)
¼   teaspoon baking soda
⅛   teaspoon salt
4   tablespoons butter, softened
⅔   cup sugar
1   teaspoon vanilla extract
1   large egg white
  Cooking spray

1. Weigh or lightly spoon flour into a dry measuring cup; level with a knife. Combine first 3 ingredients in a bowl.
2. Beat butter with a mixer at medium speed until light and fluffy. Gradually add sugar, beating at medium speed until well blended. Add vanilla and egg white, and beat well. Add flour mixture; stir until well blended. Turn dough out onto wax paper; shape into a 6-inch log. Wrap log in wax paper; freeze 3 hours or until very firm.
3. Preheat oven to 350°.
4. Cut log into 24 (¼-inch) slices, and place slices 1 inch apart on a baking sheet coated with cooking spray. Bake at 350° for 8 to 10 minutes. Remove from pan; cool on wire racks. **Yield: 24 cookies (serving size: 1 cookie).**

CALORIES 58; FAT 2g (sat 1g, mono 0.8g, poly 0.1g); PROTEIN 0.7g; CARB 9.6g; FIBER 0.1g; CHOL 5mg; IRON 0.2mg; SODIUM 41mg; CALC 2mg

Ginger-Lemon Pinwheel Cookies

Ginger Dough:
- ¼ cup unsalted butter, softened
- ⅓ cup packed dark brown sugar
- ¼ cup molasses
- 1 large egg yolk
- 6 ounces all-purpose flour (about 1⅓ cups)
- ¾ teaspoon ground ginger
- ¾ teaspoon ground cinnamon
- ¼ teaspoon salt
- ⅛ teaspoon ground nutmeg

Dash of ground allspice

Lemon Dough:
- 5 tablespoons unsalted butter, softened
- ⅔ cup granulated sugar
- 1 large egg white
- 2 teaspoons grated lemon rind
- ¾ teaspoon vanilla extract
- 6 ounces all-purpose flour (about 1⅓ cups)
- ¼ teaspoon salt

1. To prepare ginger dough, place ¼ cup butter and brown sugar in a medium bowl; beat with a mixer at medium speed until well combined (about 3 minutes). Add molasses and egg yolk; beat until well blended. Weigh or lightly spoon 6 ounces flour (about 1⅓ cups) into dry measuring cups; level with a knife. Combine 6 ounces flour, ginger, and next 4 ingredients; stir with a whisk. Add flour mixture to butter mixture; beat at low speed just until combined. Wrap dough in plastic wrap; chill 30 minutes.

2. To prepare lemon dough, place 5 tablespoons butter and granulated sugar in a medium bowl; beat with a mixer at medium speed until blended (about 3 minutes). Add egg white; beat until blended. Beat in rind and vanilla. Weigh or lightly spoon 6 ounces flour (about 1⅓ cups) into dry measuring cups; level with a knife. Combine 6 ounces flour and ¼ teaspoon salt. Add flour mixture to butter mixture; beat at low speed just until combined. Wrap dough in plastic wrap; chill 30 minutes.

3. Unwrap ginger dough. Roll ginger dough between sheets of plastic wrap into a 13 x 8½–inch rectangle (³⁄₁₆ inch thick); chill 10 minutes. Unwrap lemon dough. Roll lemon dough between sheets of plastic wrap into a 13 x 9–inch rectangle (³⁄₁₆ inch thick); chill 10 minutes. Carefully stack ginger dough on top of lemon dough, leaving a ½-inch border along 1 long edge. Starting with the long side without a border, roll up dough, jelly-roll fashion. Seal edges (do not seal ends of roll). Cover with plastic wrap; freeze 30 minutes.

4. Preheat oven to 350°.

5. Unwrap dough. Cut with a sharp knife into 40 slices (about ¼ inch thick). Reshape rounds, if necessary. Arrange slices 1 inch apart on baking sheets lined with parchment paper. Bake, 1 batch at a time, at 350° for 8 to 9 minutes or until set and lightly browned. Cool on wire racks. **Yield: 40 cookies (serving size: 1 cookie).**

CALORIES 81; FAT 2.8g (sat 1.7g, mono 0.7g, poly 0.2g); PROTEIN 1.1g; CARB 13.1g; FIBER 0.3g; CHOL 12mg; IRON 0.6mg; SODIUM 33mg; CALC 9mg

make perfect pinwheel cookies

The chilling and freezing steps in this method are important for making perfect pinwheel cookies.

1. Stack the doughs on top of each other, leaving a ½-inch border along 1 of the long edges.

2. Start with the long side with no border, and roll up the dough jelly-roll fashion.

3. Place the dough in the freezer, and chill it for 30 minutes, allowing it to firm up for easier slicing. Then, working quickly, cut the dough into thin rounds.

hand-shaped cookies

A step beyond drop cookies, this variety is the ultimate hands-on project.

kitchen how-to:
make hand-shaped cookies

Before getting started, coat your hands with cooking spray to prevent the dough from sticking. You may want to use a ruler or measuring spoons for the first few cookies to help you determine the correct size, and then eyeball the rest. To ensure thumbprint cookies hold their shape so that they can be filled, chill the dough after making the indentations, and then spoon the filling in only after the baked cookies have cooled completely.

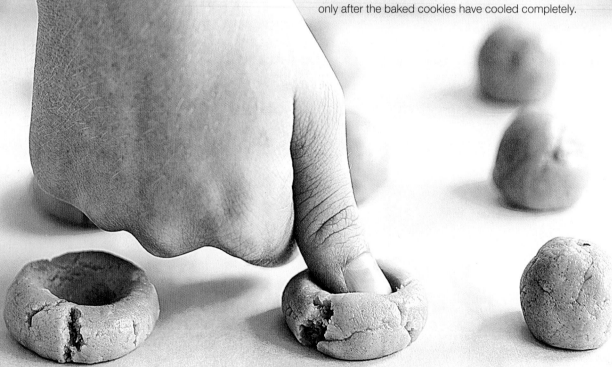

Peanut Butter and Jelly Thumbprints

- 9 ounces all-purpose flour (about 2 cups)
- ¼ teaspoon salt
- ¾ cup packed brown sugar
- ⅔ cup granulated sugar
- ½ cup chunky peanut butter
- ¼ cup butter, softened
- 2 large eggs
- 1 teaspoon vanilla extract
- Cooking spray
- 7 tablespoons seedless raspberry preserves
- 1 tablespoon fresh lemon juice

1. Weigh or lightly spoon flour into dry measuring cups; level with a knife. Combine flour and salt, stirring well with a whisk.

2. Place sugars, peanut butter, and butter in a large bowl; beat with a mixer at medium speed until well combined. Add eggs, 1 at a time, beating well after each addition. Beat in vanilla. Gradually add flour mixture to sugar mixture, beating at low speed just until combined.

3. Lightly coat hands with cooking spray. Shape dough into 36 balls (about 2½ teaspoons each). Place balls 2 inches apart on baking sheets lined with parchment paper. Press thumb into center of each dough ball, leaving an indentation. Cover and chill 1 hour.

4. Preheat oven to 350°.

5. Uncover dough. Bake at 350° for 14 minutes or until lightly browned. Remove cookies from pans; cool on a wire rack.

6. Place preserves in a small microwave-safe bowl, and microwave at HIGH 20 seconds, stirring once. Add juice, stirring until smooth. Spoon about ½ teaspoon preserves mixture into center of each cookie. **Yield: 36 cookies (serving size: 1 cookie).**

CALORIES 103; FAT 3.4g (sat 1.2g, mono 1.3g, poly 0.6g); PROTEIN 1.9g; CARB 16.9g; FIBER 0.5g; CHOL 15mg; IRON 0.5mg; SODIUM 48mg; CALC 8mg

Chocolate-Hazelnut Thumbprints

4.5 ounces all-purpose flour (about 1 cup)
 1 cup powdered sugar
 ⅓ cup unsweetened cocoa
 ¼ teaspoon salt
 ½ cup butter, softened
 2 large egg yolks
 1 teaspoon instant espresso granules (optional)
 ½ teaspoon vanilla extract
 ⅔ cup finely chopped hazelnuts, toasted
 ⅓ cup hazelnut-chocolate spread

1. Preheat oven to 350°.
2. Weigh or lightly spoon flour into a dry measuring cup; level with a knife. Combine flour, sugar, cocoa, and salt; stir with a whisk. Place butter in a large bowl, and beat with a mixer at medium speed until light and fluffy (about 2 minutes). Stir egg yolks with a whisk, adding espresso granules, if desired. Add yolk mixture and vanilla to butter; beat well. Add flour mixture to butter mixture; beat at low speed just until combined.
3. Turn dough out onto a sheet of wax paper; knead 6 times or until smooth and shiny. Shape dough into 28 (1-inch) balls. Roll sides of balls in nuts, pressing gently. Arrange balls 1 inch apart on baking sheets lined with parchment paper. Press thumb into center of each cookie, leaving an indentation. Bake, 1 batch at a time, at 350° for 10 minutes. Remove cookies from pans; cool completely on wire racks. Spoon a scant ½ teaspoon hazelnut-chocolate spread into center of each cookie. Drag a wooden pick through the spread to make a swirl.
Yield: 28 cookies (serving size: 1 cookie).

CALORIES 104; FAT 6.5g (sat 2.7g, mono 2.3g, poly 0.4g); PROTEIN 1.6g; CARB 10.9g; FIBER 0.8g; CHOL 23mg; IRON 0.6mg; SODIUM 46mg; CALC 11mg

kitchen how-to:
make chocolate-hazelnut thumbprint cookies

The espresso granules are optional, but they intensify the chocolate flavor.

1. Roll the dough into balls, and then roll the sides in nuts, leaving tops and bottoms uncovered.

2. Press your thumb into each dough ball to create a small well.
3. Let the baked cookies cool completely; spoon the hazelnut-chocolate spread into each cookie. Drag a wooden pick through the spread to make a swirl.

Crunchy Sesame Cookies

Roasted sesame seed paste and dark sesame oil deliver a deep, nutty flavor. A touch of corn syrup and cornstarch ensure crispness.

6.75 ounces all-purpose flour (about 1½ cups)
 1½ tablespoons cornstarch
  1 teaspoon baking powder
  ½ teaspoon baking soda
  ¼ teaspoon salt
  1 cup packed brown sugar
  ⅓ cup tahini (roasted sesame seed paste)
  2 tablespoons dark sesame oil
  1 tablespoon light-colored corn syrup
  2 teaspoons vanilla extract
  1 large egg
Cooking spray
  2 tablespoons granulated sugar

1. Preheat oven to 375°.
2. Weigh or lightly spoon flour into dry measuring cups; level with a knife. Combine flour and next 4 ingredients, stirring with a whisk.

3. Place brown sugar, tahini, and oil in a large bowl; beat with a mixer at medium speed until well blended. Add syrup, vanilla, and egg; beat well. Gradually add flour mixture to sugar mixture, beating at low speed just until combined.
4. Lightly coat hands with cooking spray. Shape dough into 36 balls (about 1 inch each). Place granulated sugar in a shallow bowl. Roll dough balls in granulated sugar; place 2 inches apart on baking sheets lined with parchment paper. Flatten balls slightly with the bottom of a glass. Bake at 375° for 10 minutes or until lightly browned. Cool on pans 2 minutes. Remove cookies from pans; cool completely on a wire rack. **Yield: 36 cookies (serving size: 1 cookie).**

CALORIES 71; FAT 2.1g (sat 0.3g, mono 0.8g, poly 0.9g); PROTEIN 1.1g; CARB 11.9g; FIBER 0.3g; CHOL 6mg; IRON 0.5mg; SODIUM 53mg; CALC 17mg

kitchen how-to:
shape crunchy sesame cookies

Prepare dough. Lightly coat hands with cooking spray, and shape dough into 36 balls (about 1 inch each). Place granulated sugar in a shallow bowl. Roll dough balls in granulated sugar; place 2 inches apart on baking sheets lined with parchment paper. Flatten balls slightly with the bottom of a glass.

Fortune Cookies

- 2.3 **ounces bread flour (about ½ cup)**
- ½ **cup sugar**
- 1 **teaspoon vanilla extract**
- 2 **large egg whites**

1. Weigh or lightly spoon flour into a dry measuring cup; level with a knife. Place flour and remaining ingredients in a food processor; process until blended. Scrape batter into a bowl using a rubber spatula; cover and chill 1 hour.

2. Preheat oven to 400°.

3. Cover 2 large baking sheets with parchment paper. Draw 3 (3-inch) circles on paper. Turn paper over; secure with masking tape. Spoon 1 teaspoon batter into center of each of the 3 drawn circles; spread evenly to fill circle. Bake 1 sheet at 400° for 5 minutes or until

cookies are brown just around edges. Remove from oven. Working quickly, loosen edges of cookies with a spatula, and turn over.

4. Lay handle of a wooden spoon and a prepared fortune along center of 1 cookie. Fold cookie over so edges meet over spoon handle; press edges together. Remove spoon. Gently pull ends of cookie down over rim of a small bowl or jar; hold for a few seconds or until set. Repeat procedure with remaining cookies.

5. Repeat procedure until all batter is used. Cool cookies completely; store in an airtight container.

Yield: 18 cookies (serving size: 1 cookie).

CALORIES 37; FAT 0.1g (sat 0g, mono 0g, poly 0g); PROTEIN 0g; CARB 8.4g; FIBER 0.1g; CHOL 0mg; IRON 0.2mg; SODIUM 6mg; CALC 1mg

kitchen how-to: shape fortune cookies

Bake three cookies at a time so they'll be soft enough to shape. Tuck your message into the cookie while shaping. If the cookies become too brittle, return them to the oven for a few seconds to soften.

1. Cover 2 large baking sheets with parchment paper. Draw 3 (3-inch) circles on paper. Turn paper over; secure with masking tape. Spoon 1 teaspoon batter into center of each of the 3 drawn circles; spread evenly to fill circle. Bake 1 sheet at 400° for 5 minutes or until the cookies are

brown just around the edges. Remove from oven. Working quickly, loosen the edges of the cookies with a spatula, and turn over.

2. Lay the handle of a wooden spoon and a prepared paper fortune along the center of 1 cookie. Fold cookie over so the edges meet over the spoon handle; press edges together. Remove spoon.

3. Gently pull the ends of the cookie down over the rim of a small bowl or jar; hold for a few seconds or until set. Repeat procedure with remaining cookies.

Anise Tea Crescents

Rolling the cookies in powdered sugar while they're still warm results in a deliciously sweet, snowy coating.

6.75 ounces all-purpose flour (about 1½ cups)
 ¼ cup cornstarch
 ½ teaspoon salt
1¼ cups powdered sugar, divided
 5 tablespoons butter, softened
 2 tablespoons canola oil
 2 tablespoons 2% reduced-fat milk
1½ teaspoons vanilla extract
 1 teaspoon aniseed, crushed

1. Preheat oven to 350°.
2. Weigh or lightly spoon flour into dry measuring cups; level with a knife. Combine flour, cornstarch, and salt in a medium bowl, stirring with a whisk.
3. Beat ¾ cup sugar, butter, and oil with a mixer at medium speed until light and fluffy. Add milk and vanilla; beat until well blended. Add flour mixture and aniseed; beat at low speed until blended. Chill 30 minutes. Shape dough into 32 (2-inch) logs; bend logs to form crescent shape. Arrange 16 crescents 1 inch apart on a baking sheet. Bake at 350° for 14 minutes or until edges are golden. Remove from oven; cool on pan 3 minutes. Repeat procedure with remaining 16 crescents.
4. Sift remaining ½ cup sugar into a medium bowl; toss warm cookies in sugar to coat. Cool completely on a wire rack. **Yield: 32 cookies (serving size: 2 cookies).**

CALORIES 131; FAT 5.4g (sat 2.4g, mono 2g, poly 0.7g); PROTEIN 1.3g; CARB 19.2g; FIBER 0.3g; CHOL 10mg; IRON 0.6mg; SODIUM 100mg; CALC 4mg

kitchen how-to:
shape anise tea crescents

Anise cookies are traditional in international cuisines, including Italian, Mexican, and German.

1. After dough has chilled, shape it into 32 (2-inch) logs.
2. Bend each log to form a crescent shape.

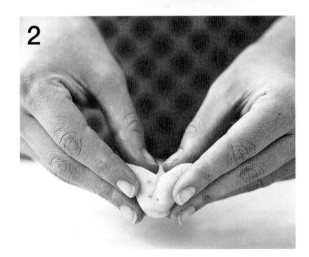

meringue cookies

Egg whites and sugar make these cookies light and airy; the resulting treats are far from ordinary.

Double Vanilla Meringues

The expense of the vanilla bean is worth it—the delicate flavor shines through in these cookies, which taste like toasted marshmallows.

- 1 **vanilla bean, split lengthwise**
- 4 **large egg whites**
- ¼ **teaspoon cream of tartar**
- ½ **cup granulated sugar**
- ⅔ **cup powdered sugar**
- 1 **tablespoon vanilla extract**

1. Preheat oven to 225°.
2. Cover 2 large baking sheets with parchment paper, and secure paper with masking tape.
3. Scrape seeds from vanilla bean. Reserve vanilla bean for another use.
4. Place egg whites and cream of tartar in a large bowl; beat with a mixer at medium speed until soft peaks form. Increase speed to high, and gradually add granulated sugar and then powdered sugar, 1 tablespoon at a time, beating until stiff peaks form. Add vanilla seeds and extract; beat just until blended.
5. Spoon batter into a pastry bag fitted with a large star tip. Pipe 60 mounds onto prepared baking sheets.
6. Bake at 225° for 1½ hours. Turn oven off; cool meringues in closed oven 1½ hours or until dry. Carefully remove meringues from paper. **Yield: 60 cookies (serving size: 1 cookie).**

CALORIES 13; FAT 0g (sat 0g, mono 0g, poly 0g); PROTEIN 0.2g; CARB 3.1g; FIBER 0g; CHOL 0mg; IRON 0mg; SODIUM 4mg; CALC 0mg

kitchen how-to:
make meringue cookies

Meringues are unlike any other cookie. They melt in your mouth, and the basic formula—stiffly beaten egg whites and sugar—is virtually fat free and a blank canvas waiting to take on a variety of flavors.

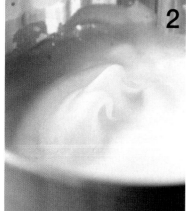

1. Start with chilled eggs, since they're easier to separate without breaking the yolks. Gently crack the egg, keeping the shell together. Hold a cupped hand over a bowl. With the other, gently separate the shell along the crack, letting the yolk and white drip into your waiting hand. Keeping the solid yolk in your hand, allow the white to fall through your fingers into the bowl below. Fat, which is found in yolks, is the enemy of light, airy, stiffly beaten egg whites. Reserve the yolk in a separate bowl for another use, and throw away the shell.
2. Place the egg whites and cream of tartar (added to stabilize the egg whites) in a large, clean bowl; beat with a mixer with clean, dry

beaters at medium speed until soft peaks form.
3. Increase the mixer speed to high, and gradually add granulated sugar and then powdered sugar, 1 tablespoon at a time, beating until stiff peaks form. Add vanilla seeds and extract; beat just until blended.
4. For picture-perfect meringues, spoon the batter into a pastry bag fitted with a large star tip; pipe 60 mounds onto prepared baking sheets.
5. Or, you can scoop the batter with a spoon, using your finger to transfer the batter onto the baking sheets. Bake the meringues slowly at 225° for 1½ hours. Turn the oven off, and leave the meringues in the oven with the door closed for 1½ hours or until the meringues are dry.

biscotti

These Italian cookies are baked twice to give them their characteristic texture and crunch.

kitchen how-to:
make biscotti

These twice-baked cookies are meant to be hard and crunchy, perfect for dipping into coffee or hot chocolate.

1. Once the ingredients are combined, the finished dough will be slightly sticky, so you may want to lightly coat your hands with cooking spray or flour before shaping it on a lightly floured work surface or baking sheet coated with cooking spray.
2. Shape the dough into a long roll, and pat to the thickness specified in the recipe. If you're making multiple rolls, leave plenty of space between the dough rolls so they don't spread and bake together.
3. After the first baking, the rolls will be slightly hardened. Use a serrated knife to slice them without crumbling them. Then place them in the oven for the second round of baking.

Double-Chocolate Biscotti

Vanilla extract enhances the dusky mix of cocoa and minichips in these twice-baked sliced cookies.

6.75 **ounces all-purpose flour (about 1½ cups)**
  1 **cup sugar**
  ½ **cup unsweetened cocoa**
  ½ **cup semisweet chocolate minichips**
  ½ **teaspoon baking powder**
  ½ **teaspoon baking soda**
  ½ **teaspoon salt**
  1 **teaspoon vanilla extract**
  2 **large eggs**
  1 **large egg white**
  Cooking spray

1. Preheat oven to 350°.
2. Weigh or lightly spoon flour into dry measuring cups; level with a knife. Combine flour and next 6 ingredients in a medium bowl, stirring with a whisk. Combine vanilla, eggs, and egg white in a large bowl, stirring with a whisk. Add flour mixture to egg mixture; stir until well blended. Divide dough in half. Turn dough out onto a baking sheet coated with cooking spray. With floured hands, shape each dough half into a 12-inch-long roll; pat to ½-inch thickness.
3. Bake at 350° for 22 minutes. Remove rolls from baking sheet, and cool 10 minutes on a wire rack. Cut each roll diagonally into 18 (½-inch) slices. Carefully stand slices upright on baking sheet. Bake an additional 15 minutes or until almost firm (cookies will be slightly soft in center but will harden as they cool). Remove from baking sheet, and cool completely on wire rack. **Yield: 36 biscotti (serving size: 2 biscotti).**

CALORIES 117; FAT 2.2g (sat 1g, mono 0.7g, poly 0.1g); PROTEIN 2.5g; CARB 22.5g; FIBER 1g; CHOL 24mg; IRON 1.1mg; SODIUM 125mg; CALC 12mg

Savory Two-Cheese Biscotti

These savory biscotti are great for dipping into chili. Make these a couple days ahead, and store in an airtight container.

12.4 ounces all-purpose flour (about 2¾ cups)
¾ cup (3 ounces) shredded extrasharp cheddar cheese
½ cup (2 ounces) grated fresh Parmesan cheese
2 teaspoons baking powder
¾ teaspoon salt
¼ teaspoon ground red pepper
¼ cup fat-free milk
2 teaspoons olive oil
3 large eggs
Cooking spray

1. Preheat oven to 350°.
2. Weigh or lightly spoon flour into dry measuring cups; level with a knife. Combine flour and next 5 ingredients in a large bowl. Combine milk, oil, and eggs; stir with a whisk. Add milk mixture to flour mixture, stirring until well blended (dough will be dry and crumbly). Turn out onto a lightly floured surface; knead 8 times. Divide dough in half. Shape each portion into an 8-inch-long roll. Place rolls, 6 inches apart, on a baking sheet coated with cooking spray; flatten to 1-inch thickness. Bake at 350° for 30 minutes. Remove from baking sheet; cool 10 minutes on a wire rack.
3. Reduce oven temperature to 325°.
4. Cut each roll diagonally into 12 (⅔-inch) slices. Place slices, cut sides down, on baking sheet. Bake at 325° for 10 minutes. Turn cookies over; bake an additional 10 minutes (cookies will be slightly soft in center but will harden as they cool). Remove from baking sheet; cool completely on wire rack. **Yield: 24 biscotti (serving size: 1 biscotto).**

CALORIES 83; FAT 2.8g (sat 1.5g, mono 0.5g, poly 0.1g); PROTEIN 3.9g; CARB 10.8g; FIBER 0.4g; CHOL 32mg; IRON 0.8mg; SODIUM 160mg; CALC 80mg

kitchen how-to:
bake biscotti another way

Instead of flipping the slices, you can stand the slices up on their flat sides on the baking sheet. This allows you to bake the sliced cookies without opening the oven to flip them. We've called for both techniques in our recipes, but you can try this and see if you like the result.

Deep Dark Chocolate Biscotti

9.5 ounces whole-wheat flour (about 2 cups)
  2 tablespoons flaxseed
  ½ teaspoon baking soda
  ¼ teaspoon salt
  ⅓ cup granulated sugar
  ⅓ cup packed dark brown sugar
  2 large egg whites
  1 large egg
1½ teaspoons vanilla extract
  ⅔ cup dark chocolate chips
  ¾ cup unsalted almonds

1. Preheat oven to 350°.
2. Weigh or lightly spoon flour into dry measuring cups; level with a knife. Combine flour, flaxseed, baking soda, and salt in a bowl, stirring with a whisk. Combine sugars, egg whites, and egg in a bowl; beat with a mixer at high speed 2 minutes. Add vanilla; mix well. Add flour mixture to egg mixture; stir until combined. Fold in chocolate chips and almonds. Divide dough into 3 equal portions. Shape each portion into a 6-inch-long roll. Arrange rolls 3 inches apart on a baking sheet lined with parchment paper. Pat to 1-inch thickness. Bake at 350° for 28 minutes or until firm.
3. Remove rolls from baking sheet; cool 10 minutes on a wire rack. Cut rolls diagonally into 30 (½-inch) slices. Place, cut sides down, on baking sheet. Reduce oven temperature to 325°; bake 7 minutes. Turn cookies over; bake 7 minutes (cookies will be slightly soft in center but will harden as they cool). Remove from baking sheet; cool on wire rack. **Yield: 30 biscotti (serving size: 1 biscotto).**

CALORIES 94; FAT 3.5g (sat 0.9g, mono 1.7g, poly 0.7g); PROTEIN 2.7g; CARB 14.4g; FIBER 1.9g; CHOL 7mg; IRON 0.7mg; SODIUM 49mg; CALC 18mg

Flaxseed
What it adds: Flaxseed is one of the only plant sources of omega-3 fatty acids and the richest plant source of lignans (antioxidants). To reap the nutritional benefits, make sure the flaxseed is ground. If left whole, the seeds pass through the body undigested.

Whole-Wheat Flour
What it adds: Using this flour as the base of the biscotti ensures you get whole grains and fiber in each bite.

Almonds

What they add: These nuts are delicately flavored and versatile. They're high in heart-healthy monounsaturated fats, the antioxidant vitamin E, and magnesium, which plays a role in hundreds of bodily processes and contributes to bone health.

way to bake

bars & squares

bars & squares

From simple batters spread in a pan to fancy treats with fillings, toppings, and glazes, bars and squares are the perfect casual, portable dessert.

One vs. Two Layers

Bars and squares can be classified into two types—one layer and two layers. An example of a one-layer bar is the classic brownie. The process is simple: Mix the batter, and pour it into the pan. Two-layer bars and squares are generally those that have a crust and a filling, like the Key Lime Squares on page 194.

Proper Pans

Make sure you use the size pan called for in each recipe. If you don't, you'll need to adjust the baking time to arrive at the desired texture of the bar or square. Most bars and squares are baked in shiny metal pans. Glass baking dishes conduct heat differently, so follow the doneness test in each recipe to avoid overbaking.

Easy Removal

Bars and squares can sometimes stick to the pan, which makes getting them out in a pretty form difficult. For easier removal, you may find it helpful to line the entire pan—bottom and sides—with parchment paper, and then cut off the excess paper around the top edge of the pan. Cool completely in the pan before cutting into portions.

Storage Strategy

Bars and squares will stay fresh up to 4 days at room temperature. Simply store them in the baking pan, and cover with plastic wrap or foil, or transfer them to an airtight container. If you need to layer them in the container, place a sheet of parchment paper between layers to prevent them from sticking together.

bars & squares

While bars bake in a pan like a cake, their dense texture is what categorizes them as cookies. They're made by spreading batter into a pan with sides, baking, and then cutting them into pieces once the batch has cooled.

Fudgy Brownies

- 4.5 ounces all-purpose flour (about 1 cup)
- ½ cup unsweetened cocoa
- ¼ teaspoon salt
- ⅓ cup butter
- 2 ounces dark chocolate, chopped
- 1 cup sugar
- ¼ cup 1% low-fat milk
- 1 teaspoon vanilla extract
- 2 large egg yolks
- 1 large egg
- Cooking spray

1. Preheat oven to 350°.

2. Weigh or lightly spoon flour into a dry measuring cup; level with a knife. Combine flour, cocoa, and salt in a medium bowl; stir with a whisk.

3. Place butter and chocolate in a medium microwave-safe bowl, and microwave at HIGH 45 seconds, stirring every 15 seconds. Stir until smooth. Cool slightly. Add sugar, milk, vanilla, egg yolks, and egg; stir with a whisk to combine. Add butter mixture to flour mixture, stirring just until combined. Pour batter into an 8-inch square metal baking pan coated with cooking spray. Bake at 350° for 20 minutes or until a wooden pick inserted in center comes out almost clean. **Yield: 16 servings (serving size: 1 square).**

CALORIES 147; FAT 6.1g (sat 3.6g, mono 1.5g, poly 0.3g); PROTEIN 2.3g; CARB 22.4g; FIBER 1.3g; CHOL 47mg; IRON 1mg; SODIUM 73mg; CALC 15mg

kitchen how-to:
make delicious light brownies

Rich, dense brownies include melted chocolate (preferably no more than 60% cacao) and bake just long enough to prevent them from drying out. Here are some foolproof tips for fudgy success.

1. It's OK if a few chocolate pieces remain intact after microwaving. Stir the chocolate after heating to help smooth out those last few bits.

2. Always check your baked goods a minute or two early to avoid overbaking. For a fudgy texture, a few crumbs should cling to the tester.

Peppermint Cheesecake Brownies

Cheesecake Batter:
- 1 (8-ounce) block ⅓-less-fat cream cheese
- ⅓ cup granulated sugar
- ¼ teaspoon peppermint extract
- 1 large egg
- 1 large egg white
- 1 tablespoon all-purpose flour

Brownie Batter:
- 4.5 ounces all-purpose flour (about 1 cup)
- ½ cup unsweetened cocoa
- ½ teaspoon salt
- 1½ cups packed brown sugar
- ¼ cup canola oil
- ¼ cup buttermilk
- 2 teaspoons vanilla extract
- 2 large egg whites
- 1 large egg

1. Preheat oven to 350°.
2. Line the bottom and sides of a 9-inch square metal baking pan with parchment paper; cut off excess parchment paper around the top edge of pan.
3. To prepare cheesecake batter, place cream cheese in a medium bowl; beat with a mixer at medium speed until smooth. Add granulated sugar and peppermint extract; beat well. Add 1 egg and 1 egg white; beat well. Add 1 tablespoon flour; beat mixture just until blended.

4. To prepare brownie batter, weigh or lightly spoon 4.5 ounces flour (about 1 cup) into a dry measuring cup; level with a knife. Combine 4.5 ounces flour, cocoa, and salt in a medium bowl, stirring with a whisk. Combine brown sugar, oil, buttermilk, vanilla, 2 egg whites, and 1 egg in a large bowl; beat with a mixer at medium-high speed until well blended. Add flour mixture to brown sugar mixture; beat at low speed just until blended.
5. Reserve ½ cup brownie batter. Pour remaining batter into prepared pan. Carefully pour cheesecake batter over top; spread evenly to edges. Dot cheesecake batter with reserved brownie batter. Swirl top 2 layers of batter together using the tip of a knife. Bake at 350° for 26 minutes or until top is set. Cool completely in pan on a wire rack. **Yield: 16 servings (serving size: 1 square).**

CALORIES 213; FAT 7.5g (sat 2.6g, mono 2.3g, poly 1.1g); PROTEIN 4.4g; CARB 32.3g; FIBER 0.7g; CHOL 37mg; IRON 1.3mg; SODIUM 169mg; CALC 32mg

kitchen how-to:
make swirled brownies

Spoon the first batter into the prepared pan (either lined with parchment paper or coated with cooking spray for easier removal). Spoon the second batter evenly over the first. Swirl batters together using the tip of a knife.

Chocolate-Mint Bars

Bottom Layer:
- 4.5 ounces all-purpose flour (about 1 cup)
- ½ teaspoon salt
- 1 cup granulated sugar
- 4 large egg whites
- ¼ cup butter, melted
- 2 tablespoons water
- 1 teaspoon vanilla extract
- 2 large eggs, beaten
- 1 (16-ounce) can chocolate syrup
- Cooking spray

Mint Layer:
- 2 cups powdered sugar
- ¼ cup butter, melted
- 2 tablespoons fat-free milk
- ½ teaspoon peppermint extract
- 2 drops green food coloring

Glaze:
- ¾ cup semisweet chocolate chips
- 3 tablespoons butter

1. Preheat oven to 350°.

2. To prepare bottom layer, weigh or lightly spoon flour into a dry measuring cup; level with a knife. Combine flour and salt; stir with a whisk. Combine granulated sugar, 4 egg whites, ¼ cup melted butter, 2 tablespoons water, vanilla, eggs, and chocolate syrup in a medium bowl; stir until smooth. Add flour mixture to chocolate mixture, stirring until blended. Pour batter into a 13 x 9–inch metal baking pan coated with cooking spray. Bake at 350° for 23 minutes or until a wooden pick inserted in center comes out almost clean. Cool completely in pan on a wire rack.

3. To prepare mint layer, combine powdered sugar, ¼ cup melted butter, and next 3 ingredients in a medium bowl; beat with a mixer until smooth. Spread mint mixture over cooled cake.

4. To prepare glaze, combine chocolate chips and 3 tablespoons butter in a medium microwave-safe bowl. Microwave at HIGH 1 minute or until melted, stirring after 30 seconds. Let stand 2 minutes. Spread chocolate mixture evenly over top. Cover and refrigerate until ready to serve. **Yield: 24 servings (serving size: 1 bar).**

CALORIES 220; FAT 7.3g (sat 4.3g, mono 2.1g, poly 0.3g); PROTEIN 2.3g; CARB 37.5g; FIBER 0.4g; CHOL 32mg; IRON 0.8mg; SODIUM 116mg; CALC 10mg

Glaze
What it adds: The top layer adds a smooth, chocolaty finish. Refrigerating the bars allows this layer to set properly. For a more grown-up taste, you can also use dark chocolate chips for some or all of the semisweet chocolate chips in the glaze.

Peppermint Extract
What it adds: Just a touch of peppermint extract gives this thin layer a burst of minty flavor. Don't overdo the extract, or it could overpower the flavor of these bars.

Bottom Layer
What it adds: The dense base layer is like a rich, fudgy brownie, so don't overcook it, or the dessert bars will be dry.

Chai Latte Brownies

If you love the rich flavor of Mexican hot chocolate spiced with cinnamon, this dessert will delight you. These brownies are best served warm and gooey.

- ¼ cup 1% low-fat milk
- 3 cardamom pods, crushed
- 3 whole allspice, crushed
- 3 whole cloves
- 1 cinnamon stick
- ¼ cup semisweet chocolate chips
- ¼ cup butter
- 2 large eggs
- 6.75 ounces all-purpose flour (about 1½ cups)
- 1 cup granulated sugar
- ½ cup unsweetened cocoa
- ⅓ cup packed brown sugar
- 1 teaspoon baking powder
- ½ teaspoon salt
- Cooking spray

1. Preheat oven to 350°.

2. Combine first 5 ingredients in a small saucepan; bring to a boil. Cover, remove from heat, and let stand 15 minutes. Strain milk mixture through a fine sieve into a large microwave-safe bowl; discard solids. Add chocolate chips and butter to milk mixture; microwave at HIGH 20 seconds or until chips and butter melt, stirring until smooth. Cool slightly; add eggs, stirring with a whisk.

3. Weigh or lightly spoon flour into dry measuring cups; level with a knife. Combine flour and next 5 ingredients in a medium bowl, stirring with a whisk. Add flour mixture to chocolate mixture, stirring just until combined. Spread evenly in a 9-inch square metal baking pan coated with cooking spray. Bake at 350° for 30 minutes or until center is set. Cool 10 minutes in pan on a wire rack. **Yield: 20 servings (serving size: 1 bar).**

CALORIES 130; FAT 3.8g (sat 1.9g, mono 1.5g, poly 0.2g); PROTEIN 2.2g; CARB 23.5g; FIBER 1.1g; CHOL 27mg; IRON 1mg; SODIUM 110mg; CALC 29mg

all about chai

The origin of chai stretches back thousands of years to ancient Nepal, Tibet, and India. "Chai" is the Indian word for tea. The fragrantly spiced, sweetened black tea served in India is often called masala (meaning "spice blend") chai. The blend typically includes combinations of cinnamon, cloves, cardamom, and black peppercorns, though masala chai can also contain fresh ginger, vanilla beans, white peppercorns, aniseed, bay leaves, mace, fennel seeds, and nutmeg. Chai has no single authentic recipe; flavors vary from region to region and even kitchen to kitchen, but regardless of the blend, chai spices bring warm, exotic flavors to a variety of dishes.

Butterscotch Blondies

We wanted just enough salt to heighten the flavor, so we opted for unsalted butter here.

- 9 ounces all-purpose flour (about 2 cups)
- 2½ cups firmly packed light brown sugar
- 2 teaspoons baking powder
- ½ teaspoon salt
- 10 tablespoons unsalted butter
- 6 large egg whites
- Cooking spray

1. Preheat oven to 350°.

2. Weigh or lightly spoon flour into dry measuring cups; level with a knife. Combine flour, sugar, baking powder, and salt in a large bowl.

3. Place butter in a small skillet over medium heat. Cook 6 minutes or until lightly browned, stirring occasionally. Pour into a small bowl, and cool 10 minutes. Combine butter and egg whites, stirring with a whisk. Pour butter mixture over flour mixture; stir just until moistened. Spoon batter into a 13 x 9–inch metal baking pan coated with cooking spray; smooth top using a spatula. Bake at 350° for 30 minutes or until a wooden pick inserted in center comes out clean. Cool in pan on a wire rack. **Yield: 24 servings (serving size: 1 square).**

CALORIES 170; FAT 4.8g (sat 3g, mono 1.2g, poly 0.2g); PROTEIN 1.9g; CARB 30.5g; FIBER 0.3g; CHOL 13mg; IRON 1.1mg; SODIUM 108mg; CALC 45mg

brown butter

Browning the butter deepens its flavor and gives it a nutty taste and aroma. Be sure to watch the butter closely, since it can quickly go from perfectly browned to burned.

1. Place butter in a small skillet over medium heat. It's best not to use a black or dark-colored pan, since you won't be able to see the butter browning.
2. Cook butter 6 minutes or until lightly browned.

Piña Colada Cheesecake Bars

This recipe uses a small amount of coconut flour, which is slightly sweet and high in fiber (3 grams per tablespoon). You also can substitute an equal amount of all-purpose flour. Standard lemons work well in this recipe, but Meyer lemons, which have a sweeter flavor, are a good substitute.

Crust:
- 1 cup graham cracker crumbs
- 2 tablespoons coconut flour or all-purpose flour
- 2 tablespoons turbinado sugar or granulated sugar
- ½ teaspoon ground ginger
- 2 tablespoons butter, melted
- 1 tablespoon canola oil
- 1 tablespoon water
- Cooking spray

Filling:
- 1 cup 2% low-fat cottage cheese
- ½ cup granulated sugar
- ¼ cup (2 ounces) block-style fat-free cream cheese, softened
- 1½ tablespoons grated lemon rind
- 1 tablespoon fresh lemon juice
- 1 tablespoon pineapple juice
- ½ teaspoon vanilla extract
- Dash of salt
- 6 large egg whites

Remaining Ingredients:
- 1 cup chopped fresh pineapple
- ¼ cup unsweetened shredded coconut, toasted

1. Preheat oven to 350°.

2. To prepare crust, combine first 4 ingredients in a bowl. Add butter, oil, and 1 tablespoon water; toss well. Press mixture into bottom of an 8-inch square metal baking pan coated with cooking spray. Bake at 350° for 10 minutes. Cool completely on a wire rack.

3. To prepare filling, place cottage cheese and next 7 ingredients in a food processor; process until smooth. Add egg whites; process until blended. Spread cheese mixture over cooled crust. Bake at 350° for 33 minutes or until set. Cool 10 minutes on wire rack. Refrigerate 2 hours or until thoroughly chilled. Top with pineapple and coconut. **Yield: 16 servings (serving size: 1 bar).**

CALORIES 117; FAT 4.6g (sat 2.2g, mono 1.2g, poly 0.7g); PROTEIN 4.1g; CARB 15.4g; FIBER 0.9g; CHOL 6mg; IRON 0.5mg; SODIUM 142mg; CALC 27mg

kitchen how-to:
chop fresh pineapple

1

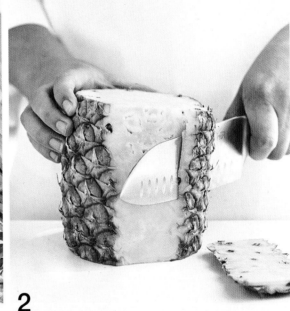

2

The prickly exterior of fresh pineapple may tempt you to reach for the precut variety, but you can easily cut your own following these steps.

1. Lay the pineapple on its side on a cutting board, and cut off the leafy top (the plume) and the base.
2. Stand the pineapple upright, and cut down the sides to remove the rind. Try to remove as little of the flesh as possible.
3. Cut the pineapple into thirds by carefully slicing downward, avoiding the fibrous core at the center. You can then slice the thirds into cubes.

3

Pumpkin
What it adds: Pumpkin's bright-orange flesh signals rich amounts of beta-carotene, which, translated into vitamin A, helps keep your eyesight sharp.

Blend of Cream Cheese
What it adds: Using a mix of ⅓-less-fat cream cheese and fat-free, we're able to get a creamy consistency while keeping calories and saturated fat in check.

Pumpkin Cheesecake Bars

When buying canned pumpkin, make sure you buy unsweetened pumpkin with just one ingredient: pumpkin.

Crust:
6.75	ounces all-purpose flour (about 1½ cups)
½	cup packed dark brown sugar
⅛	teaspoon salt
8	teaspoons chilled butter, cut into small pieces
	Cooking spray

Filling:
1¼	cups canned unsweetened pumpkin
½	cup granulated sugar
½	cup packed dark brown sugar
1	(8-ounce) block fat-free cream cheese, softened
1	(8-ounce) block ⅓-less-fat cream cheese, softened
6	large egg whites
1	teaspoon ground cinnamon
1½	teaspoons vanilla extract
¼	teaspoon ground allspice
1	large egg

Remaining Ingredients:
¼	cup chopped pecans
2	teaspoons water

1. Preheat oven to 350°.

2. To prepare crust, weigh or lightly spoon flour into dry measuring cups; level with a knife. Heat a nonstick skillet over medium-high heat. Add flour to pan; cook 5 minutes or until light brown, stirring often. Remove pan from heat. Transfer flour to a bowl; cool completely.

3. Place cooled flour, ½ cup brown sugar, and salt in a food processor; pulse 5 times or until combined. Add chilled butter; pulse until mixture resembles fine meal. Press 1 cup flour mixture evenly into bottom of a 13 x 9–inch glass or ceramic baking dish coated with cooking spray; reserve remaining flour mixture. Bake at 350° for 10 minutes or until crust is lightly browned.

4. To prepare filling, spread pumpkin evenly on several layers of paper towels; cover with additional paper towels. Let stand 5 minutes.

5. Combine granulated sugar, ½ cup brown sugar, and cream cheeses in a bowl. Beat with a mixer at medium speed 2 minutes or until smooth. Scrape pumpkin into bowl using a rubber spatula. Add egg whites and next 4 ingredients; beat until smooth. Scrape batter into baked crust.

6. Combine reserved flour mixture and pecans in a small bowl; sprinkle with 2 teaspoons water. Squeeze handfuls of topping to form large pieces. Crumble over filling. Bake at 350° for 40 minutes or until filling is firmly set. Remove from heat; cool in pan on a wire rack to room temperature. Serve at room temperature. **Yield: 16 servings (serving size: 1 bar).**

CALORIES 216; FAT 7g (sat 3.6g, mono 2.3g, poly 0.7g); PROTEIN 6.7g; CARB 32.2g; FIBER 1.1g; CHOL 29mg; IRON 1.5mg; SODIUM 207mg; CALC 65mg

Apple-Date Bars

9	ounces all-purpose flour (about 2 cups)
1	teaspoon baking soda
1	teaspoon baking powder
½	teaspoon ground cinnamon
¼	teaspoon salt
2	cups sugar
7	tablespoons butter, softened
1	large egg
2	large egg whites
¼	cup applesauce
1	teaspoon vanilla extract
1	cup chopped pitted dates
1	teaspoon all-purpose flour
1½	cups chopped peeled Granny Smith apple (about 1 large)
1½	cups chopped peeled Red Delicious apple (about 1 large)
½	teaspoon fresh lemon juice
⅔	cup chopped pecans
	Cooking spray

1. Preheat oven to 325°.

2. Weigh or lightly spoon 9 ounces flour (about 2 cups) into dry measuring cups; level with a knife. Combine 9 ounces flour and next 4 ingredients in a large bowl; stir with a whisk.

3. Place sugar and butter in a large bowl, and beat with a mixer at high speed 2 minutes or until light and fluffy. Add egg and egg whites, beating well after each addition. Stir in applesauce and vanilla. Gradually add flour mixture to sugar mixture; stir just until combined to form a stiff batter. Toss dates with 1 teaspoon flour. Toss apples with juice. Add dates, apples, and pecans to flour mixture, stirring just until combined. Pour batter into a 13 x 9–inch glass or ceramic baking dish coated with cooking spray. Bake at 325° for 1 hour and 5 minutes or until a wooden pick inserted in center comes out clean. Cool completely on a wire rack.

Yield: 20 servings (serving size: 1 bar).

CALORIES 223; FAT 7.2g (sat 2.9g, mono 2.7g, poly 1.1g); PROTEIN 2.6g; CARB 38.8g; FIBER 1.6g; CHOL 21mg; IRON 0.9mg; SODIUM 154mg; CALC 26mg

Mix of Apples

What it adds: Each apple variety offers its own sweet or tart flavor. Red Delicious has a mildly sweet flavor, while Granny Smith is more tart.

Butter
What it adds: The butter contributes to the golden crust and rich flavor of these dense, moist, fruit-studded bars.

Lemon Juice
What it adds: Tossing the apples with a bit of lemon juice perks up their flavor.

Roasted Banana Bars with Browned Butter–Pecan Frosting

You can use walnuts instead of pecans, if you'd like. For more information about how to brown butter, see page 181.

Bars:
- 2 cups sliced ripe banana (about 3 medium)
- ⅓ cup packed dark brown sugar
- 1 tablespoon chilled butter, cut into small pieces
- 9 ounces cake flour (about 2¼ cups)
- ¾ teaspoon baking soda
- ½ teaspoon baking powder
- ¼ cup nonfat buttermilk
- 1 teaspoon vanilla extract
- ½ cup butter, softened
- 1¼ cups granulated sugar
- 2 large eggs
- Baking spray with flour

Frosting:
- ¼ cup butter
- 2 cups powdered sugar
- ⅓ cup (3 ounces) ⅓-less-fat cream cheese, softened
- 1 teaspoon vanilla extract
- ¼ cup chopped pecans, toasted

1. Preheat oven to 400°.
2. To prepare bars, combine banana, brown sugar, and 1 tablespoon butter in an 8-inch square glass or ceramic baking dish. Bake at 400° for 35 minutes, stirring after 17 minutes. Cool slightly.
3. Reduce oven temperature to 375°.
4. Weigh or lightly spoon flour into dry measuring cups; level with a knife. Combine flour, baking soda, and baking powder in a medium bowl. Combine banana mixture, buttermilk, and 1 teaspoon vanilla in another medium bowl. Place ½ cup butter and granulated sugar in a large bowl; beat with a mixer at medium speed until well blended. Add eggs to granulated sugar mixture; mix well. Add flour mixture and banana mixture alternately to sugar mixture, beginning and ending with flour mixture.
5. Pour batter into a 13 x 9–inch metal baking pan coated with baking spray. Bake at 375° for 20 minutes or until a wooden pick inserted in center comes out clean. Cool completely in pan on a wire rack.
6. To prepare frosting, place ¼ cup butter in a small saucepan over medium heat; cook 4 minutes or until lightly browned. Cool slightly. Combine browned butter, powdered sugar, cream cheese, and 1 teaspoon vanilla in a medium bowl; beat with a mixer until smooth. Spread frosting over cooled bars. Sprinkle with pecans.
Yield: 24 servings (serving size: 1 bar).

CALORIES 221; FAT 8.4g (sat 4.7g, mono 2.3g, poly 0.6g); PROTEIN 2.3g; CARB 35.1g; FIBER 0.6g; CHOL 39mg; IRON 1mg; SODIUM 117mg; CALC 23mg

all about pecans

Pecans are a delicious, crunchy source of healthy fats. You can buy them in many forms—halves, pieces, chopped—but whole pecans in the shell provide the best flavor and are the best bet for freshness. One pound of unshelled pecans will yield about half a pound (or about 2 cups) of nuts. Any leftover unshelled pecans can be stored in a cool, dry place for up to 6 months.

Cherry-Oatmeal Bars

Crust:
4.5 ounces all-purpose flour (about 1 cup)
  1 cup quick-cooking oats
  ½ cup packed brown sugar
  ¼ teaspoon salt
  ¼ teaspoon baking soda
  ¼ teaspoon ground cinnamon
  6 tablespoons butter, melted
  3 tablespoons orange juice
Cooking spray

Filling:
1⅓ cups dried cherries (about 6 ounces)
  ¾ cup sour cream
  ½ cup granulated sugar
  2 tablespoons all-purpose flour
  1 teaspoon vanilla extract
  ½ teaspoon grated lemon rind
  1 large egg white, lightly beaten

1. Preheat oven to 325°.
2. To prepare crust, weigh or lightly spoon flour into a dry measuring cup; level with a knife. Combine flour and next 5 ingredients in a medium bowl, stirring well with a whisk. Drizzle butter and juice over flour mixture, stirring until moistened (mixture will be crumbly). Reserve ½ cup oat mixture. Press remaining oat mixture into bottom of an 11 x 7–inch glass or ceramic baking dish coated with cooking spray.
3. To prepare filling, combine cherries, sour cream, granulated sugar, and remaining ingredients in a medium bowl, stirring well. Spread cherry mixture over prepared crust; sprinkle reserved oat mixture evenly over filling. Bake at 325° for 40 minutes or until edges are golden. Cool completely in pan on a wire rack. **Yield: 24 servings (serving size: 1 bar).**

CALORIES 135; FAT 4.6g (sat 2.6g, mono 0.8g, poly 0.2g); PROTEIN 1.7g; CARB 21.5g; FIBER 1.3g; CHOL 13mg; IRON 0.7mg; SODIUM 68mg; CALC 27mg

all about oats

Regular, or old-fashioned, oats (shown at left) are the type that many of us know as oatmeal. This type is made of whole groats that have been steamed, and then flattened by large rollers; they take about 5 minutes to cook. Quick oats (shown at right) are regular oats that have been flattened even more, and then cooked and dried, which speeds up their cooking process—often they take only a minute to cook. Don't confuse quick oats with the pulverized oats mixed with sugar and other flavorings in the instant oat packets.

Fig and Almond Squares

Bake these chewy, blondie-like treats up to 2 days ahead, and store in an airtight container.

 Cooking spray
3.4 ounces all-purpose flour (about ¾ cup)
 ½ teaspoon baking powder
 ⅛ teaspoon salt
 ¾ cup packed brown sugar
 ¼ cup butter, melted
 1 tablespoon amaretto (almond-flavored liqueur)
 1 teaspoon vanilla extract
 1 large egg
 1 large egg white
 ½ cup chopped dried figs
 ¼ cup flaked sweetened coconut
 2 tablespoons sliced almonds, toasted
 ½ cup powdered sugar
2½ teaspoons hot water
 ¼ teaspoon amaretto (almond-flavored liqueur)

1. Preheat oven to 350°.
2. Coat bottom of an 8-inch square metal baking pan with cooking spray (do not coat sides of pan).
3. Weigh or lightly spoon flour into dry measuring cups; level with a knife. Combine flour, baking powder, and salt in a large bowl, stirring well with a whisk. Combine brown sugar and next 5 ingredients in a medium bowl, stirring with a whisk until well blended. Add brown sugar mixture, figs, coconut, and almonds to flour mixture; stir until blended. Spoon batter into prepared pan. Bake at 350° for 25 minutes or until a wooden pick inserted in center comes out clean. Cool in pan on a wire rack.
4. Combine powdered sugar, 2½ teaspoons hot water, and ¼ teaspoon amaretto in a small bowl, stirring with a whisk until smooth. Drizzle over squares. **Yield: 16 servings (serving size: 1 square).**

CALORIES 138; FAT 4.2g (sat 2.4g, mono 1.3g, poly 0.3g); PROTEIN 1.6g; CARB 23.7g; FIBER 1g; CHOL 21mg; IRON 0.7mg; SODIUM 79mg; CALC 32mg

kitchen how-to: toast nuts

Toasting nuts gives them a richer flavor and enhances their nuttiness. Spread the nuts in a single layer on a baking sheet, and bake at 350° for 6 to 8 minutes. Or for a stovetop method, place the nuts in a dry skillet, and cook over medium heat, stirring frequently, 1 to 2 minutes or until they're toasted. Whichever method you choose, you need to watch them carefully—they can go from perfectly toasted to burned *very* quickly.

Key Lime Squares

Crust:
2.25 ounces all-purpose flour (about ½ cup)
⅓ cup toasted wheat germ
⅓ cup packed brown sugar
¼ cup butter, softened
Cooking spray

Filling:
1 cup granulated sugar
2 tablespoons all-purpose flour
½ teaspoon baking powder
2 tablespoons tub-style light cream cheese
2 large eggs
1 teaspoon grated Key lime rind or lime rind
¼ cup Key lime juice or lime juice
1 cup frozen reduced-calorie whipped topping, thawed

Remaining Ingredient:
Grated fresh lime rind

1. Preheat oven to 350°.
2. To prepare crust, weigh or lightly spoon 2.25 ounces flour (about ½ cup) into a dry measuring cup; level with a knife. Combine 2.25 ounces flour, wheat germ, and brown sugar in a small bowl; cut in butter with a pastry blender or 2 knives until well blended. Press mixture into a 9-inch square metal baking pan coated with cooking spray. Bake at 350° for 15 minutes. Cool on a wire rack.
3. To prepare filling, combine granulated sugar, 2 tablespoons flour, and baking powder in a medium bowl. Add cream cheese and eggs; beat with a mixer at high speed until well blended. Stir in rind and juice. Spread filling over crust. Bake at 350° for 25 minutes or until filling is set. Cool on a wire rack. Spread whipped topping evenly over filling. Sprinkle rind over topping. **Yield: 9 servings (serving size: 1 square).**

CALORIES 251; FAT 8.3g (sat 2.7g, mono 2.7g, poly 2.1g); PROTEIN 3.9g; CARB 41.8g; FIBER 0.9g; CHOL 51mg; IRON 1.1mg; SODIUM 128mg; CALC 43mg

kitchen how-to: juice citrus fruits

The juice of citrus fruits can add a burst of citrus flavor to a variety of dishes. To get the juice, you'll want the fruit to be at room temperature—if the fruit is cold, it won't release as much juice. To extract even more, firmly roll the fruit between your palm and work surface several times before juicing. Simply cut the fruit in half and squeeze, or place the cut half in a handheld press. This gadget releases the most juice while trapping the seeds.

kitchen how-to: store extra juice

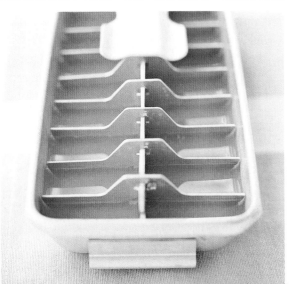

If you have leftover juice that didn't make it into a recipe, pour it into a clean, empty ice cube tray. The frozen cubes can then be transferred to a zip-top plastic freezer bag and be used as ice for fruit punches without watering them down, or as a time-saver for later.

Two-Layer Caramel-Pecan Bars

Try cutting the panful into four equal strips, using firm pressure with a large, heavy knife. Remove the strips from the pan, and cut each crosswise into five pieces. Then drizzle with chocolate.

⅓   cup packed brown sugar
3   tablespoons butter, softened
2   teaspoons vanilla extract, divided
¼   teaspoon salt
3.4   ounces all-purpose flour (about ¾ cup)
     Cooking spray
3   tablespoons fat-free milk, divided
40   small soft caramel candies
3   tablespoons finely chopped pecans
⅓   cup semisweet chocolate chips

1. Preheat oven to 375°.
2. Place brown sugar, butter, 1 teaspoon vanilla, and salt in a large bowl; beat with a mixer at medium speed until well blended. Weigh or lightly spoon flour into dry measuring cups; level with a knife. Add flour to sugar mixture, stirring until well blended. (Mixture will be crumbly.) Firmly press mixture into bottom of an 8-inch square metal baking pan coated with cooking spray. Bake at 375° for 15 minutes.
3. While crust bakes, combine 2 tablespoons milk and caramel candies in a medium saucepan. Place over medium heat; cook 10 minutes or until candies melt, stirring occasionally. Stir in remaining 1 teaspoon vanilla; remove from heat.
4. Remove crust from oven. Pour caramel mixture evenly over hot crust. Sprinkle with pecans. Bake at 375° for 15 minutes. Cool completely in pan on a wire rack. Cut into 20 bars. Combine remaining 1 tablespoon milk and chocolate chips in a microwave-safe bowl; microwave at HIGH 45 seconds or until melted, stirring until smooth. Drizzle over bars. **Yield: 20 servings (serving size: 1 bar).**

CALORIES 142; FAT 4.7g (sat 2g, mono 1.1g, poly 0.3g); PROTEIN 1.8g; CARB 22.6g; FIBER 0.5g; CHOL 7mg; IRON 0.3mg; SODIUM 89mg; CALC 39mg

kitchen how-to:
make the base of two-layer caramel-pecan bars

Use your fingers to press the flour mixture evenly and firmly into the bottom of a baking pan coated with cooking spray. Compacting the layer means it will hold together better when cut.

Chocolate Shortbread

4.5 ounces all-purpose flour (about 1 cup)
3 tablespoons unsweetened premium dark cocoa
¼ teaspoon salt
½ cup powdered sugar
5 tablespoons butter, softened
¼ cup canola oil
Cooking spray

1. Weigh or lightly spoon flour into a dry measuring cup; level with a knife. Combine flour, cocoa, and salt in a small bowl; stir with a whisk.
2. Place sugar, butter, and oil in a medium bowl; mix with hands until combined. Add flour mixture, and mix with hands until combined; wrap in plastic wrap. Refrigerate 30 minutes.
3. Preheat oven to 325°.
4. Place dough on a baking sheet coated with cooking spray; press dough into an 8 x 5–inch rectangle about ⅜ inch thick. Pierce entire surface liberally with a fork. Bake at 325° for 30 minutes or just until set. Cut shortbread into 24 squares. Cool completely. **Yield: 24 servings (serving size: 1 square).**

CALORIES 72; FAT 4.8g (sat 1.7g, mono 2.1g, poly 0.8g); PROTEIN 0.7g; CARB 7g; FIBER 0.3g; CHOL 6mg; IRON 0.3mg; SODIUM 42mg; CALC 2mg

Lemon Shortbread: You can also use grated orange rind in place of lemon. A little bit of cornstarch ensures a short texture in the cookies. Substitute 3 tablespoons cornstarch for the unsweetened cocoa. Add ½ teaspoon grated lemon rind to flour mixture. Knead dough lightly 4 times or just until smooth before chilling. Bake 30 minutes or just until set and edges are golden. **Yield: 24 servings (serving size: 1 square).**

CALORIES 74; FAT 4.8g (sat 1.7g, mono 2g, poly 0.8g); PROTEIN 0.6g; CARB 7.5g; FIBER 0.2g; CHOL 6mg; IRON 0.3mg; SODIUM 42mg; CALC 2mg

Brown Sugar Shortbread: Using light brown sugar yields sweet treats with caramel notes. These double easily; just bake each batch separately for the best results. Use 5.5 ounces all-purpose flour (about 1¼ cups), and substitute 3 tablespoons cornstarch for the cocoa. Omit powdered sugar and oil, and use ½ cup packed light brown sugar and 7 tablespoons butter, softened. Sprinkle dough with 1½ teaspoons ice water; knead dough lightly 4 times or just until smooth before chilling. Bake 25 minutes or just until set and edges are golden. **Yield: 24 servings (serving size: 1 square).**

CALORIES 74; FAT 3.4g (sat 2.1g, mono 0.9g, poly 0.2g); PROTEIN 0.7g; CARB 10.4g; FIBER 0.2g; CHOL 9mg; IRON 0.4mg; SODIUM 50mg; CALC 6mg

kitchen how-to:
make shortbread

Shortbread has a wonderful buttery, rich, and short (or crisp) texture. Traditional shortbread recipes use a lot of butter to create that texture, but we lowered the saturated fat in our versions by replacing some of the butter with canola oil, which is high in healthy fats and lower in saturated fat. To prepare shortbread, use your hands to incorporate the ingredients. Then place the dough in plastic wrap, and chill it in the refrigerator to let it firm up. Pat the dough out onto a baking sheet coated with cooking spray, and pierce the surface with a fork to prevent the dough from rising. Bake just until the shortbread is set.

Raisin-Cranberry Granola Bars

3.4 ounces all-purpose flour (about ¾ cup)
½ cup packed light brown sugar
2 tablespoons chilled butter, cut into small pieces
1½ cups uncooked old-fashioned rolled oats
⅓ cup chopped pitted dates
⅓ cup raisins
⅓ cup dried cranberries
2 teaspoons grated orange rind
1 teaspoon ground cinnamon
2 large egg whites, lightly beaten
¼ cup applesauce
1 teaspoon vanilla extract
Cooking spray

1. Preheat oven to 350°.
2. Weigh or lightly spoon flour into dry measuring cups; level with a knife. Place brown sugar in a medium bowl. Cut in butter with a pastry blender or 2 knives until crumbly. Stir in flour, oats, and next 5 ingredients.
3. Add egg whites, applesauce, and vanilla to oat mixture; stir well.
4. Press mixture into a 9-inch square metal baking pan coated with cooking spray. Bake at 350° for 15 to 18 minutes. Cool completely on a wire rack. **Yield: 12 servings (serving size: 1 bar).**

CALORIES 165; FAT 2.8g (sat 1.2g, mono 0.7g, poly 0.4g); PROTEIN 3.5g; CARB 32.3g; FIBER 2.1g; CHOL 5mg; IRON 1.1mg; SODIUM 26mg; CALC 22mg

make raisin-cranberry granola bars

Granola bars are easily adaptable. You can use any type of dried fruit you like or change it up by mixing in nuts, chocolate chips, or butterscotch morsels. There are plenty of options to keep your palate pleased.

1. Weigh or lightly spoon flour into dry measuring cups; level with a knife. Cut butter into brown sugar with a pastry blender or 2 knives until the mixture is crumbly.

2. Stir in flour, oats, dried fruit, orange rind, and ground cinnamon.

3. Add egg whites, applesauce, and vanilla to oat mixture; stir well.

4. Press the mixture into a 9-inch square metal baking pan coated with cooking spray, and bake. If you prefer a chewier texture, bake the granola bars only 15 minutes. For a crispier bar, bake 18 minutes.

5. Cool completely on a wire rack, and then cut into bars. Wrap individual bars in heavy-duty plastic wrap, and store in an airtight container.

way to bake

cakes &
cupcakes

cakes & cupcakes

You can have your cake (or cupcake)—and eat the crumbs, too.

Equipment

Good-quality cake pans are important. Choose aluminum pans with a dull finish, since this metal absorbs and conducts heat efficiently. Avoid shiny pans, which deflect heat, and dark metal pans, which cause the outer edges of the cake to cook more quickly than the center and overbrown, making the cake dry and tough.

A stand mixer is ideal for mixing most cakes and cupcakes, since the powerful motor aerates the butter, sugar, and egg mixture, which helps the cake rise nicely while it bakes. A handheld mixer works just fine, though you should mix the butter and sugar a minute or two longer to incorporate as much air as the stand mixer does.

In the Oven

Avoid baking cake layers on different levels in the oven if possible, and place them at least 2 inches apart in the oven and 2 inches away from the oven walls to promote even baking and allow maximum air circulation. If you have to bake the layers on different racks, rotate the pans halfway through the baking time so they'll cook evenly.

Once the cake layers or cupcakes are in the oven, don't

open the oven door—turn on the oven light if you need to take a peek. Opening the door causes temperature fluctuations that can lead to a variety of problems. If the temperature in the oven drops, the cake or cupcakes will likely bake more slowly, and they may sink in the center. Then, as the oven reheats to the required temperature, the edges of the cake will be exposed to more extreme temperatures, possibly resulting in a tough, dry cake.

Testing for Doneness

Overbaking is more of a problem for lighter cakes and cupcakes that use less butter and sugar, and it can result in a dry-textured cake. To prevent it, we suggest testing for doneness about 5 to 10 minutes before the recipe states the cake should finish baking. Test the cake's doneness by inserting a wooden pick into the center of the cake and pulling it straight out. If the wooden pick comes out clean (or almost clean, depending on the recipe's instructions), the cake is done. If you see the sides of the cake pulling away from the pan, this is another sign of doneness.

layer cakes

Layer cakes from scratch are not only tastier than anything that comes from a box, but they're also surprisingly easy to make.

Pecan Spice Cake with Maple Frosting

Work quickly to spread frosting over first layer, stack second on top, and then spread remaining frosting over top and sides before it sets.

Cake:

  Cooking spray
  2 teaspoons all-purpose flour
  9 ounces all-purpose flour (about 2 cups)
  ½ teaspoon baking soda
  ½ teaspoon salt
  ½ teaspoon ground cinnamon
  ¼ teaspoon ground nutmeg
  Dash of ground cloves
  1 cup packed brown sugar
  ½ cup butter, softened
  3 large eggs
  1 teaspoon vanilla extract
  1 cup buttermilk
  ⅓ cup chopped pecans, toasted

Frosting:

  ½ cup packed brown sugar
  ¼ cup heavy whipping cream
  ¼ cup maple syrup
  1 tablespoon butter
  Dash of salt
  2 cups powdered sugar
  ½ teaspoon vanilla extract
  2 tablespoons chopped pecans, toasted

1. Preheat oven to 350°.
2. To prepare cake, coat 2 (8-inch) round cake pans with cooking spray. Line bottoms of pans with wax paper; coat wax paper with cooking spray. Dust each pan with 1 teaspoon flour. Weigh or lightly spoon 9 ounces flour (about 2 cups) into dry measuring cups; level with a knife. Combine 9 ounces flour, baking soda, and next 4 ingredients, stirring well with a whisk.
3. Place 1 cup brown sugar and ½ cup butter in a large mixing bowl; beat with a mixer at medium-high speed until light and fluffy (about 3 minutes). Add eggs, 1 at a time, beating well after each addition. Beat in 1 teaspoon vanilla. Add flour mixture and buttermilk alternately to sugar mixture, beginning and ending with flour mixture and beating just until combined. Fold in ⅓ cup pecans. Pour batter into prepared pans.
4. Bake at 350° for 24 minutes or until a wooden pick inserted in center comes out clean. Cool in pans 5 minutes on wire racks. Invert cake layers onto racks; cool completely. Discard wax paper.
5. To prepare frosting, place ½ cup brown sugar and next 4 ingredients in a heavy saucepan over medium-high heat; bring to a boil, stirring just until sugar dissolves. Cook, without stirring, 3 minutes. Scrape brown sugar mixture into a bowl. Add powdered sugar; beat with a mixer at high speed 2 minutes or until slightly cooled and thick. Beat in ½ teaspoon vanilla. Place 1 cake layer on a plate; spread with ¾ cup frosting. Top with remaining cake layer. Spread remaining frosting over top and sides of cake; sprinkle with 2 tablespoons pecans. Let cake stand until frosting is set. **Yield: 16 servings (serving size: 1 slice).**

CALORIES 325; FAT 11.8g (sat 5.7g, mono 3.8g, poly 1.2g); PROTEIN 3.8g; CARB 52.1g; FIBER 0.8g; CHOL 64mg; IRON 1.5mg; SODIUM 209mg; CALC 36mg

kitchen how-to: bake a layer cake

Our lighter cakes save on calories and fat,
which is no small thing in baking—and eating—decadent
desserts. There are, naturally, a few tricks to coaxing
great taste and texture from a cake that relies on less
butter and sugar. We'll share our secrets.

1. Prevent the cake layers from sticking to the pan and
crumbling when you try to remove them by spraying the
pan with cooking spray, lining it with wax paper,
spraying again, and dusting with flour.

2. Precision is important when baking, especially light
baking, where there's less margin for error. For absolute
accuracy, weigh the flour instead of scooping and
measuring with a cup.

3. Fluffy batter will result in a moist cake with a fine
crumb. The first step of the mixing process—creaming
butter with sugar—whips air into the batter. More air is
added as you incorporate eggs into the batter by
beating it.

4. Slow the mixer speed before adding flour and milk.
Start with flour, then alternate with liquid (often milk).
Finish with flour as well. Beat only until combined. If
overbeaten at this stage, the cake will become tough.

Espresso Layer Cake

Cake:
  Cooking spray
  ¼ cup hot water
  2 tablespoons finely ground espresso
10.13 ounces all-purpose flour (about 2¼ cups)
  1 teaspoon baking soda
  ½ teaspoon salt
  1 cup granulated sugar
  ¼ cup packed brown sugar
  ½ cup vegetable shortening
  1 teaspoon vanilla extract
  3 large eggs
  1 cup low-fat buttermilk

Frosting:
  ¼ cup butter
  ½ cup packed brown sugar
  7 tablespoons evaporated fat-free milk

  2 teaspoons finely ground espresso
1½ teaspoons vanilla extract
  3 cups powdered sugar
Whole coffee beans (optional)

1. Preheat oven to 350°.
2. To prepare cake, coat 2 (9-inch) round cake pans with cooking spray; line bottoms of pans with wax paper. Coat wax paper with cooking spray.
3. Combine ¼ cup hot water and 2 tablespoons espresso in a small bowl, stirring to dissolve. Weigh or lightly spoon flour into dry measuring cups; level with a knife. Sift together flour, baking soda, and salt.
4. Combine granulated sugar and ¼ cup brown sugar. Place ¼ cup sugar mixture, shortening, and 1 teaspoon vanilla in a large bowl; beat with a mixer at low speed for 30 seconds or until well combined. Increase speed to medium; add remaining sugar mixture, ¼ cup at a time, beating for 15 seconds after each addition. Scrape sides of bowl; beat an additional 5 minutes. Add eggs, 1 at a time, beating for 1 minute after each addition. Add espresso mixture, beating until well combined. Add flour mixture and buttermilk alternately to egg mixture, beginning and ending with flour mixture. Pour batter into prepared pans. Bake at 350° for 30 minutes or until a wooden pick inserted in center comes out clean. Cool in pans 10 minutes on wire racks; remove from pans. Cool completely on wire racks. Discard wax paper.

5. To prepare frosting, melt butter in a medium, heavy saucepan over medium heat. Add ½ cup brown sugar; cook 3 minutes or until mixture is smooth, stirring frequently with a whisk. Stir in evaporated milk, 1 tablespoon at a time; cook 3 minutes or until mixture resembles caramel sauce.

Remove from heat; stir in 2 teaspoons espresso. Cool to room temperature. Stir in 1½ teaspoons vanilla. Gradually add powdered sugar, stirring with a whisk until smooth.

6. Place 1 cake layer on a plate; spread with ½ cup frosting. Top with remaining cake layer; spread

remaining frosting over top and sides of cake. Arrange coffee beans on top of cake, if desired. Let cake stand 1 hour or until frosting is set. **Yield: 18 servings (serving size: 1 slice).**

CALORIES 309; FAT 9g (sat 3.3g, mono 2.9g, poly 1.6g); PROTEIN 3.7g; CARB 53.4g; FIBER 0.4g; CHOL 43mg; IRON 1.1mg; SODIUM 197mg; CALC 50mg

kitchen how-to: frost a cake

1

2

3

Frosting adds moisture to a cake and helps hold moisture in. Since a cake is more likely to crumble if you frost it while it's still warm, you should let the layer (or layers) cool in the pan and then on a wire rack.

1. Unwrap the cake layers, and place 1 layer on a cake stand. Slip strips of wax paper beneath the edges to keep the stand clean.
2. To frost between the layers, place about 1 cup of frosting onto the center of the layer, and sweep outward with a spatula—an offset spatula, which allows for even spreading and keeps your hand away from the cake, is best.

4

5

3. Place an unfrosted layer bottom-side up on the frosted layer. Apply a thin layer of frosting (known as a crumb coat) to the entire cake to seal in any loose crumbs. Allow it to set in the refrigerator for about 15 minutes.
4. To frost the top of the cake, place about 1 cup of frosting onto the center of the cake, and spread to

the edge. Cover the top with an even layer of frosting
5. For the sides, load the spatula with frosting, and lightly push into the cake as you turn the cake stand. Continue spreading until the cake is evenly coated. Let the cake set in the refrigerator for 15 minutes before decorating it.

Lemon Cake

Cake:
  Cooking spray
  2 tablespoons all-purpose flour
  9 ounces all-purpose flour (about 2 cups)
  1 teaspoon baking powder
  ½ teaspoon baking soda
  ½ teaspoon salt
  1½ cups granulated sugar
  ½ cup unsalted butter, softened
  3 large eggs
  1 cup nonfat buttermilk
  2 tablespoons finely grated lemon rind
  2 tablespoons fresh lemon juice

Frosting:
  3 cups powdered sugar
  ¼ cup unsalted butter, melted
  1 tablespoon finely grated lemon rind
  ¼ cup fresh lemon juice
  Lemon rind strips (optional)

1. Preheat oven to 350°.
2. To prepare cake, coat 2 (8-inch) round cake pans with cooking spray; line bottoms of pans with wax paper. Coat wax paper with cooking spray. Dust each pan with 1 tablespoon flour.

3. Weigh or lightly spoon 9 ounces flour (about 2 cups) into dry measuring cups, and level with a knife. Combine 9 ounces flour, baking powder, baking soda, and salt, stirring with a whisk.
4. Place granulated sugar and ½ cup butter in a large bowl; beat with a mixer at medium speed until well blended (about 5 minutes). Add eggs, 1 at a time, beating well after each addition. Add flour mixture and buttermilk alternately to sugar mixture, beginning and ending with flour mixture. Beat in 2 tablespoons lemon rind and 2 tablespoons lemon juice.
5. Pour batter into prepared pans; sharply tap pans once on counter to remove air bubbles. Bake at 350° for 32 minutes or until a wooden pick inserted in center comes out clean. Cool in pans 10 minutes on wire racks; remove from pans. Cool completely on wire racks; discard wax paper.
6. To prepare frosting, combine powdered sugar and next 3 ingredients in a large bowl; stir with a whisk until smooth. Place 1 cake layer on a plate; spread half of frosting over top of cake. Top with remaining cake layer. Spread remaining half of frosting over top of cake. Garnish, if desired. Store cake loosely covered in refrigerator. **Yield: 16 servings (serving size: 1 slice).**

CALORIES 317; FAT 9.5g (sat 5.6g, mono 2.6g, poly 0.5g); PROTEIN 3.6g; CARB 55.7g; FIBER 0.6g; CHOL 56mg; IRON 1mg; SODIUM 165mg; CALC 52mg

kitchen how-to: zest fresh citrus

If you plan on also using the juice of the fruit, you'll want to zest the fruit before juicing it. To zest, gently run the fruit up and down the fine holes of a box grater or a handheld grater, also called a Microplane®. Avoid grating the white pith—it can add bitterness rather than tartness to a recipe. One medium lemon will yield about 1 teaspoon grated rind.

Italian Cream Cake

Cake:
  Cooking spray
  2 teaspoons cake flour
  ⅓ cup butter, softened
  1¼ cups granulated sugar
  2 large egg yolks
  8 ounces cake flour (about 2 cups)
  1 teaspoon baking soda
  ¼ teaspoon salt
  1 cup low-fat buttermilk
  ¼ cup finely chopped pecans, toasted
  1 teaspoon coconut extract
  1 teaspoon vanilla extract
  6 large egg whites

Frosting:
  1 tablespoon butter
  ½ cup (4 ounces) ⅓-less-fat cream cheese
  3½ cups powdered sugar
  1 teaspoon vanilla extract

1. Preheat oven to 350°.
2. To prepare cake, coat bottoms of 2 (9-inch) round cake pans with cooking spray (do not coat sides of pans). Line bottoms of pans with wax paper. Coat wax paper with cooking spray, and dust each pan with 1 teaspoon flour.
3. Place ⅓ cup butter in a large bowl; beat with a mixer at medium speed until creamy. Gradually add granulated sugar, beating well. Add egg yolks, 1 at a time, beating well after each addition.
4. Weigh or lightly spoon 8 ounces flour (about 2 cups) into dry measuring cups; level with a knife. Combine 8 ounces flour, baking soda, and salt; stir well. Add flour mixture and buttermilk alternately to sugar mixture, beginning and ending with flour mixture. Stir in pecans, coconut extract, and 1 teaspoon vanilla.
5. Beat egg whites with a mixer at high speed until stiff peaks form (do not overbeat). Fold egg whites into batter; pour batter into prepared pans. Bake at 350° for 23 minutes or until a wooden pick inserted in center comes

out clean. Cool in pans 5 minutes on wire racks. Loosen cake layers from sides of pans; remove from pans. Cool completely on wire racks. Discard wax paper.
6. To prepare frosting, place 1 tablespoon butter and cream cheese in a large bowl; beat with a mixer at high speed until fluffy. Gradually add powdered sugar, beating at low speed until smooth (do not overbeat). Add 1 teaspoon vanilla; beat well.
7. Place 1 cake layer on a plate; spread with one-third of frosting. Top with remaining cake layer. Spread remaining frosting over top and sides of cake. **Yield: 16 servings (serving size: 1 slice).**

CALORIES 322; FAT 8.8g (sat 4.6g, mono 2.8g, poly 0.8g); PROTEIN 4.7g; CARB 56.6g; FIBER 0.5g; CHOL 45mg; IRON 1.4mg; SODIUM 221mg; CALC 33mg

kitchen how-to:
easily remove & cool cake layers

After removing the cake from the oven, let it cool in the pan for 5 to 10 minutes (15 minutes for tube or Bundt pans). Run a knife around the sides of the pan to loosen the cake, if necessary. Then, invert the cake onto a wire rack to cool completely.

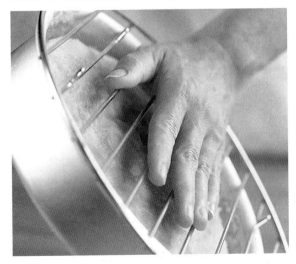

Fresh Coconut Cake

If your coconut water does not measure 1 cup (8 fluid ounces), add enough tap water so the liquid measures 1 cup. Even though fresh coconut is sublime, you can use store-bought coconut water in place of fresh coconut water and buy coconut flakes in the baking aisle.

Cake:
Cooking spray
1 tablespoon cake flour
12 ounces sifted cake flour (about 3 cups)
2 teaspoons baking powder
¼ teaspoon salt
1¾ cups sugar, divided
⅔ cup butter, softened

1 cup warm coconut water (from 1 small brown coconut)
1 teaspoon vanilla extract
6 large egg whites

Frosting:
4 large egg whites
¼ teaspoon cream of tartar
⅛ teaspoon salt
2 tablespoons sugar
1¼ cups sugar
¼ cup water
1 teaspoon vanilla extract
1½ cups shaved fresh coconut, toasted

1. Preheat oven to 350°.

2. To prepare cake, lightly coat 3 (9-inch) round cake pans with cooking spray; line bottoms of pans with wax paper. Lightly coat wax paper with cooking spray; dust each pan with 1 teaspoon flour.

3. Weigh or lightly spoon 12 ounces flour (about 3 cups) into dry measuring cups; level with a knife. Combine 12 ounces flour, baking powder, and salt; stir with a whisk. Place 1½ cups plus 2 tablespoons sugar and butter in a large bowl; beat with a mixer at medium speed for 2½ minutes or until well blended. Add flour mixture and coconut water alternately to sugar mixture, beginning and ending with flour mixture. Beat in 1 teaspoon vanilla. In a separate bowl, beat 6 egg whites at high speed until foamy using clean, dry beaters. Add remaining 2 tablespoons sugar, 1 tablespoon at a time, beating until stiff peaks form (do not overbeat). Carefully fold egg white mixture into batter; pour batter into prepared pans. Bake at 350° for 18 minutes or until a wooden pick inserted in center comes out clean. Cool in pans 10 minutes on wire racks; remove from pans. Cool completely on wire racks. Discard wax paper.

4. To prepare frosting, combine 4 egg whites, cream of tartar, and ⅛ teaspoon salt in a large bowl; beat with a mixer at high speed until foamy. Add 2 tablespoons sugar, 1 tablespoon at a time, beating until stiff peaks form. Combine 1¼ cups sugar and ¼ cup water in a saucepan; bring to a boil. Cook, without stirring, until candy thermometer registers 250°. With mixer at low speed, pour hot sugar syrup in a thin stream over egg whites. Gradually increase speed to high; beat 8 minutes or until thick and cool. Stir in 1 teaspoon vanilla.

5. Place 1 cake layer on a serving plate; spread with 1 cup frosting. Top with another cake layer. Repeat procedure with 1 cup frosting and remaining cake layer, ending with cake. Spread remaining frosting over top and sides of cake. Gently press shaved coconut onto top and sides of cake. Store cake loosely covered in refrigerator. **Yield: 16 servings (serving size: 1 slice).**

CALORIES 323; FAT 10g (sat 6.8g, mono 2.1g, poly 0.4g); PROTEIN 4.2g; CARB 55.4g;
FIBER 1.1g; CHOL 20mg; IRON 1.6mg; SODIUM 206mg; CALC 54mg

kitchen how-to:
cut fresh coconut

The soft meat of a fresh coconut and its water are more fun and easier to obtain than you might think.

1. Use a clean nail and small hammer to make 3 holes in the eyes of the coconut; pour the coconut water into a measuring cup.

2. Warm the coconut in a preheated 350° oven for 25 to 30 minutes. Wrap the whole coconut in a kitchen towel. On a steady, hard surface, give the coconut several good raps all over to crack it open. Warming the coconut helps separate the coconut meat from the shell.

3. With a small, sharp knife, cut the creamy white flesh from the shell and tough inner brown layer. Shave into large, thin pieces.

Sticky Date and Coconut Cake

Coat the bottom and sides of the pan with cooking spray so this puddinglike cake doesn't stick. Prepare the topping while the cake bakes.

Cake:
- 1 cup chopped pitted dates
- 1 cup water
- 1 teaspoon baking soda
- 3 tablespoons butter
- Dash of salt
- 6.75 ounces all-purpose flour (about 1½ cups)
- 1 teaspoon baking powder
- ½ teaspoon salt
- 1 cup granulated sugar
- 1 teaspoon vanilla extract
- 1 large egg, lightly beaten
- Cooking spray

Topping:
- ⅔ cup packed light brown sugar
- ½ cup flaked sweetened coconut
- 2½ tablespoons butter
- 2 teaspoons fat-free milk

1. Preheat oven to 350°.

2. To prepare cake, combine first 5 ingredients in a small saucepan; bring to a boil, stirring occasionally. Remove from heat, and let stand 10 minutes or until dates are tender.

3. Weigh or lightly spoon flour into dry measuring cups; level with a knife. Combine flour, baking powder, and ½ teaspoon salt in a bowl. Stir in date mixture, granulated sugar, vanilla, and egg until well combined. Pour batter into a 9-inch springform pan coated with cooking spray. Bake at 350° for 20 minutes.

4. To prepare topping, combine brown sugar and remaining ingredients in a small saucepan; bring to a boil. Reduce heat, and simmer 1 minute. Pour brown sugar mixture over cake; bake at 350° for an additional 13 minutes or until a wooden pick inserted in center comes out clean. Cool in pan 5 minutes on a wire rack. Run a knife around outside edge; remove cake from pan. Cool cake completely on wire rack.

Yield: 12 servings (serving size: 1 wedge).

CALORIES 268; FAT 6.5g (sat 4.2g, mono 1.6g, poly 0.3g); PROTEIN 2.5g; CARB 51.6g; FIBER 1.7g; CHOL 31mg; IRON 1.2mg; SODIUM 313mg; CALC 46mg

kitchen how-to:
pack brown sugar

The difference between packed and unpacked brown sugar can make a substantial difference in a recipe. When a recipe calls for packed brown sugar (shown on the top left), spoon it into a dry measuring cup in the size specified in the recipe, and press the sugar into the cup with the back of a spoon. Continue to add and pack more sugar until it reaches the rim of the measuring cup. Level with the flat side of a knife, scraping off any excess. For an unpacked cup (shown on the bottom left), lightly spoon the brown sugar into the cup; level it with a knife.

Pureed Carrots
What they add: Using pureed carrot baby food was one way we cut back on oil—we use only ¼ cup—to keep calories in check while ensuring a moist cake.

Flaked Sweetened Coconut
What it adds: Adding toasted coconut to the frosting is a delicious flavor variation on this classic cake, but you can omit it, if you like, for a more traditional version.

Carrot Cake with Toasted Coconut Cream Cheese Frosting

Quick Oats

What they add: Pulsing the oats with the flour in the food processor is an easy and inconspicuous way to add extra fiber and whole grains to this dessert.

This cake keeps for up to 3 days in the refrigerator and also freezes well.

Cake:
- 3.4 ounces all-purpose flour (about ¾ cup)
- ¼ cup quick-cooking oats
- 1½ teaspoons ground cinnamon
- 1 teaspoon baking powder
- ½ teaspoon baking soda
- ¼ teaspoon salt
- 1 cup granulated sugar
- ¼ cup canola oil
- 1 (2½-ounce) jar carrot baby food
- 2 large eggs, lightly beaten
- 1¼ cups finely shredded carrot (about 4 ounces)
- ½ cup golden raisins
- Cooking spray

Frosting:
- ⅓ cup (3 ounces) ⅓-less-fat cream cheese, softened
- 1 tablespoon butter, softened
- 1¼ cups powdered sugar, sifted
- ½ teaspoon vanilla extract
- ¼ cup flaked sweetened coconut, toasted

1. Preheat oven to 325°.

2. To prepare cake, weigh or lightly spoon flour into dry measuring cups; level with a knife. Place flour and next 5 ingredients in a food processor; pulse 6 times or until well blended. Place flour mixture in a large bowl. Combine granulated sugar, oil, baby food, and eggs; stir with a whisk. Add to flour mixture; stir just until moist. Stir in shredded carrot and raisins. Spoon batter into an 8-inch square metal baking pan coated with cooking spray.

3. Bake at 325° for 40 minutes or until a wooden pick inserted in center comes out clean. Cool in pan on a wire rack.

4. To prepare frosting, combine cream cheese and butter in a large bowl. Beat with a mixer at high speed until creamy. Gradually add powdered sugar and vanilla, beating at low speed until smooth (do not overbeat). Spread over cake; sprinkle with coconut. Cover and chill. **Yield: 12 servings (serving size: 1 piece).**

CALORIES 262; FAT 8.8g (sat 2.7g, mono 3.6g, poly 1.6g); PROTEIN 3.2g; CARB 44.1g; FIBER 1.2g; CHOL 44mg; IRON 0.9mg; SODIUM 201mg; CALC 47mg

220

Dark Chocolate

What it adds: High-quality dark chocolate, specifically a 71 percent cocoa bar, lends just the right amount of bitterness to amplify the flavor of espresso in the cakes.

Espresso Powder

What it adds: Espresso powder adds a subtle flavor to these cakes while enhancing the rich flavor of the chocolate. The powder dissolves easily during mixing.

Unsweetened Cocoa

What it adds: On its own, unsweetened cocoa tastes bitter, but it gives these cakes a deep chocolate flavor.

Hot Chocolate Fudge Cakes

These hot-from-the-oven desserts are ideal for a holiday celebration and can be mostly made up to 2 days ahead.

3.4 ounces all-purpose flour (about ¾ cup)
⅔ cup unsweetened cocoa
5 teaspoons instant espresso powder
1½ teaspoons baking powder
¼ teaspoon salt
¼ cup unsalted butter, softened
⅔ cup granulated sugar
⅔ cup packed brown sugar
8 large egg whites
1½ teaspoons vanilla extract
1 (2.6-ounce) bar dark (71 percent cocoa) chocolate, finely chopped
2 tablespoons powdered sugar

1. Weigh or lightly spoon flour into dry measuring cups; level with a knife. Sift together flour, cocoa, espresso powder, baking powder, and salt.
2. Place butter in a large bowl; beat with a mixer at medium speed for 1 minute. Add granulated and brown sugars, beating until well blended (about 5 minutes). Add egg whites and vanilla, beating until well blended. Fold flour mixture into sugar mixture; fold in chocolate. Divide batter evenly among 10 (4-ounce) ramekins; arrange ramekins on a jelly-roll pan. Cover and refrigerate 4 hours or up to 2 days.
3. Preheat oven to 350°.
4. Let ramekins stand at room temperature 10 minutes. Uncover and bake at 350° for 21 minutes or until cakes are puffy and slightly crusty on top. Sprinkle evenly with powdered sugar; serve immediately. **Yield: 10 servings (serving size: 1 cake).**

CALORIES 260; FAT 8.2g (sat 4.5g, mono 2.3g, poly 0.2g); PROTEIN 5.1g; CARB 43.9g; FIBER 1.8g; CHOL 12mg; IRON 2.3mg; SODIUM 189mg; CALC 63mg

pound cakes

Pound cakes are wonderfully rich with a golden crust and moist interior. Our lighter versions use less butter but are still packed with flavor.

kitchen how-to: make a pound cake

Using butter and whole eggs instead of egg whites gives pound cake a rich texture.

1. Combine butter and sugar in a large mixing bowl.
2. Beat at medium speed until well blended and creamy.
3. Add eggs, 1 at a time, beating well after each addition. Adding them 1 at a time incorporates more air, resulting in a great rise. Add flour and milk or buttermilk alternately to the sugar mixture.
4. Spoon the batter into a pan coated with cooking spray and lightly dusted with flour. The batter should have a velvety, thick texture.

Pumpkin Pound Cake with Buttermilk Glaze

Drain the canned pumpkin before making the cake batter to keep the cake's texture light.

Cake:
  Cooking spray
   1 tablespoon all-purpose flour
   1 (15-ounce) can pumpkin
  ¾ cup granulated sugar
  ¾ cup packed dark brown sugar
  ½ cup butter, softened
   4 large eggs
   1 teaspoon vanilla extract
13.5 ounces all-purpose flour (about 3 cups)
1½ teaspoons pumpkin pie spice
   1 teaspoon baking powder
  ½ teaspoon baking soda
  ½ teaspoon salt
  ¾ cup nonfat buttermilk

Glaze:
  ⅓ cup nonfat buttermilk
  ¼ cup granulated sugar
   2 tablespoons butter
   2 teaspoons cornstarch
  ⅛ teaspoon baking soda

1. Preheat oven to 350°.
2. To prepare cake, lightly coat a 10-inch tube pan with cooking spray; dust with 1 tablespoon flour. Spread pumpkin over 2 layers of paper towels; cover with 2 additional layers of paper towels. Let stand about 10 minutes. Scrape drained pumpkin into a bowl.
3. Place ¾ cup granulated sugar, brown sugar, and ½ cup butter in a large bowl; beat with a mixer at medium speed for 3 minutes or until well blended. Add eggs, 1 at a time, beating well after each addition. Beat in pumpkin and vanilla. Weigh or lightly spoon 13.5 ounces flour (about 3 cups) into dry measuring cups; level with a knife. Combine 13.5 ounces flour and next 4 ingredients in a bowl, stirring well with a whisk. Add flour mixture and ¾ cup buttermilk alternately to sugar mixture, beginning and ending with flour mixture.
4. Spoon batter into prepared pan. Bake at 350° for 55 minutes or until a wooden pick inserted in center comes out clean. Cool in pan 10 minutes on a wire rack. Remove from pan; cool completely on wire rack.
5. To prepare glaze, combine ⅓ cup buttermilk and remaining ingredients in a small saucepan over medium heat; bring to a boil. Cook 1 minute or until thick, stirring constantly; remove from heat. Drizzle glaze over cake. **Yield: 16 servings (serving size: 1 slice).**

CALORIES 273; FAT 8.7g (sat 5g, mono 2.4g, poly 0.5g); PROTEIN 5g; CARB 44.6g; FIBER 1.4g; CHOL 72mg; IRON 2mg; SODIUM 243mg; CALC 66mg

Lemon Pound Cake with Cherry Compote

Cake:
 Cooking spray
  2 tablespoons all-purpose flour
13.5 ounces all-purpose flour (about 3 cups)
  2 teaspoons baking powder
  ½ teaspoon baking soda
  ½ teaspoon salt
  2 cups granulated sugar
  ¾ cup butter, softened
  2 large eggs
  1 cup low-fat buttermilk
  1 tablespoon grated lemon rind
  3 tablespoons fresh lemon juice
  1 teaspoon chopped fresh mint
  1 tablespoon powdered sugar

Compote:
  4 cups pitted sweet cherries (about 1½ pounds)
  ¼ cup granulated sugar
  2 tablespoons water
  2 teaspoons cornstarch
  ¼ teaspoon almond extract

1. Preheat oven to 350°.
2. To prepare cake, coat a 10-inch tube pan with cooking spray; dust with 2 tablespoons flour.
3. Weigh or lightly spoon 13.5 ounces flour (about 3 cups) into dry measuring cups; level with a knife. Combine flour and next 3 ingredients in a bowl, stirring well with a whisk. Combine 2 cups granulated sugar and butter in a large bowl; beat with a mixer at medium speed until light and fluffy. Add eggs, 1 at a time, beating well after each addition. Add flour mixture to sugar mixture alternately with buttermilk, beating at low speed, beginning and ending with flour mixture. Add rind, juice, and mint; beat just until blended.
4. Spoon batter into prepared pan; sharply tap pan once on counter to remove air bubbles. Bake at 350° for 45 minutes or until a wooden pick inserted in center comes out clean. Cool in pan 10 minutes on a wire rack; remove from pan. Cool completely on wire rack.

Sift powdered sugar over top of cake. Cut cake into 16 slices.
5. To prepare compote, combine cherries, ¼ cup granulated sugar, 2 tablespoons water, and cornstarch in a medium saucepan; bring to a boil. Cook 1 minute, stirring constantly. Remove from heat; stir in extract. Cool. Serve with cake. **Yield: 16 servings (serving size: 1 cake slice and ¼ cup compote).**

CALORIES 319; FAT 9.9g (sat 5.8g, mono 2.6g, poly 0.6g); PROTEIN 4.4g; CARB 54.8g; FIBER 1.6g; CHOL 50mg; IRON 1.5mg; SODIUM 260mg; CALC 68mg

all about cherries

Cherry season runs from early June through August. Cherries can be whitish-yellow to bright red to nearly black in color, and they come in two types: sweet, such as Bing, Royal Ann, and Rainier, and sour cherries (also called pie or tart cherries) like Montmorency. Fresh cherries are usually sold with their stems still intact as this helps them last longer. The stems should be green and snap back when bent. Choose large, plump cherries with smooth, shiny skins and no discolored, wrinkled, or mushy spots. Keep whole cherries, unwashed, in a breathable plastic bag in the refrigerator. Wash them before serving, and eat them as soon as possible, since they can deteriorate quickly.

bundt cakes

Bundt cakes are cakes baked in the classic Bundt pan. The beautiful shape makes extra adornment and decoration unnecessary.

Decadent Double-Chocolate Bundt Cake

Glaze:
- ⅔ **cup granulated sugar**
- ¼ **cup water**
- ¼ **cup chocolate-flavored liqueur**
- 2 **tablespoons butter**

Cake:
- 1½ **teaspoons canola oil**
- 2 **tablespoons all-purpose flour**
- **Cooking spray**
- 1½ **cups granulated sugar**
- 6 **tablespoons butter, softened**
- 2 **large eggs**
- 2 **large egg whites**
- 2 **teaspoons vanilla extract**
- 13.5 **ounces all-purpose flour (about 3 cups)**
- ½ **cup unsweetened cocoa**
- 1 **teaspoon baking powder**
- ½ **teaspoon baking soda**
- ½ **teaspoon salt**
- 1½ **cups 1% low-fat milk**
- ⅔ **cup semisweet chocolate minichips**
- 2 **tablespoons powdered sugar**

1. To prepare glaze, combine first 4 ingredients in small saucepan. Bring to a boil over medium-high heat, stirring constantly. Cool completely.

2. Preheat oven to 350°.

3. To prepare cake, drizzle oil into a 12-cup Bundt pan; coat pan thoroughly using a pastry brush. Sprinkle with 2 tablespoons flour, shaking out excess. Coat prepared pan with cooking spray.

4. Place 1½ cups granulated sugar and 6 tablespoons butter in a large bowl; beat with a mixer at medium speed until well blended (about 5 minutes). Add eggs and egg whites, 1 at a time, beating well after each addition. Beat in vanilla.

5. Weigh or lightly spoon 13.5 ounces flour (about 3 cups) into dry measuring cups; level with a knife. Combine 13.5 ounces flour and next 4 ingredients, stirring with a whisk. Add flour mixture and milk alternately to sugar mixture, beginning and ending with flour mixture; mix after each addition.

Beat at medium speed for 2 minutes. Fold in chips. Spoon batter into prepared pan. Swirl batter using a knife.

6. Bake at 350° for 45 minutes or until a wooden pick inserted in center comes out clean. Immediately pour glaze over cake. Cool cake in pan on a wire rack 30 minutes. Invert cake onto a serving plate; cool completely. Sprinkle with powdered sugar. **Yield: 16 servings (serving size: 1 slice).**

CALORIES 326; FAT 10.3g (sat 5.8g, mono 2.7g, poly 0.5g); PROTEIN 5.5g; CARB 54.8g; FIBER 2g; CHOL 43mg; IRON 1.9mg; SODIUM 211mg; CALC 59mg

all about bundt pans

Cake recipes often yield different amounts of batter, so it's a good idea to double-check the size of your Bundt pan by filling it to the rim with water and measuring the amount. Depending on the brand, a 10-inch pan may hold 10, 12, or 14 cups. If you use a smaller pan than is called for in the recipe, fill the pan no more than one-half to two-thirds full.

shortcakes

Shortcakes are small biscuitlike cakes generally filled and topped with sweetened fruit. They're easy to assemble and make a beautiful presentation.

kitchen how-to: make shortcakes

You can bake shortcakes up to a day ahead. Cool completely, and store at room temperature in a large zip-top plastic bag.

1. Combine the dry ingredients in a large bowl, stirring with a whisk.
2. Cut in butter with a pastry blender or 2 knives until mixture resembles coarse meal. Some recipes use a food processor to speed up this process.
3. Add milk or buttermilk, stirring just until moist. When mixing the dough for shortcakes, use a light hand and work quickly for the most tender cakes. If the recipe calls for kneading the dough, knead lightly only a few times so the dough doesn't become overworked.
4. Turn the dough out onto a lightly floured surface, and pat dough into the size specified in the recipe. Some recipes call for the dough to be cut into wedges, cutting into but not through the dough, much like making scones, while others require that the shortcakes bake separately. Either way works, so just follow the recipe's instructions. Bake, and then cool on a wire rack.
5. Use a serrated knife to split the shortcakes in half; it will cut through the cakes without crumbling them. Add the filling and toppings. To freeze shortcakes, cool them completely, place in a heavy-duty zip-top plastic bag, and freeze for up to 2 months. Thaw at room temperature. To reheat, wrap them in foil, and heat at 350° for 10 minutes.

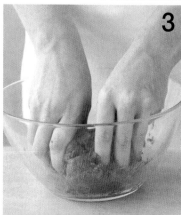

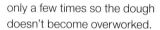

Chocolate Shortcakes with Bananas and Caramel

These dusky cakes are enriched with cocoa and butter. Patting the dough into a single disk keeps it from being overworked, so the shortcake stays tender.

Shortcakes:
6.75 ounces all-purpose flour (about 1½ cups)
 ½ cup sugar
 ⅓ cup unsweetened cocoa
 1 teaspoon baking soda
 ½ teaspoon baking powder
 ¼ teaspoon salt
 ¼ cup chilled butter, cut into small pieces
 ½ cup nonfat buttermilk

Filling:
 ¼ cup sugar
 2 tablespoons water
 2 tablespoons whipping cream
 1 teaspoon butter
 1 cup frozen fat-free whipped topping, thawed
 ⅛ teaspoon unsweetened cocoa
 2 medium bananas, cut into ¼-inch-thick slices (about 2 cups)

1. Preheat oven to 375°.
2. To prepare shortcakes, weigh or lightly spoon flour into dry measuring cups; level with a knife. Combine flour and next 5 ingredients in a large bowl, stirring with a whisk. Cut in ¼ cup butter with a pastry blender or 2 knives until mixture resembles coarse meal. Add buttermilk; stir just until moist. Knead lightly in bowl 5 or 6 times. Turn dough out onto a lightly floured surface; pat dough into an 8-inch circle on a baking sheet lined with parchment paper. Cut dough into 8 wedges, cutting into, but not through, dough. Bake at 375° for 18 minutes or until just firm to the touch. Remove from pan; cool on a wire rack. Place shortcake on a cutting board or work surface; cut along score lines with a serrated knife to form 8 wedges.
3. To prepare filling, combine ¼ cup sugar and 2 tablespoons water in a small saucepan over medium-high heat; stir gently just until sugar dissolves. Cook, without stirring, until pale golden (about 4 minutes), gently swirling pan, if needed, to cook sugar evenly. Remove from heat; add cream and 1 teaspoon butter, stirring with a whisk until smooth. Cool 5 minutes.
4. Place whipped topping in a medium bowl; fold in ⅛ teaspoon cocoa just until combined. Split shortcakes in half horizontally using a serrated knife. Arrange about ¼ cup banana slices over bottom half of each shortcake; top each serving with about 1 teaspoon caramel sauce, about 2 tablespoons whipped topping mixture, and top of shortcake. Drizzle ½ teaspoon caramel sauce over top of each shortcake. **Yield: 8 servings (serving size: 1 filled shortcake).**

CALORIES 282; FAT 8.3g (sat 4.9g, mono 2.1g, poly 0.4g); PROTEIN 4.3g; CARB 49.2g; FIBER 2.1g; CHOL 22mg; IRON 1.7mg; SODIUM 320mg; CALC 48mg

Fat-Free Whipped Topping
What it adds: A dollop of whipped topping adds a creamy contrast to the shortcakes and berries.

Crystallized Ginger
What it adds: The sweet, spicy flavor of the crystallized ginger (dried gingerroot preserved in sugar) amps up the taste of these shortcakes.

Gingered Blueberry Shortcakes

Sweet, juicy, peak-season berries make this dish shine. For convenience, make the berry mixture and shortcakes in advance, and then assemble just before serving. Prepare the berry mixture earlier in the day, and refrigerate; bring the berry mixture to room temperature or warm slightly in a pan before serving. Make the shortcakes as time permits, freeze them, and then defrost at room temperature when ready to serve.

4   cups blueberries
3   tablespoons granulated
    sugar
1   tablespoon fresh lime juice
9   ounces all-purpose flour
    (about 2 cups)
1   tablespoon baking powder
½   teaspoon salt
6   tablespoons chilled butter,
    cut into small pieces
3   tablespoons minced
    crystallized ginger
¾   cup 2% reduced-fat milk
1   large egg white
1   tablespoon water
1   tablespoon turbinado sugar
    or granulated sugar
¾   cup frozen fat-free whipped
    topping, thawed

1. Preheat oven to 400°.
2. Combine first 3 ingredients in a medium saucepan over medium-low heat; cook 3 minutes or until berries begin to pop, stirring frequently. Set aside.
3. Weigh or lightly spoon flour into dry measuring cups; level with a knife. Place flour, baking powder, and salt in a food processor; pulse 3 times to combine. Add butter and ginger to processor; pulse until mixture resembles coarse meal. Place mixture in a large bowl; add milk, stirring just until moist. Turn dough out onto a lightly floured surface. Press dough into a 7-inch circle; cut into 8 wedges. Place wedges 1 inch apart on a baking sheet. Combine egg white and 1 tablespoon water in a small bowl. Lightly brush tops of wedges with egg white mixture; sprinkle evenly with turbinado sugar. Bake at 400° for 20 minutes or until golden brown. Remove from pan; cool on a wire rack.
4. Split shortcakes in half horizontally; spoon ⅓ cup berry mixture over each bottom half. Top each with 1½ tablespoons whipped topping; cover with shortcake tops.
Yield: 8 servings (serving size: 1 filled shortcake).

CALORIES 294; FAT 9.7g (sat 5.8g, mono 2.4g, poly 0.6g); PROTEIN 5.2g; CARB 47.5g; FIBER 2.6g; CHOL 25mg; IRON 1.8mg; SODIUM 381mg; CALC 134mg

upside-down cakes

The sweetened fruit base of an upside-down cake, which eventually becomes the top of the cake, caramelizes during baking, creating a delectable, gooey glaze.

kitchen how-to: make an upside-down cake

Upside-down cakes start with fruit on the bottom and a cake batter poured over the top.

1. Upside-down cakes can be made with a variety of fruits—from pears or pineapples to apples or cherries. Cook the fruit with sugar and any spices and seasonings you like until softened.

2. Arrange the fruit in the bottom of a pan coated with cooking spray.

3. Prepare the batter, and carefully spoon it over the fruit in the prepared pan.

4. Bake until golden brown. Place a plate upside down on top of the cake, and invert onto the plate.

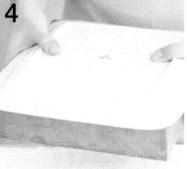

Cherry-Almond Upside-Down Cake

If you're pitting the cherries, be sure to work over a bowl and save any accumulated juice, which should be added to the recipe with the cherries.

- 1¼ cups sugar, divided
- ¼ cup dry red wine
- 2 pounds dark sweet cherries, pitted
- 1 teaspoon fresh lemon juice
- Cooking spray
- ¾ cup whole blanched almonds, toasted
- 2 large eggs
- 2 large egg whites
- 4.5 ounces all-purpose flour (about 1 cup)
- ½ teaspoon salt

1. Preheat oven to 375°.

2. Combine ¼ cup sugar and wine in a large saucepan over low heat; stir until sugar dissolves. Increase heat to medium-high; bring to a boil. Stir in cherries. Reduce heat to low, and cook 5 minutes or until cherries just begin to soften, stirring frequently. Remove cherries from pan with a slotted spoon, reserving liquid in pan. Place cherries in a bowl; stir in lemon juice. Arrange cherries in an even layer in bottom of a 9-inch square metal baking pan coated with cooking spray.

3. Cook wine mixture over medium-high heat 3 minutes or until reduced to ¼ cup. Remove from heat; drizzle over cherries in prepared pan.

4. Place almonds and 2 tablespoons sugar in a food processor; process until finely ground (do not process to a paste).

5. Place eggs and egg whites in a large bowl. Beat with a mixer at high speed until foamy; slowly add remaining ¾ cup plus 2 tablespoons sugar. Beat until thick and lemon-colored (about 2 minutes).

6. Weigh or lightly spoon flour into a dry measuring cup; level with a knife. Combine flour and salt. Gradually sift flour mixture over egg mixture; fold in. Fold in ground almond mixture. Carefully spoon batter over cherries in prepared pan. Bake at 375° for 30 minutes or until golden brown. Cool in pan 15 minutes on a wire rack. Place a plate upside down on top of cake; invert onto plate. **Yield: 9 servings (serving size: 1 piece).**

CALORIES 322; FAT 8.3g (sat 1.1g, mono 4.6g, poly 2g); PROTEIN 7.5g; CARB 57.8g; FIBER 3.9g; CHOL 47mg; IRON 1.7mg; SODIUM 163mg; CALC 51mg

Apple Upside-Down Cake

Topping:
  Cooking spray
  ¾ cup sugar
  ¼ cup water
  3 cups (¼-inch-thick) slices
     peeled Rome apple (about
     2 large)
  ¼ cup chopped walnuts

Cake:
  5.3 ounces cake flour (about
       1⅓ cups)
  1½ teaspoons baking powder
  ¼ teaspoon salt
  ⅔ cup sugar
  3 tablespoons butter, softened
  2 large egg yolks
  1 teaspoon vanilla extract
  ½ cup 1% low-fat milk
  3 large egg whites

1. Preheat oven to 350°. Coat a 9-inch round cake pan with cooking spray.

2. To prepare topping, combine ¾ cup sugar and ¼ cup water in a small heavy saucepan over medium-high heat; cook until sugar dissolves, stirring gently as needed to dissolve sugar evenly (about 3 minutes). Continue cooking 4 minutes or until golden (do not stir). Immediately pour into prepared cake pan, tipping pan quickly to coat bottom. Arrange apple slices in concentric circles over warm caramel in pan. Sprinkle with nuts; set aside.

3. To prepare cake, weigh or lightly spoon flour into dry measuring cups; level with a knife. Combine flour, baking powder, and salt; stir with a whisk.

4. Combine ⅔ cup sugar and butter in a large bowl; beat with a mixer at medium speed until light and fluffy. Add egg yolks and vanilla to sugar mixture; beat until combined. Add flour mixture and milk alternately to sugar mixture, beginning and ending with flour mixture; mix after each addition.

5. Place egg whites in a large, clean bowl. Beat egg whites with mixer at high speed until stiff peaks form using clean, dry beaters. Gently fold egg whites into batter. Spread batter over apples. Bake at 350° for 35 minutes or until a wooden pick inserted in center comes out clean. Cool in pan 5 minutes on a wire rack. Loosen cake from sides of pan with a knife; invert cake onto a serving plate. Serve warm or at room temperature. **Yield: 10 servings (serving size: 1 slice).**

CALORIES 253; FAT 6.6g (sat 2.8g, mono 1.6g, poly 1.7g); PROTEIN 3.9g; CARB 45.8g; FIBER 0.9g; CHOL 52mg; IRON 1.5mg; SODIUM 163mg; CALC 79mg

kitchen how-to:
peel & slice an apple

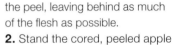

Be sure to peel apples just before using them since they can start to turn brown quickly.

1. Use an apple corer to remove the stem, tough center, and seeds and either a vegetable peeler or sharp paring knife to carefully remove the peel, leaving behind as much of the flesh as possible.

2. Stand the cored, peeled apple upright, and slice vertically in half. For slices or wedges, place halves cut side down, and cut toward the core to make slices as thick or as thin as you like.

coffee cakes

These cakes are the perfect accompaniment to coffee and make an ideal breakfast or afternoon snack.

Turbinado Sugar
What it adds: The coarse crystals of this sugar add a sweet crunch and pretty finish.

Blueberries
What they add: Fresh blueberries create plump, juicy pockets of flavor in this cake.

Blueberry Coffee Cake

This moist, tender blueberry coffee cake scored high in our Test Kitchens, where tasters unanimously considered it a delicious way to use the first blueberries of the season. Ideal for breakfast, brunch, dessert, or as a snack to savor with coffee, it's a recipe you'll make more than once.

6.75 **ounces all-purpose flour (about 1½ cups)**
 1 **teaspoon baking powder**
 ¼ **teaspoon baking soda**
 ¼ **teaspoon salt**
 ¾ **cup granulated sugar**
 6 **tablespoons butter, softened**
 1 **teaspoon vanilla extract**
 1 **large egg**
 1 **large egg white**
 1⅓ **cups low-fat buttermilk**
Cooking spray
 2 **cups blueberries**
 1 **tablespoon turbinado sugar or granulated sugar**

1. Preheat oven to 350°.
2. Weigh or lightly spoon flour into dry measuring cups; level with a knife. Combine flour, baking powder, baking soda, and salt, stirring with a whisk.

3. Place granulated sugar and butter in a large bowl; beat with a mixer at medium speed until well blended (about 2 minutes). Add vanilla, egg, and egg white; beat well. Add flour mixture and buttermilk alternately to sugar mixture, beginning and ending with flour mixture; mix after each addition.
4. Spoon half of batter into a 9-inch round cake pan coated with cooking spray. Sprinkle evenly with 1 cup blueberries. Spoon remaining batter over blueberries; sprinkle evenly with remaining 1 cup blueberries. Sprinkle top evenly with turbinado sugar. Bake at 350° for 50 minutes or until a wooden pick inserted in center comes out clean. Cool in pan 10 minutes on a wire rack; remove from pan. Cool completely on wire rack.
Yield: 8 servings (serving size: 1 wedge).

Note: If using peak-season fruit, use 1½ cups blueberries instead of 2 cups and only 1 cup buttermilk instead of 1⅓ cups. This will thicken the batter so the berries won't sink to the bottom.

CALORIES 287; FAT 9.9g (sat 5.9g, mono 2.6g, poly 0.6g); PROTEIN 5.4g; CARB 45.4g; FIBER 1.5g; CHOL 51mg; IRON 1.4mg; SODIUM 294mg; CALC 93mg

angel food cakes

Angel food cakes are light in texture, weight, calories, and fat, but they're certainly not light on flavor.

kitchen how-to: **make an angel food cake**

Angel food cakes rely on egg whites to give them their light texture and flavor. Follow these tips to get the best results.

1. Separate the eggs while they're still cold—the yolks and whites will be firmer and separate more easily. Don't allow any of the yolk to mix with the whites, or they won't beat to full volume.

2. Place the egg whites in a large bowl, and beat with a mixer at high speed until foamy. Make sure the beaters are clean and dry. Add cream of tartar and salt; beat until soft peaks form. The whites will look shiny, moist, and snowy, and the peaks will hold high when you lift the beaters. Don't overbeat the whites— lightly underbeaten egg whites will work, but overbeaten ones will make a tough cake.

3. Combine the dry ingredients, and sprinkle over the beaten egg whites ¼ cup at a time. With a spatula, fold the flour mixture into the egg whites using large sweeping motions. This will incorporate the dry ingredients without deflating the whites.

4. Spoon the batter into an ungreased tube pan. Run a knife through the batter to break up any air pockets. Don't open the oven door as the cake bakes—the egg whites can deflate as cool air rushes into the oven.

5. Cool the cake upside down so it doesn't deflate while still warm. If your pan doesn't have "feet," you can invert it by placing the center hole on the neck of a wine bottle.

6. To remove the cake from the pan, run a knife around the edges, including the center hole.

Café au Lait Angel Food Cake

Cake:

3.75 ounces sifted cake flour (about 1 cup)
1½ cups sugar, divided
¼ teaspoon ground cinnamon
2 tablespoons instant espresso granules
2 tablespoons hot water
12 large egg whites
1 teaspoon cream of tartar
¼ teaspoon salt
1½ teaspoons vanilla extract

Sauce:

3 large egg yolks, lightly beaten
½ cup sugar
1 tablespoon cornstarch
⅛ teaspoon salt
3 cups 2% reduced-fat milk, divided
1 vanilla bean, split lengthwise
3 tablespoons Frangelico (hazelnut-flavored liqueur)

Remaining Ingredient:

½ cup chopped hazelnuts, toasted

1. Preheat oven to 350°.
2. To prepare cake, weigh or lightly spoon flour into a dry measuring cup; level with a knife. Combine flour, ¾ cup sugar, and cinnamon, stirring with a whisk, and set aside. Combine espresso granules and 2 tablespoons hot water, stirring until granules dissolve; set aside.
3. Place egg whites in large bowl; beat with a mixer at high speed until foamy. Add cream of tartar and ¼ teaspoon salt; beat until soft peaks form. Add ¾ cup sugar, 2 tablespoons at a time, beating until stiff peaks form.
4. Beat in espresso mixture and vanilla. Sift ¼ cup flour mixture over egg white mixture; fold in. Repeat procedure with remaining flour mixture, ¼ cup at a time.
5. Spoon batter into an ungreased 10-inch tube pan, spreading evenly. Break air pockets by cutting through batter with a knife. Bake at 350° for 50 minutes or until cake springs back when lightly touched. Invert pan; cool

completely. Loosen cake from sides of pan using a narrow metal spatula. Invert cake onto plate.
6. To prepare sauce, place egg yolks in a large bowl. Combine ½ cup sugar, cornstarch, and ⅛ teaspoon salt in a medium saucepan. Gradually add ½ cup milk, stirring with a whisk until smooth. Stir in remaining 2½ cups milk. Scrape seeds from vanilla bean into milk mixture; add bean to mixture. Bring milk mixture to a boil over medium heat. Remove from heat; gradually add hot milk mixture to egg yolks, stirring constantly with a whisk.
7. Return milk mixture to pan. Cook mixture over medium heat until thick and bubbly (about 4 minutes), stirring constantly. Remove from heat. Spoon milk mixture into a bowl; place bowl in a large ice-filled bowl, and let stand 10 minutes or until milk mixture comes to room temperature, stirring occasionally. Remove bowl from ice; stir in liqueur. Cover and chill completely.
8. Remove and discard vanilla bean. Drizzle angel food cake with sauce, and sprinkle with toasted hazelnuts.
Yield: 12 servings (serving size: 1 cake slice, about 3 tablespoons sauce, and 2 teaspoons hazelnuts).

CALORIES 271; FAT 5.5g (sat 1.4g, mono 3g, poly 0.6g); PROTEIN 7.7g; CARB 46.8g; FIBER 0.6g; CHOL 58mg; IRON 1.1mg; SODIUM 162mg; CALC 90mg

Angel Food Cake Stuffed with Whipped Cream and Berries

Berries:
  2 **cups raspberries**
1½ **cups fresh blackberries**
1½ **cups fresh blueberries**
  ¼ **cup granulated sugar**
  2 **tablespoons fresh orange juice**

Cake:
  4 **ounces cake flour (about 1 cup)**
  1 **cup powdered sugar, divided**
  ½ **teaspoon ground ginger**
  ¾ **cup granulated sugar**
12 **large egg whites**
  1 **teaspoon cream of tartar**
  ½ **teaspoon salt**
  2 **tablespoons fresh orange juice**

Whipped Cream:
  ¾ **cup whipping cream, chilled**
  ½ **vanilla bean, split lengthwise**
  ¾ **cup powdered sugar**

Remaining Ingredients:
  2 **tablespoons powdered sugar**
  Grated orange rind (optional)

1. To prepare berries, combine first 5 ingredients; toss to combine. Cover and chill 1 hour.
2. Preheat oven to 375°.
3. To prepare cake, place a rack in lower third of oven. Weigh or lightly spoon flour into a dry measuring cup; level with a knife. Sift together flour, ½ cup powdered sugar, and ginger in a medium bowl. Sift together ½ cup powdered sugar and ¾ cup granulated sugar in another bowl. Place egg whites in a large bowl; beat with a mixer at high speed until foamy. Add cream of tartar and salt; beat until soft peaks form. Add sugar mixture, 1 tablespoon at a time, beating until stiff peaks form. Sift flour mixture over egg white mixture, ¼ cup at a time; fold in. Fold in 2 tablespoons juice.
4. Spoon batter into an ungreased 10-inch tube pan, spreading evenly. Break air pockets by cutting through batter with a knife. Bake at 375° for 30 minutes or until cake springs back when lightly touched. Invert pan; cool completely. Loosen cake from sides of pan using a narrow metal spatula. Invert cake onto plate.
5. Cut 1 inch off top of cake using a serrated knife; set top of cake aside. Hollow out bottom of cake using a small knife, leaving a 1-inch-thick shell; reserve torn cake for another use.
6. To prepare whipped cream, place cream in a medium bowl; beat with a mixer at high speed until soft peaks form. Scrape seeds from vanilla bean into bowl; discard bean. Gradually add ¾ cup powdered sugar, beating at high speed until stiff peaks form.
7. Spoon all but 1 cup berry mixture into cake shell; top with whipped cream. Replace top of cake; sprinkle with 2 tablespoons powdered sugar. Serve immediately with additional berry mixture; garnish with orange rind, if desired. **Yield: 12 servings (serving size: 1 stuffed cake slice and 4 teaspoons berry mixture).**

CALORIES 269; FAT 6g (sat 3.5g, mono 1.6g, poly 0.4g); PROTEIN 5.2g; CARB 50.2g; FIBER 2.9g; CHOL 20mg; IRON 1.2mg; SODIUM 149mg; CALC 26mg

stuff an angel food cake

Stuffing angel food cake is an easy way to make an everyday angel food cake extraordinary.

1. Using a serrated knife, cut 1 inch off the top of the cake, and set the top aside.
2. Hollow out the bottom half of the cake using a small knife, leaving a 1-inch-thick shell; reserve torn cake for another use. Spoon the filling into the cake shell, and replace the top of the cake.

tea cakes

Tea cakes are an easy way to make desserts with the comforting flavors and aromas of your favorite teas.

all about:
tea cakes

Tea cakes are subtly flavored with brewed tea. Every cake contains liquid (milk, buttermilk, or water), and replacing some or all of that with strong brewed tea—stronger than you'd drink—infuses the cake with a delicate flavor and colors the batter. Just about any tea will work, but those with pronounced flavors, such as English breakfast or Darjeeling, are best. Many herbal and spiced teas also make good flavorings.

English Breakfast Angel Food Cake

English breakfast tea is actually a combination of several black teas; it imparts full-bodied flavor to this classic angel food cake. We tested with supermarket brands—there's no need to visit a specialty shop. If you can't find loose tea, cut tea bags open and measure out the amount specified.

　½ **cup boiling water**
　¼ **cup loose English breakfast tea leaves**
4.25 **ounces sifted cake flour (about 1 cup plus 2 tablespoons)**
　1½ **cups sugar, divided**
　12 **large egg whites**
　1 **teaspoon cream of tartar**
　¼ **teaspoon salt**

1. Preheat oven to 325°.
2. Pour ½ cup boiling water over tea leaves in a bowl; steep 5 minutes. Strain through a fine sieve into a bowl; cool tea to room temperature.

3. Weigh or lightly spoon flour into a dry measuring cup; level with a knife. Combine flour and ¾ cup sugar, stirring with a whisk. Place egg whites in a large bowl; beat with a mixer at high speed until foamy. Add cream of tartar and salt; beat until soft peaks form. Add remaining ¾ cup sugar, 2 tablespoons at a time, beating until stiff peaks form. Beat in brewed tea.
4. Sift about ¼ cup flour mixture over egg white mixture; fold in. Repeat procedure with remaining flour mixture, ¼ cup at a time.
5. Spoon batter into an ungreased 10-inch tube pan, spreading evenly. Break air pockets by cutting through batter with a knife. Bake at 325° for 50 minutes or until cake springs back when lightly touched. Invert pan; cool completely. Loosen cake from sides of pan using a narrow metal spatula. Invert cake onto a plate. **Yield: 12 servings (serving size: 1 slice).**

CALORIES 147; FAT 0.1g (sat 0g, mono 0g, poly 0.1g); PROTEIN 4.3g; CARB 32.5g; FIBER 0.2g; CHOL 0mg; IRON 0.7mg; SODIUM 105mg; CALC 3.6mg

jelly-roll cakes

Spread with a variety of fillings and rolled into a log, jelly-roll cakes are not as complicated as they look.

Five-Spice Toasted-Coconut Cake Roll with Tropical Fruit Compote

Angel food cake batter makes a delicate base for a sorbet or ice cream cake roll. This is a great make-ahead dessert because you can freeze the rolled cake for up to 2 days before serving it with the compote. To soften the sorbet for spreading on the cake, let it stand at room temperature 30 to 45 minutes.

1.88 ounces sifted cake flour (about ½ cup)
 ¾ cup granulated sugar, divided
 ¾ teaspoon five-spice powder
 6 large egg whites
 ½ teaspoon cream of tartar
Dash of salt
 1 teaspoon fresh lemon juice
 1 teaspoon vanilla extract
 ½ teaspoon coconut extract
 ⅓ cup flaked sweetened coconut
 2 tablespoons powdered sugar
 1 pint mandarin orange with passion fruit sorbet, softened
 1 cup (½-inch) cubed peeled ripe mango
 1 cup (½-inch) cubed fresh pineapple
 1 cup (½-inch) cubed peeled kiwifruit
 2 tablespoons brown sugar
 2 tablespoons dark rum
 ¼ cup flaked sweetened coconut, toasted

1. Preheat oven to 325°.
2. Line bottom of a 15 x 10–inch jelly-roll pan with wax paper.

3. Weigh or lightly spoon flour into a dry measuring cup; level with a knife. Combine flour, 6 tablespoons granulated sugar, and five-spice powder, stirring with a whisk.
4. Place egg whites in a large bowl; beat with a mixer at high speed until foamy. Add cream of tartar and salt, and beat until soft peaks form. Add remaining 6 tablespoons granulated sugar, 2 tablespoons at a time, beating until stiff peaks form. Beat in juice and extracts.
5. Sift ¼ cup flour mixture over egg white mixture; fold in. Repeat procedure with remaining flour mixture, ¼ cup at a time. Spread batter into prepared pan. Sprinkle with ⅓ cup coconut. Bake at 325° for 20 minutes or until cake springs back when touched lightly.
6. Place a clean dish towel over a large wire rack; dust with powdered sugar. Loosen cake from sides of pan; turn out onto towel. Carefully peel off wax paper; cool 3 minutes. Starting at narrow end, roll up cake and towel together. Place, seam side down, on wire rack; cool cake completely. Unroll cake, and remove towel. Spread sorbet over cake, leaving a ½-inch border around outside edges. Reroll cake. Wrap cake in plastic wrap; freeze 1 hour or until firm.
7. Combine mango, pineapple, kiwifruit, brown sugar, and rum; let stand 20 minutes. Cut cake into 16 slices; place 2 slices on each of 8 plates. Spoon about ¼ cup compote over each serving, and sprinkle each serving with 1½ teaspoons toasted coconut. **Yield: 8 servings.**

CALORIES 245; FAT 2.1g (sat 1.6g, mono 0.1g, poly 0.1g); PROTEIN 4g; CARB 51.6g; FIBER 1.7g; CHOL 0mg; IRON 1.2mg; SODIUM 80mg; CALC 22mg

kitchen how-to:
roll a jelly-roll cake

To make a jelly-roll cake, jam, frosting, whipped cream, or any of a variety of fillings is spread onto a thin, flat cake baked on a jelly-roll pan. The cake is then rolled into a log and cut into slices. While the cake bakes, lay a dry rectangular terry cloth or tea towel that's slightly larger than the jelly-roll pan on a flat surface, and lightly dust it with powdered sugar. This prevents the cake from sticking. Remove the cake from the oven, and invert the cake onto the towel. Remove the wax paper from the cake, and roll the cake and the towel together, pressing gently. Be sure to move carefully during the rolling process—otherwise, the towel will end up rolled inside the cake. Cool the cake on a wire rack, seam side down. Unroll and remove the towel—the cake will be slightly wavy. Spread the filling as directed in the recipe, and reroll the cake.

cheesecakes

Cheesecakes are rich and creamy, and despite their sophisticated reputation, they're not difficult to make.

kitchen how-to: make a swirled cheesecake

To make a cheesecake, you'll need a springform pan—a round pan with high, straight sides that expand with the aid of a spring or clamp. The separate bottom of the pan can easily be removed from the sides when the clamp is opened. This allows the cheesecake to be removed by simply removing the sides of the pan.

1. Bring cranberry mixture to a boil, and cook 8 minutes or until cranberries pop and mixture is syrupy. Cool 20 minutes.
2. Puree the cranberry mixture in a food processor 1 minute or until smooth.

3. Prepare cheesecake batter, and pour filling over crust. Spoon the cranberry mixture over the filling.

4. Swirl together using the tip of a knife. Make just a few passes with the knife for a bold design or several for an intricate, feathery effect.

Cranberry Swirled Cheesecake

If the cranberry mixture gets too thick, add a tablespoon of water and whirl it around in the food processor. You can also make this in an 8-inch springform pan; it'll be very full, so be sure to bake over a foil-lined baking sheet. The cook time will be the same.

4 ounces chocolate graham crackers
3 tablespoons canola oil
Cooking spray
1½ cups fresh cranberries
½ cup sugar
¼ cup Chambord (raspberry-flavored liqueur)
3 tablespoons water
1 cup sugar
2 (8-ounce) blocks ⅓-less-fat cream cheese, softened
½ cup (4 ounces) block-style fat-free cream cheese, softened
1 cup plain fat-free Greek yogurt
2 teaspoons vanilla extract
⅛ teaspoon salt
3 large eggs
2 large egg whites

1. Preheat oven to 375°.
2. Wrap outside and bottom of a 9-inch springform pan tightly with a double layer of heavy-duty foil.
3. Place crackers in a food processor; process until finely ground. Drizzle with oil; pulse until combined. Press mixture into bottom and ½ inch up sides of prepared pan coated with cooking spray. Bake at 375° for 8 minutes; cool on a wire rack.
4. Reduce oven temperature to 325°.
5. Place cranberries and next 3 ingredients in a saucepan; bring to a boil. Cook 8 minutes or until cranberries pop and mixture is syrupy. Cool 20 minutes. Place mixture in a food processor; process 1 minute or until smooth.
6. Combine 1 cup sugar and cheeses in a large bowl; beat with a mixer at medium speed until smooth. Beat in yogurt, vanilla, and salt. Add whole eggs, 1 at a time, beating well after each addition.
7. Place 2 egg whites in a medium bowl; beat with a mixer at high speed until soft peaks form using clean, dry beaters. Fold beaten egg whites into cream cheese mixture. Pour filling over crust. Spoon cranberry mixture over filling; swirl together using the tip of a knife. Place springform pan in a 13 x 9–inch metal baking pan. Add hot water to pan to a depth of 2 inches. Bake at 325° for 50 minutes or until center of cheesecake barely moves when pan is touched.
8. Turn oven off. Cool cheesecake in closed oven 30 minutes. Remove cheesecake from oven. Run a knife around outside edge. Cool on a wire rack. Cover and chill 8 hours. **Yield: 14 servings (serving size: 1 wedge).**

CALORIES 275; FAT 12.1g (sat 5.2g, mono 4.3g, poly 1.3g); PROTEIN 8.6g; CARB 32.4g; FIBER 0.8g; CHOL 69mg; IRON 0.4mg; SODIUM 285mg; CALC 69mg

Nectarine Cheesecake with Pistachio Brittle

Once you add the eggs to the cheesecake batter, pulse just until combined. Incorporating too much air at this stage can cause the cheesecake to puff up as it bakes and sink as it cools, leaving a cracked or sunken appearance.

Crust:
Cooking spray
 6 graham cracker sheets
 2 tablespoons shelled dry-roasted unsalted pistachios
 1 tablespoon canola oil

Filling:
 2 cups diced, peeled, pitted nectarine (about 2 nectarines)
 1 cup plus 1 tablespoon sugar, divided
 1 (16-ounce) container 2% low-fat cottage cheese
 1½ cups (12 ounces) ⅓-less-fat cream cheese, softened
 ¼ cup cornstarch
 1 cup reduced-fat sour cream
 1½ teaspoons vanilla extract
 2 large egg whites
 1 large egg

Brittle:
 ½ cup sugar
 ⅓ cup water
 ¼ cup coarsely chopped shelled dry-roasted unsalted pistachios

Sauce:
 2 cups chopped, peeled, pitted nectarine (about 2 nectarines)
 2 tablespoons sugar
 1 teaspoon fresh lemon juice

1. Preheat oven to 325°.
2. To prepare crust, wrap outside and bottom of a 10-inch springform pan tightly with a double layer of heavy-duty foil. Lightly coat pan with cooking spray.

3. Place graham crackers and 2 tablespoons pistachios in a food processor; process until finely ground. Add oil; process until moist. Firmly press crumb mixture into bottom and 1 inch up sides of prepared pan.
4. To prepare filling, combine diced nectarine and 1 tablespoon sugar in a small saucepan. Cover and cook over low heat 5 minutes or until sugar dissolves. Uncover and cook 5 minutes or until mixture thickens. Cool.
5. Place cottage cheese in food processor; process until smooth. Add nectarine mixture, remaining 1 cup sugar, cream cheese, and cornstarch; process until smooth. Add sour cream, vanilla, egg whites, and egg; pulse just until combined. Pour cheese mixture into prepared pan. Place pan in a shallow roasting pan; add enough boiling water to come halfway up sides of pan.
6. Bake at 325° for 50 minutes or until center barely moves when pan is touched. Turn oven off, and open oven door; cool cheesecake in oven 1 hour. Remove cheesecake from roasting pan; run a knife around outside edge. Discard foil. Cool completely on a wire rack. Cover and chill at least 8 hours.
7. To prepare brittle, coat a baking sheet with cooking spray. Combine ½ cup sugar and ⅓ cup water in a small saucepan over medium-high heat; bring to a boil. Cook 1 minute or until sugar dissolves. Continue cooking 4 minutes or until golden (do not stir). Remove from heat; carefully stir in ¼ cup chopped pistachios. Quickly spread mixture in a thin layer onto prepared baking sheet. Cool completely; break into small pieces. Sprinkle brittle around edge of cheesecake.
8. To prepare sauce, combine chopped nectarine, 2 tablespoons sugar, and juice in a blender; process until smooth. Serve with cheesecake. **Yield: 16 servings (serving size: 1 cheesecake wedge and 1 tablespoon sauce).**

CALORIES 263; FAT 10.3g (sat 5g, mono 2.3g, poly 1g); PROTEIN 9.3g; CARB 34.4g; FIBER 1g; CHOL 36mg; IRON 0.5mg; SODIUM 263mg; CALC 61mg

kitchen how-to: avoid cheesecake cracks

Some cracks in cheesecakes are normal and can even make them look prettier.

1. Generally, the more slowly the cheesecake is cooked, the less chance there is for cracking. Use an oven thermometer to make sure your oven stays at the correct temperature.

2. After the cheesecake has cooled in the oven, remove it, and run a knife around the edge. Cool completely on a wire rack, then cover and chill at least 8 hours.

cupcakes

Cupcakes are a great small treat. Topped with frosting or a glaze or even left plain, they're perfect for satisfying a sweet tooth.

kitchen how-to: bake cupcakes

If you have only one pan and a recipe calls for more cupcakes than your pan will hold, simply cover the batter with plastic wrap and refrigerate while the first batch bakes. Once the first batch is baked, you'll need to allow the pan to cool or run it under cool water, and then dry it. For the second batch, you may need to add a minute or two to the bake time to account for the cooler batter.

1. Place muffin cup liners in muffin cups, and coat them with cooking spray. Some recipes don't require cooking spray. Follow the recipe's instructions for the best results.

2. Prepare the batter. You can mix the batter by hand using a whisk or with a hand mixer for ease.

3. Divide the batter evenly among the prepared muffin cups, filling them no more than two-thirds full. You'll want to leave room for the batter to expand and rise as it cooks and to prevent it from overflowing.

Fresh Apple Cupcakes with Almond Streusel

You can replace the amaretto with the same amount of 2% reduced-fat milk, if you like.

Cooking spray
6.75 ounces all-purpose flour (about 1½ cups)
½ teaspoon baking powder
¼ teaspoon salt
¼ teaspoon baking soda
¾ cup granulated sugar
¼ cup (2 ounces) ⅓-less-fat cream cheese, softened
¼ cup butter, softened
2 tablespoons amaretto (almond-flavored liqueur)
1 teaspoon vanilla extract
1 large egg
½ cup reduced-fat sour cream
¼ cup 2% reduced-fat milk
¾ cup finely chopped Gala apple
3 tablespoons all-purpose flour, divided
2 tablespoons brown sugar
¼ teaspoon ground cinnamon
2 tablespoons chilled butter
2 tablespoons sliced almonds
1 cup powdered sugar
4 teaspoons 2% reduced-fat milk

1. Preheat oven to 350°.
2. Place 12 paper muffin cup liners in muffin cups; coat liners with cooking spray.
3. Weigh or lightly spoon 6.75 ounces flour (about 1½ cups) into dry measuring cups; level with a knife. Combine 6.75 ounces flour, baking powder, salt, and baking soda in a small bowl, stirring with a whisk. Combine granulated sugar, cream cheese, and ¼ cup butter in a large bowl; beat with a mixer at high speed until well blended. Add amaretto, vanilla, and egg to sugar mixture; beat with a mixer at medium speed until well blended. Combine sour cream and ¼ cup milk in a small bowl; stir with a whisk until well blended. Combine apple and 1 tablespoon flour in a small bowl; toss well.
4. Add flour mixture and sour cream mixture alternately to sugar mixture, beginning and ending with flour mixture. Beat just until blended. Fold in apple mixture. Divide batter evenly among muffin cups.

5. Combine remaining 2 tablespoons flour, brown sugar, and cinnamon in a small bowl. Cut in 2 tablespoons butter with a pastry blender or 2 knives until mixture resembles coarse meal; stir in almonds. Sprinkle streusel evenly over cupcakes. Bake at 350° for 27 minutes or until a wooden pick inserted in center comes out clean. Cool in pan 15 minutes on a wire rack; remove cupcakes from pan.
6. Combine powdered sugar and 4 teaspoons milk in a small bowl, stirring with a whisk. Drizzle glaze over cupcakes. **Yield: 12 servings (serving size: 1 cupcake).**

CALORIES 256; FAT 9g (sat 5.3g, mono 2.3g, poly 0.5g); PROTEIN 3.5g; CARB 39.9g; FIBER 0.8g; CHOL 40mg; IRON 1mg; SODIUM 172mg; CALC 43mg

Blueberry Cupcakes with Lemon Cream Cheese Frosting

Cupcakes:

Cooking spray

6.75 ounces all-purpose flour (about 1½ cups)

2 tablespoons all-purpose flour, divided

10 tablespoons granulated sugar

1½ teaspoons baking powder

¼ teaspoon salt

⅛ teaspoon baking soda

¼ cup butter, melted

1 large egg

½ cup nonfat buttermilk

½ cup 2% reduced-fat milk

1 teaspoon grated lemon rind

¾ cup blueberries

Frosting:

¼ cup (2 ounces) ⅓-less-fat cream cheese, softened

2 tablespoons butter, softened

1 teaspoon grated lemon rind

1 teaspoon vanilla extract

⅛ teaspoon salt

1½ cups powdered sugar, sifted

2 teaspoons fresh lemon juice

1. Preheat oven to 350°.

2. Place 12 paper muffin cup liners in muffin cups; coat liners with cooking spray.

3. To prepare cupcakes, weigh or lightly spoon 6.75 ounces flour (about 1½ cups) into dry measuring cups; level with a knife. Measure 1 tablespoon flour; level with a knife. Sift together 6.75 ounces flour plus 1 tablespoon flour, granulated sugar, baking powder, ¼ teaspoon salt, and baking soda in a large bowl. Combine melted butter and egg in another large bowl; stir with a whisk. Add buttermilk, milk, and 1 teaspoon rind to butter mixture; stir with a whisk. Add buttermilk mixture to flour mixture, stirring just until moist. Toss blueberries with remaining 1 tablespoon flour. Fold blueberries into batter. Spoon batter into prepared muffin cups. Bake at 350° for 25 minutes or until a wooden pick inserted in center comes out clean. Cool in pan 5 minutes on a wire rack; remove from pan. Cool completely on wire rack.

4. To prepare frosting, place cream cheese, 2 tablespoons butter, 1 teaspoon rind, vanilla, and ⅛ teaspoon salt in a bowl; beat with a mixer at medium speed just until blended. Gradually add powdered sugar (do not overbeat). Stir in juice. Spread frosting evenly over cupcakes. Cover and store in refrigerator. **Yield: 12 servings (serving size: 1 cupcake).**

CALORIES 236; FAT 7.7g (sat 4.6g, mono 2g, poly 0.4g); PROTEIN 3.7g; CARB 38.7g; FIBER 0.7g; CHOL 38mg; IRON 1mg; SODIUM 230mg; CALC 71mg

all about salted and unsalted butter

The difference between salted and unsalted butter is simple: about 80 milligrams of sodium per tablespoon. Salt acts as a preservative and prolongs the shelf life of butter. Most people use salted butter, and we often use it in our recipes, but some cooks prefer unsalted because it allows them to control the amount of salt in a dish and preserves the mellow sweetness of butter. If you want unsalted butter, look for the words "sweet butter" or "unsalted." The term "sweet cream butter" is used for both salted and unsalted butter.

Coconut Cupcakes with Lime Buttercream Frosting

Texture can suffer when you lighten cakes by using less butter and sugar. Mild-flavored potato starch, available on the baking aisle of most grocery stores, is a fine powder that ensures a moist, light result. Make sure you purchase potato *starch* and not potato *flour*, which is heavier and denser. Use lemon rind and fresh lemon juice in place of the lime for a variation.

Cupcakes:
Cooking spray
4.5 ounces all-purpose flour (about 1 cup)
  3 tablespoons potato starch
  1 teaspoon baking powder
  ½ teaspoon salt
  ¾ cup granulated sugar
  2 tablespoons butter, softened
  1 large egg
  1 large egg white
  ⅔ cup fat-free milk
  2 tablespoons flaked sweetened coconut
  ½ teaspoon vanilla extract

Frosting:
  3 tablespoons butter, softened
  1 teaspoon half-and-half
  ½ teaspoon grated lime rind
  1 tablespoon fresh lime juice
4.75 ounces powdered sugar (about 1⅓ cups), sifted

1. Preheat oven to 350°.
2. To prepare cupcakes, place 2 paper muffin cup liners in each of 12 muffin cups; coat liners with cooking spray.
3. Weigh or lightly spoon flour into a dry measuring cup; level with a knife. Combine flour and next 3 ingredients in a small bowl; stir with a whisk.
4. Combine granulated sugar and 2 tablespoons butter in a large bowl; beat with a mixer at medium speed until blended (mixture will be the consistency of damp sand). Add egg and egg white, 1 at a time, beating well after

each addition. Add flour mixture and milk alternately to egg mixture, beginning and ending with flour mixture. Fold in coconut and vanilla.
5. Spoon batter evenly into prepared muffin cups. Bake at 350° for 18 minutes or until cupcakes spring back when touched lightly in center. Cool in pan 2 minutes on a wire rack; remove from pan. Cool completely on wire rack.
6. To prepare frosting, combine 3 tablespoons butter and next 3 ingredients in a medium bowl; beat with a mixer at medium speed until smooth. Gradually add powdered sugar, beating just until smooth. Spread about 2½ teaspoons frosting on each cupcake. **Yield: 12 servings (serving size: 1 cupcake).**

CALORIES 196; FAT 5.6g (sat 3.4g, mono 1.4g, poly 0.3g); PROTEIN 2.5g; CARB 34.8g; FIBER 0.3g; CHOL 31mg; IRON 0.7mg; SODIUM 179mg; CALC 52mg

kitchen how-to:
make & frost cupcakes

Homemade frostings are easy to make, and at their simplest require only a handful of ingredients. A mixer makes quick work of beating butter or cream cheese until smooth and fluffy and slowly incorporating the powdered sugar. A small, flat spatula makes frosting cupcakes easy, but you can also use a knife. Or, pipe the frosting with a pastry bag fitted with a star tip for a fun, swirled topping.

Double-Chocolate Cupcakes

These cupcakes are easy to make. Because the recipe calls for simple ingredients, it's best to purchase premium cocoa and dark chocolate. Since they're studded with dark chocolate chunks, just dusting them with powdered sugar is enough to decorate these treats. Bake them in muffin cup liners.

Cooking spray
4.5 ounces all-purpose flour (about 1 cup)
⅓ cup unsweetened cocoa
1 teaspoon baking soda
⅛ teaspoon salt
⅔ cup granulated sugar
¼ cup butter, softened
½ cup egg substitute
1 teaspoon vanilla extract
½ cup low-fat buttermilk
1.25 ounces dark (70 percent cocoa) chocolate, finely chopped
2 tablespoons powdered sugar

1. Preheat oven to 350°.
2. Place 12 paper muffin cup liners in muffin cups; coat liners with cooking spray.
3. Weigh or lightly spoon flour into a dry measuring cup; level with a knife. Combine flour, cocoa, baking soda, and salt; stir with a whisk.
4. Place granulated sugar and butter in a large bowl; beat with a mixer at medium speed until well combined (about 3 minutes). Add egg substitute and vanilla, beating well. Add flour mixture and buttermilk alternately to sugar mixture, beginning and ending with flour mixture. Fold in chocolate. Spoon batter into prepared muffin cups. Bake at 350° for 18 minutes or until cupcakes spring back when touched lightly in center or until wooden pick inserted in center comes out clean. Remove from pan; cool completely on a wire rack. Sprinkle with powdered sugar just before serving.
Yield: 12 servings (serving size: 1 cupcake).

CALORIES 150; FAT 5.2g (sat 3.2g, mono 1.2g, poly 0.2g); PROTEIN 3.1g; CARB 24g; FIBER 1.1g; CHOL 11mg; IRON 1mg; SODIUM 125mg; CALC 42mg

all about cupcake liners

Paper liners can be a fun way to add color and interest to your cupcakes, but their purpose is also functional—they keep these sweet treats from sticking to the pan and also make cleanup quick and easy. If you're using liners, there's no need to coat the pan with cooking spray, but you should coat the liners with cooking spray to make them easier to peel off.

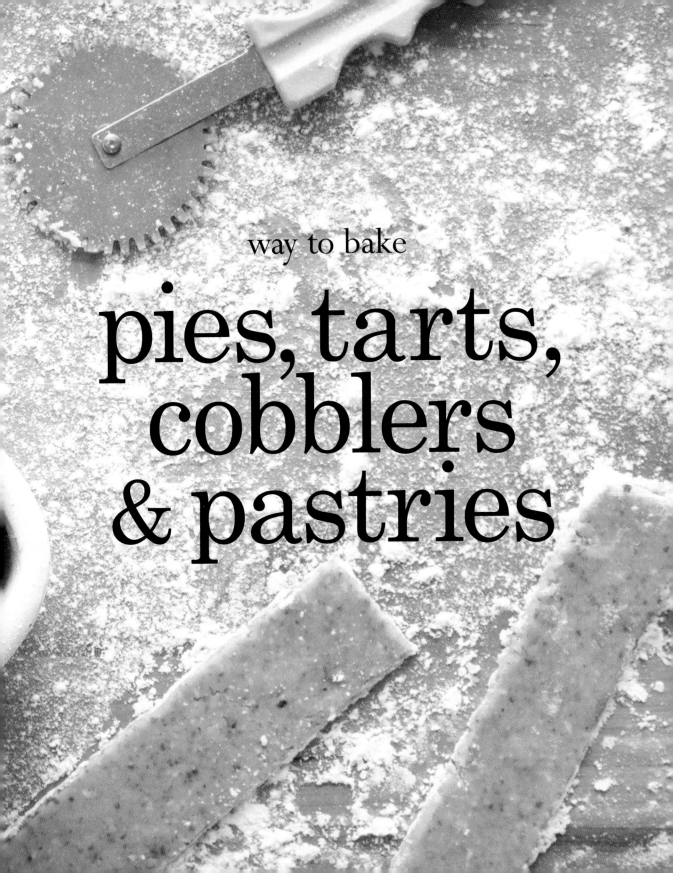

way to bake

pies, tarts, cobblers & pastries

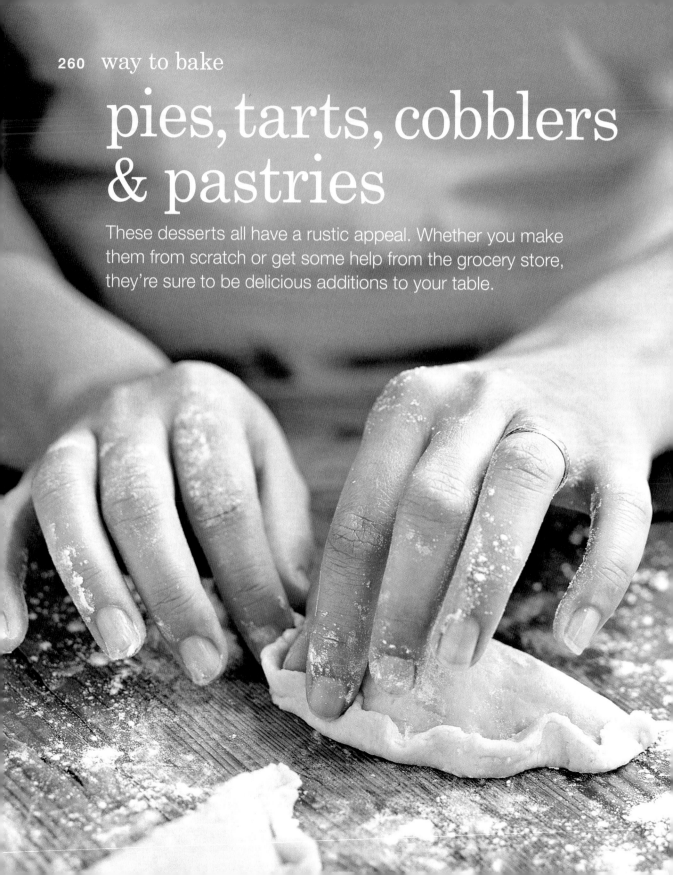

pies, tarts, cobblers & pastries

These desserts all have a rustic appeal. Whether you make them from scratch or get some help from the grocery store, they're sure to be delicious additions to your table.

Pies vs. Tarts

The difference between a pie and a tart is simple: It's all about the pan in which it is baked. Pies, served from the pan, tend to be homey. Tarts often bake in scallop-edged pans and are frequently removed from the pan for a special-occasion presentation.

Getting a Great Crust

What makes many of these desserts so tasty is the base of flaky piecrust. When making piecrust from scratch, follow these tips:

• Be patient when cutting in the vegetable shortening or butter with a pastry blender or 2 knives; it may take as long as 5 minutes for the mixture to look like coarse meal. This is how the fat gets distributed in the flour, creating pockets that make the pastry flaky when heated.

• Chill the flour in the freezer 1 hour prior to preparing the dough. This makes the piecrust flakier by preventing the fat cut into the flour from melting, which makes for tough crusts.

• Freeze the dough to make it easier to handle. You want to handle the dough as little as possible, since overworking can make the crust tough. Place the rolled-out pastry in the freezer 10 minutes before transferring it to your baking dish or tart pan, or using it to make individual pastries.

Baking Crusts for Refrigerated Pies

For refrigerated pies, the pastry is baked without the filling; this is also called blind baking. Place the dough in a pie plate, prick it with a fork, and then cover with foil or wax paper and fill it with pie weights or uncooked dried beans, which work just as well. (Make sure you use the dried beans for this purpose only, since they can't be cooked afterwards.) This weighs down the pastry and prevents it from bubbling up as it bakes in the oven. In place of pie weights or beans, you can also weigh the crust down with a glass pie dish. To brown the crust, uncover it a few minutes before it's done baking. We show you how to make delicious, light piecrust on page 262.

piecrust

There's something so satisfying and comforting about a homemade pie, but success starts with—and depends on—the crust. Once you master the shell, you can easily bake a pie (or tart) for any occasion.

kitchen how-to: **make flaky, delicious, light piecrust**

To bake the crust, simply roll out your pastry dough, fit it into your pan, pierce it with a fork to minimize shrinkage as it bakes, weigh it down with pie weights or dried beans, and bake until it's done. Then allow the crust to cool, and spoon in your filling.

1. Weigh or measure the flour carefully. Too much flour, and you'll have a dense, dry, and floury-tasting crust. Invest in an inexpensive scale, which will ensure success every time you bake.

2. After weighing the flour, combine it with other dry ingredients, such as salt and baking powder, stirring well. Separately combine wet ingredients. Using a flexible spatula, slowly incorporate the dry ingredients into the wet, and stir just until mixture is evenly moistened throughout.

3. The dough will be clumpy at this point, just as it should be. Don't knead it, but simply gather it up, gently press it into a disk, wrap it in plastic wrap, and let it rest in the refrigerator so the gluten will relax.

4. This is a delicate dough, so it's easiest to roll it out to an even thickness between sheets of plastic wrap. This prevents the dough from sticking to the work surface and tearing as you go.

All-Purpose Light Piecrust

Add chopped fresh herbs, a pinch of ground red pepper, ground nuts, or other ingredients to customize the flavor of your piecrust. Vegetable shortening gives the piecrust a flaky texture. Make sure you buy a brand that doesn't contain trans fats. A small bit of butter adds flavor but keeps saturated fat in check.

5	ounces all-purpose flour (about 1¼ cups)
1	teaspoon sugar
¼	teaspoon salt
¼	teaspoon baking powder
¼	cup vegetable shortening
4	teaspoons unsalted butter, melted
¼	cup boiling water

1. Weigh or lightly spoon flour into dry measuring cups; level with a knife. Combine flour and next 3 ingredients in a bowl; cut in shortening with a pastry blender or 2 knives until mixture resembles coarse meal.
2. Make a well in center of flour mixture. Combine butter and boiling water. Pour butter mixture into center of well. Gently draw flour mixture into butter mixture until moist clumps form. Press dough into a 4-inch circle. Cover and chill 30 minutes.
3. Slightly overlap 2 sheets of plastic wrap. Uncover and place chilled dough on plastic wrap. Cover dough with 2 additional sheets of overlapping plastic wrap. Roll dough, still covered, into a 13-inch circle. **Yield: 1 piecrust (serving size: ⅛ of piecrust).**

CALORIES 127; FAT 7g (sat 2.8g, mono 3.1g, poly 0.7g); PROTEIN 1.9g; CARB 14.1g; FIBER 0.5g; CHOL 5mg; IRON 0.8mg; SODIUM 147mg; CALC 14mg

Chive Piecrust variation: Prepare All-Purpose Light Piecrust, omitting sugar. Add 2 tablespoons minced fresh chives to flour mixture. **Yield: 1 piecrust (serving size: ⅛ of piecrust).**

CALORIES 125; FAT 7g (sat 2.8g, mono 3.1g, poly 0.7g); PROTEIN 1.9g; CARB 13.6g; FIBER 1g; CHOL 5mg; IRON 0.9mg; SODIUM 147mg; CALC 15mg

kitchen how-to: make a graham cracker crust

A homemade graham cracker crust takes a little more time to prepare than using a commercial variety does, but the flavor and texture make it worth the effort. Once you have the crumb mixture ready, place about half of the mixture in the bottom of a pie

plate coated with cooking spray. Using both hands, firmly press the crumb mixture against the sides of the pan, rotating the pan until the sides are completely and evenly covered. Place the remaining crumb mixture in the bottom of the pan, spreading it around to cover the pan and firmly pressing down as you go.

Graham Cracker Crust

This crust is lighter than many commercial graham cracker crusts. The egg white acts as a binder for the crumbs and allows you to use less butter and sugar.

40	graham crackers (10 cookie sheets)
2	tablespoons sugar
2	tablespoons butter, melted
1	large egg white
Cooking spray	

1. Preheat oven to 350°.
2. Place crackers in a food processor; process until crumbly. Add sugar, butter, and egg white; pulse 6 times or just until moist. Press crumb mixture into a 9-inch pie plate coated with cooking spray. Bake at 350° for 8 minutes; cool on a wire rack 15 minutes. **Yield: 1 piecrust (serving size: ⅛ of piecrust).**

CALORIES 114; FAT 4.6g (sat 1.7g, mono 1.8g, poly 0.2g); PROTEIN 1.7g; CARB 16.5g; FIBER 0.6g; CHOL 8mg; IRON 0.7mg; SODIUM 194mg; CALC 142mg

pies

Great pies come in many forms. From sweet to savory and frozen to baked, the common denominators are a delicious filling and a satisfying piecrust.

kitchen how-to: make a decorative piecrust

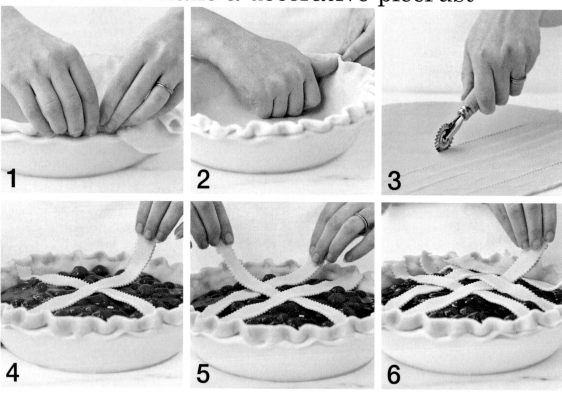

You can top your pie in a variety of ways, but this decorative lattice is sure to please.

1. Press 1 piecrust into a pie plate, making sure there are no air bubbles, and then tuck extra dough under edges.

2. Pinch dough with thumb and index finger of one hand, while pressing inward with thumb of other hand.

3. Place reserved piecrust on a work surface, and use a pastry cutter to cut the dough into 10 (½-inch-wide) strips.

4. Pour filling into pie. Working from the center outward, lay 1 strip of dough horizontally, then 1 vertically.

5. Continue alternating strips, leaving about ½ inch between each, as you weave them over and under.

6. Be sure each strip is long enough to reach the edge of the pie, and then seal dough strips to edge of crust.

Apple Pie

11.25   ounces all-purpose flour (about 2½ cups)

¾   teaspoon salt

6   tablespoons chilled butter, cut into small pieces

2   tablespoons vegetable shortening, cut into small pieces

1   tablespoon fresh lemon juice

¾   cup ice water

1.1   ounces all-purpose flour (about ¼ cup)

2½   cups thinly sliced peeled Braeburn apple (about 1 pound)

2½   cups thinly sliced peeled Cortland apple (about 1 pound)

1   cup sugar

¼   teaspoon ground cinnamon

⅛   to ¼ teaspoon ground allspice

Cooking spray

1   tablespoon chilled butter, cut into small pieces

½   teaspoon vanilla extract

1   tablespoon whole milk

1. Weigh or lightly spoon 11.25 ounces flour (about 2½ cups) into dry measuring cups; level with a knife. Combine 11.25 ounces flour and salt in a large bowl; cut in 6 tablespoons butter and vegetable shortening with a pastry blender or 2 knives until mixture resembles coarse meal. Add lemon juice. Sprinkle surface with ice water, 1 tablespoon at a time, and toss with a fork until moist and crumbly. Shape dough into a ball, and wrap in plastic wrap. Chill 1 hour.

2. Divide dough into 2 equal portions. Gently press each portion into a 1-inch-thick circle on heavy-duty plastic wrap; cover and freeze 10 minutes.

3. Preheat oven to 350°.

4. Weigh or lightly spoon 1.1 ounces flour (about ¼ cup) into a dry measuring cup; level with a knife. Place apples in a large bowl. Combine sugar, 1.1 ounces flour, cinnamon, and allspice in a small bowl. Sprinkle sugar mixture over apples; toss well to coat.

5. Working with 1 dough portion at a time, roll dough into a 12-inch circle on a lightly floured surface. Fit dough circle into a 9-inch pie plate coated with cooking spray, allowing dough to extend over edge of plate. Roll the remaining dough portion into a 10-inch circle on a lightly floured surface. Spoon apple mixture into prepared pie plate, and dot with 1 tablespoon butter. Drizzle apple mixture with vanilla. Top with 10-inch dough circle. Press edges of dough together. Fold edges under; flute. Brush surface of dough with milk. Cut 3 (1-inch) slits in top of dough to allow steam to escape. Bake at 350° for 1 hour or until apples are tender. **Yield: 12 servings (serving size: 1 slice).**

CALORIES 272; FAT 9g (sat 5g, mono 2.3g, poly 1g); PROTEIN 3.2g; CARB 45.1g; FIBER 1.9g; CHOL 18mg; IRON 1.4mg; SODIUM 194mg; CALC 12mg

Pear Pie with Streusel Topping and Caramel Sauce

Bartlett or Anjou pears work best in this pie. Be sure to purchase firm, slightly underripe fruit for this pie, since the pears soften and release juice as they cook.

Pie:
- 3 ounces all-purpose flour (about ⅔ cup), divided
- ½ cup granulated sugar
- ½ teaspoon ground cinnamon
- ⅛ teaspoon salt
- 3 tablespoons fresh lemon juice
- 6 medium-sized firm pears, peeled, cored, and cut lengthwise into ½-inch-thick wedges
- ½ (15-ounce) package refrigerated pie dough
- Cooking spray
- ⅓ cup packed brown sugar
- 3 tablespoons chilled butter, cut into small pieces

Sauce:
- ⅓ cup packed brown sugar
- 3 tablespoons heavy whipping cream
- 2 tablespoons butter, softened
- 2 teaspoons water

1. Preheat oven to 375°.

2. To prepare pie, weigh or lightly spoon flour into dry measuring cups; level with a knife. Combine 1.5 ounces flour (about ⅓ cup), granulated sugar, cinnamon, and salt in a large bowl. Add juice and pears to flour mixture; toss gently to coat. Roll dough into an 11-inch circle; fit dough into a 9-inch pie plate coated with cooking spray. Fold edges under and flute. Arrange pear mixture in an even layer in prepared crust.

3. Combine remaining 1.5 ounces flour (about ⅓ cup) and ⅓ cup brown sugar in a bowl. Cut in 3 tablespoons chilled butter with a pastry blender or 2 knives until mixture resembles coarse meal. Sprinkle butter mixture evenly over pear mixture. Bake at 375° for 1 hour or until lightly browned. Cool on a wire rack 10 minutes.

4. To prepare sauce, combine ⅓ cup brown sugar, cream, and 2 tablespoons softened butter in a small,

heavy saucepan over medium-high heat; bring to a boil. Cook 1 minute or until thickened. Remove from heat; stir in 2 teaspoons water. Serve at room temperature or slightly warmed with pie. **Yield: 12 servings (serving size: 1 slice and about 1½ teaspoons sauce).**

CALORIES 287; FAT 11g (sat 5.5g, mono 1.7g, poly 0.3g); PROTEIN 1.5g; CARB 47.5g; FIBER 2.8g; CHOL 20mg; IRON 0.7mg; SODIUM 139mg; CALC 24mg

all about
refrigerated piecrust

Premade refrigerated piecrusts are a real time-saver. The unbaked piecrusts can be frozen for up to 2 months, but you'll need to thaw them in the refrigerator. Defrosting them in the microwave can heat them unevenly, causing some parts of the crust to cook.

kitchen how-to: clean & freeze rhubarb

1

2

3

Rhubarb has a short growing season (April through May) and is a sought-after spring commodity. The best way to utilize the flavor of rhubarb for longer is to prep and freeze it. When buying, look for deep-red, crisp stalks free of blemishes and cuts.

1. Trim leaves from the top of the stalk, and cut about 1 inch from the bottom; discard.
2. After rinsing, pat the stalks dry with a paper towel and cut into 1-inch sections. You can use the stalks now or freeze them for later.
3. Lay the cut pieces of rhubarb on a lined baking sheet, and freeze for about an hour, which prevents the rhubarb from sticking together.
4. Transfer the pieces to a zip-top plastic freezer bag, and store in the freezer for up to 6 months. To thaw, defrost it overnight in the refrigerator.

4

Lattice-Topped Rhubarb Pie

If you don't feel like weaving the dough strips through one another for the lattice topping, just arrange 6 dough strips over the pie; lay the other 6 strips perpendicular to the first strips without weaving.

Crust:
- 7.88 ounces all-purpose flour (about 1¾ cups)
- 3 tablespoons sugar
- ⅛ teaspoon salt
- ¼ cup chilled unsalted butter, cut into small pieces
- 3 tablespoons vegetable shortening
- 5 tablespoons ice water
- Cooking spray

Filling:
- 6 cups (1-inch) sliced rhubarb (about 1½ pounds)
- 1 cup sugar
- 3 tablespoons cornstarch
- 1½ teaspoons grated orange rind
- ¼ teaspoon ground nutmeg

Remaining Ingredients:
- 1½ teaspoons 1% low-fat milk
- 1 tablespoon sugar

1. To prepare crust, weigh or lightly spoon flour into dry measuring cups; level with a knife. Combine flour, 3 tablespoons sugar, and salt in a large bowl; cut in butter and shortening with a pastry blender or 2 knives until mixture resembles coarse meal. Sprinkle surface with ice water, 1 tablespoon at a time; toss with a fork until moist and crumbly (do not form a ball).

2. Gently press two-thirds of dough into a 4-inch circle on heavy-duty plastic wrap, and cover with additional plastic wrap. Roll dough, still covered, into a 12-inch circle. Press remaining dough into a 4-inch circle on heavy-duty plastic wrap, and cover with additional plastic wrap. Roll dough into a 9-inch circle. Freeze both dough portions 10 minutes or until plastic wrap can be easily removed.

3. Preheat oven to 425°.

4. Remove 1 sheet of plastic wrap from 12-inch dough circle, and fit dough, plastic wrap side up, into a 9-inch pie plate coated with cooking spray, allowing dough to extend over edge of plate. Remove top sheet of plastic wrap; fold edges under, and flute.

5. To prepare filling, combine rhubarb and next 4 ingredients, tossing well. Spoon filling into crust.

6. Remove top sheet of plastic wrap from remaining dough. Cut dough into 12 (¾-inch) strips. Gently remove dough strips from bottom sheet of plastic wrap, and arrange in a lattice design over rhubarb mixture. Seal dough strips to edge of crust. Brush top and edges of dough with milk; sprinkle with 1 tablespoon sugar. Place pie on a baking sheet covered with foil. Bake at 425° for 15 minutes. Reduce oven temperature to 375° (do not remove pie from oven). Bake an additional 30 minutes or until golden (shield crust with foil if it browns too quickly). Cool on a wire rack. **Yield: 10 servings (serving size: 1 slice).**

CALORIES 276; FAT 8.8g (sat 3.9g, mono 3.1g, poly 1.3g); PROTEIN 3g; CARB 47.3g; FIBER 2g; CHOL 12mg; IRON 1.2mg; SODIUM 34mg; CALC 69mg

Harvest Pie

Butternut squash stands in for pumpkin in this pie, which received our Test Kitchens' highest rating. Prepare a day in advance, and store at room temperature.

2½   cups mashed cooked butternut squash (about 1 large)
½   cup evaporated fat-free milk
¾   cup granulated sugar
4   large egg whites
1   teaspoon vanilla extract
½   teaspoon ground cinnamon
⅛   teaspoon ground allspice
⅛   teaspoon ground cloves
1.1   ounces all-purpose flour (about ¼ cup)
¼   cup packed dark brown sugar
2   tablespoons chilled butter, cut into small pieces
3   tablespoons chopped pecans
½   (15-ounce) package refrigerated pie dough
Cooking spray
10   tablespoons frozen fat-free whipped topping, thawed (optional)

1. Preheat oven to 425°.

2. Place butternut squash and milk in a food processor; process until smooth. Add granulated sugar and next 5 ingredients; process until smooth.

3. Weigh or lightly spoon flour into a dry measuring cup; level with a knife. Combine flour and brown sugar in a medium bowl; cut in butter using a pastry blender or 2 knives. Add pecans; toss to combine.

4. Roll dough into a 13-inch circle; fit into a 9-inch deep-dish pie plate coated with cooking spray. Fold edges under; flute. Pour squash mixture into prepared crust. Place pie plate on bottom rack in oven; bake at 425° for 15 minutes. Remove pie from oven.

5. Reduce oven temperature to 350°.

6. Sprinkle flour mixture evenly over filling; shield edges of piecrust with foil. Return pie plate to bottom rack; bake an additional 40 minutes or until center is set. Cool on a wire rack. Garnish each serving with 1 tablespoon whipped topping, if desired. **Yield: 10 servings (serving size: 1 slice).**

CALORIES 294; FAT 11g (sat 3.9g, mono 4.9g, poly 1.5g); PROTEIN 4.6g; CARB 46.2g; FIBER 3.5g; CHOL 7mg; IRON 1.7mg; SODIUM 200mg; CALC 97mg

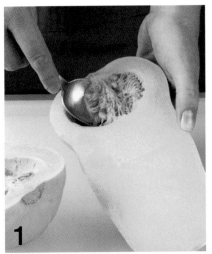

kitchen how-to:
roast & mash butternut squash

One large butternut squash (about 2¼ pounds) will be enough to yield 2½ cups of mashed cooked butternut squash.

1. Cut butternut squash in half, and scoop out seeds.
2. Place oven rack in lowest position. Preheat oven to 400°.

Place squash, cut sides down, on a foil-lined baking sheet coated with cooking spray.
3. Bake at 400° for 30 minutes or until the squash is tender. Cool squash slightly. Scoop out cooked squash.
4. Mash butternut squash with a potato masher.

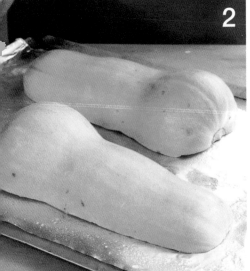

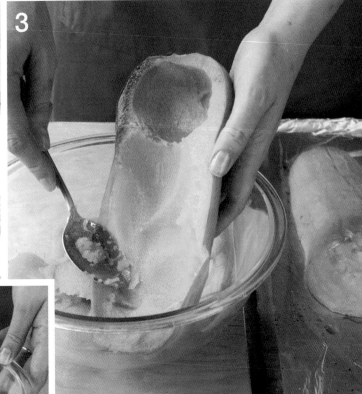

Oat-Crusted Pecan Pie with Fresh Cranberry Sauce

Cover the pie loosely with aluminum foil for the last 8 minutes of baking if it begins to brown too much.

Crust:
- 1¾ cups old-fashioned rolled oats
- 3 tablespoons granulated sugar
- ¼ teaspoon salt
- 3½ tablespoons chilled butter, cut into small pieces
- 1 tablespoon ice water
- Cooking spray

Filling:
- ¾ cup packed brown sugar
- ⅔ cup light-colored corn syrup
- 3 tablespoons all-purpose flour
- 3 tablespoons molasses
- 1 tablespoon butter, melted
- ½ teaspoon vanilla extract
- ¼ teaspoon salt
- 2 large eggs
- 1 large egg white
- ⅔ cup pecan halves

Sauce:
- 1½ cups fresh cranberries
- ⅔ cup granulated sugar
- ½ cup fresh orange juice
- ¼ cup water
- ½ teaspoon cornstarch

1. Preheat oven to 400°.
2. To prepare crust, place first 3 ingredients in a food processor; process until finely ground (about 30 seconds). Add chilled butter, and pulse 5 times or until combined. Add 1 tablespoon ice water; pulse just until combined (mixture will be crumbly). Press oat mixture into bottom and up sides of a 9-inch deep-dish pie plate coated with cooking spray. Bake at 400° for 15 minutes or until lightly browned. Cool 5 minutes on a wire rack.
3. Reduce oven temperature to 350°.
4. To prepare filling, combine brown sugar and next 8 ingredients in a medium bowl, stirring well. Stir in pecan halves. Spoon filling into prepared crust. Bake at 350° for 48 minutes or until center is set. Cool to room temperature on wire rack.
5. To prepare sauce, combine cranberries, ⅔ cup granulated sugar, and juice in a small saucepan over medium-high heat; bring to a boil. Reduce heat, and simmer until cranberries begin to pop, about 3 minutes, stirring occasionally.
6. Combine ¼ cup water and cornstarch in a small bowl, stirring with a whisk. Stir cornstarch mixture into cranberry mixture; bring to a boil. Cook 1 minute, stirring often; remove from heat. Cool completely. Cut pie into 12 slices; serve with sauce. **Yield: 12 servings (serving size: 1 slice and about 1½ tablespoons sauce).**

CALORIES 329; FAT 10.3g (sat 3.5g, mono 4.1g, poly 1.9g); PROTEIN 46.5g; CARB 58.4g; FIBER 2g; CHOL 47mg; IRON 1.4mg; SODIUM 164mg; CALC 43mg

kitchen how-to:
make fresh cranberry sauce

Fresh cranberries are in season only from October through December, which leaves a small window for making fresh cranberry sauce. Cranberries are quite tart and need to be cooked to release their full flavor and absorb the flavors of other ingredients—one of which is usually sugar. To prepare a pleasantly tart cranberry sauce, combine 1½ cups fresh cranberries, ⅔ cup granulated sugar, and ½ cup fresh orange juice in a small saucepan over medium-high heat, and bring to a boil. Reduce heat, and simmer until the cranberries begin to pop. Combine ¼ cup water and ½ teaspoon cornstarch in a bowl, and add it to the cranberry mixture. This cornstarch mixture will help thicken the sauce. Bring to a boil, and cook 1 minute, stirring often. Remove from heat, and let the sauce cool completely.

Dark Chocolate
What it adds: Dark chocolate gives the glaze a beautiful deep-brown color and a rich chocolate flavor.

Cointreau
What it adds: This orange-flavored liqueur boozes up the chocolate glaze, but feel free to omit it.

Cake Flour
What it adds: This flour is low in protein, which gives this cake a light, delicate texture.

Boston Cream Pie

Cake:
 Cooking spray
 2 teaspoons cake flour
 5 ounces sifted cake flour (about 1¼ cups)
 1½ teaspoons baking powder
 ¼ teaspoon salt
 ½ cup granulated sugar
 ¼ cup butter, softened
 1 teaspoon vanilla extract
 1 large egg
 ¾ cup 1% low-fat milk
 2 large egg whites
 3 tablespoons granulated sugar

Filling:
 ½ cup granulated sugar
 3 tablespoons cornstarch
 ⅛ teaspoon salt
 1 cup plus 2 tablespoons 1% low-fat milk
 ⅓ cup egg substitute
 1 tablespoon butter
 ½ teaspoon vanilla extract

Glaze:
 2 ounces dark chocolate
 2 tablespoons 1% low-fat milk
 ⅓ cup powdered sugar
 2 teaspoons Cointreau (orange-flavored liqueur)

1. Preheat oven to 350°.
2. To prepare cake, coat bottom of a 9-inch round cake pan with cooking spray. Dust with 2 teaspoons cake flour.
3. Weigh or lightly spoon 5 ounces cake flour (about 1¼ cups) into dry measuring cups; level with a knife. Combine 5 ounces cake flour, baking powder, and ¼ teaspoon salt in a small bowl, stirring with a whisk.

Place ½ cup granulated sugar and ¼ cup butter in a large bowl, and beat with a mixer at medium speed until light and fluffy (about 5 minutes). Add 1 teaspoon vanilla and egg, beating until well blended. Add flour mixture and ¾ cup milk alternately to sugar mixture, beginning and ending with flour mixture.
4. Place egg whites in a medium bowl; beat with a mixer at high speed until foamy using clean, dry beaters. Gradually add 3 tablespoons granulated sugar, beating until stiff peaks form. Gently fold egg white mixture into batter; pour into prepared pan. Bake at 350° for 35 minutes or until a wooden pick inserted in center comes out clean. Cool in pan 10 minutes; run a knife around outside edge. Remove from pan; cool completely on a wire rack.
5. To prepare filling, combine ½ cup granulated sugar, cornstarch, and ⅛ teaspoon salt in a medium saucepan. Gradually add 1 cup plus 2 tablespoons milk and egg substitute to pan, stirring with a whisk until well blended. Bring to a boil over medium heat, stirring constantly with a whisk until thick. Remove from heat; stir in 1 tablespoon butter and ½ teaspoon vanilla. Place pan in a large ice-filled bowl until custard cools to room temperature (about 15 minutes), stirring occasionally.
6. To prepare glaze, place chocolate and 2 tablespoons milk in a microwave-safe bowl. Microwave at HIGH 20 seconds or until chocolate melts. Add powdered sugar and liqueur, stirring with a whisk until smooth.
7. Split cake in half horizontally using a serrated knife; place bottom layer, cut side up, on a serving plate. Spread cooled filling evenly over bottom layer; top with remaining cake layer, cut side down. Spread glaze evenly over top cake layer. **Yield: 10 servings (serving size: 1 slice).**

CALORIES 281; FAT 8.7g (sat 5.2g, mono 1.9g, poly 0.4g); PROTEIN 5.1g; CARB 46.4g; FIBER 0.5g; CHOL 39mg; IRON 1.5mg; SODIUM 262mg; CALC 110mg

Mississippi Mud Pie

Don't be tempted to use Dutch process cocoa in the crust, or the pastry will be tough. However, its mild chocolate flavor and dark brown color are perfect for the filling.

Crust:
- 4.5 ounces all-purpose flour (about 1 cup)
-   2 tablespoons sugar
-   2 tablespoons unsweetened cocoa
-   ¼ teaspoon salt
- 2½ tablespoons vegetable shortening
-   2 tablespoons chilled butter, cut into small pieces
-   ¼ cup ice water
-     Cooking spray

Filling:
-   3 tablespoons butter
-   1 ounce semisweet chocolate chips
-   1 teaspoon vanilla extract
-   4 large egg whites
-   1 cup sugar
- 3.4 ounces all-purpose flour (about ¾ cup)
-   ⅓ cup Dutch process cocoa
-   ½ teaspoon baking powder
-     Dash of salt

1. To prepare crust, weigh or lightly spoon 4.5 ounces flour (about 1 cup) into a dry measuring cup; level with a knife. Combine 4.5 ounces flour, 2 tablespoons sugar,

2 tablespoons unsweetened cocoa, and ¼ teaspoon salt in a food processor; pulse 2 times or until blended. Add shortening and chilled butter; pulse 6 times or until mixture resembles coarse meal. With processor on, slowly pour ice water through food chute, processing just until blended (do not allow dough to form a ball); remove from bowl. Gently press mixture into a 4-inch circle; wrap in plastic wrap. Chill 30 minutes.

2. Preheat oven to 350°.

3. Unwrap and place chilled dough on plastic wrap. Lightly sprinkle dough with flour; roll into a 10-inch circle. Fit dough, plastic wrap side up, into a 9-inch pie plate coated with cooking spray. Remove remaining plastic wrap. Fold edges under; flute.

4. To prepare filling, place 3 tablespoons butter and chocolate in a microwave-safe bowl. Microwave at HIGH 30 seconds or until butter and chocolate melt, stirring

well to combine. Place vanilla and egg whites in a bowl; beat with a mixer at medium speed until foamy. Gradually add 1 cup sugar; beat until soft peaks form (about 2 minutes). Gently fold melted chocolate mixture into egg white mixture.

5. Weigh or lightly spoon 3.4 ounces flour (about ¾ cup) into dry measuring cups; level with a knife. Combine 3.4 ounces flour, ⅓ cup Dutch process cocoa, baking powder, and dash of salt in a small bowl, stirring with a whisk. Fold flour mixture into egg white mixture. Pour mixture into prepared crust. Bake at 350° for 40 minutes or until a wooden pick inserted in center comes out clean. Cool on a wire rack. **Yield: 10 servings (serving size: 1 slice).**

CALORIES 277; FAT 10.2g (sat 5.5g, mono 2.5g, poly 1.2g); PROTEIN 4.7g; CARB 43.5g; FIBER 1.8g; CHOL 15mg; IRON 1.7mg; SODIUM 162mg; CALC 24mg

all about Dutch process cocoa vs. unsweetened cocoa

Similar to coffee, cocoa powder starts as beans—cocoa beans, from the cacao tree. After harvest, the seeds are fermented, roasted, and ground to create chocolate liquor. To make cocoa, the chocolate liquor is pressed to remove most of its fat, or cocoa butter, and then ground again, resulting in a fine, dusky powder. Natural unsweetened cocoa powder (shown in top right) is acidic and slightly bitter, so a 19th-century Dutch scientist named Conrad van Houten found a way to neutralize the beans with alkaline chemicals, creating Dutch process cocoa (shown in bottom right), which has a smooth, mild chocolate flavor and a rich reddish-brown hue. Always check the label before purchasing. Dutch process cocoa may also be called "Dutched" or "alkalized," while natural may be labeled only "cocoa."

Spiced Pumpkin Chiffon Pie

All-Purpose Light Piecrust dough (page 263)
Cooking spray
1¼ cups canned pumpkin
½ cup packed brown sugar
¾ teaspoon ground cinnamon
½ teaspoon grated lemon rind
¼ teaspoon salt
⅛ teaspoon ground nutmeg
2 large egg yolks
⅔ cup evaporated low-fat milk
1 envelope unflavored gelatin
¼ cup fresh orange juice
2 large egg whites
⅛ teaspoon cream of tartar
5 tablespoons granulated sugar, divided
3 tablespoons water
½ cup frozen reduced-calorie whipped topping,
    thawed
½ ounce bittersweet chocolate, shaved

1. Preheat oven to 400°.
2. Remove top sheets of plastic wrap from All-Purpose Light Piecrust dough. Fit dough, plastic wrap side up, into a 9-inch pie plate coated with cooking spray. Remove remaining plastic wrap. Fold edges under; flute. Pierce bottom and sides of dough with a fork; freeze 10 minutes. Line bottom of dough with a piece of foil; arrange pie weights or dried beans on foil. Bake at 400° for 25 minutes or until browned. Remove weights and foil. Cool completely on a wire rack.
3. Combine pumpkin and next 6 ingredients in a medium saucepan, stirring with a whisk. Stir in milk; bring to a boil. Reduce heat, and simmer 4 minutes or until slightly thick, stirring frequently. Remove from heat. Sprinkle gelatin over orange juice in a small microwave-safe bowl; let stand 1 minute. Microwave at HIGH 15 seconds, stirring until gelatin dissolves. Stir gelatin mixture into pumpkin mixture. Cool.
4. Place 2 egg whites and cream of tartar in a large bowl; beat with a mixer at high speed until frothy. Gradually add 1 tablespoon granulated sugar, beating until soft peaks form. Combine remaining ¼ cup granulated sugar and 3 tablespoons water in a saucepan; bring to a boil. Cook, without stirring, until candy thermometer registers 250°. Pour hot sugar syrup in a thin stream over egg white mixture, beating at high speed until stiff peaks form. Gently stir one-fourth of egg white mixture into pumpkin mixture; gently fold in remaining egg white mixture. Pour into cooled crust. Refrigerate 4 hours or until set.
5. Spread whipped topping evenly over pie; sprinkle with chocolate. **Yield: 10 servings (serving size: 1 slice).**

CALORIES 240; FAT 9.2g (sat 3.5g, mono 2.4g, poly 1.5g); PROTEIN 4.9g; CARB 35.4g; FIBER 1.5g; CHOL 49mg; IRON 1.3mg; SODIUM 167mg; CALC 71mg

kitchen how-to:

grate & shave chocolate

To easily grate chocolate, use a handheld grater or zester or the smallest holes on a box grater. To easily shave chocolate, use a vegetable peeler. Start at the narrowest side of the chocolate to create smaller shaved pieces and curls.

Malt Shop Ice Cream Pie

Think of this no-cook pie as a deconstructed hot fudge sundae in an ice-cream cone—crushed cones form the crust, cradling the malt-flavored ice cream and toppings.

     2 **tablespoons honey**
     2 **tablespoons butter, melted**
    12 **sugar cones, crushed (about 2 cups)**
     2 **cups strawberry light ice cream, softened**
    ¼ **cup malted milk powder, divided**
    ½ **cup strawberry topping**
     2 **cups vanilla light ice cream, softened**
    ½ **cup fat-free hot fudge topping**
    1¼ **cups frozen fat-free whipped topping, thawed**

1. Combine first 3 ingredients, stirring well. Firmly press mixture into bottom and up sides of a 9-inch pie plate. Freeze 30 minutes or until firm.

2. Place softened strawberry ice cream and 2 tablespoons milk powder in a medium bowl; beat with a mixer at medium speed until smooth. Spoon mixture evenly into crust; spread with strawberry topping. Freeze 30 minutes or until firm.

3. Place softened vanilla ice cream and remaining 2 tablespoons milk powder in a medium bowl; beat with a mixer at medium speed until smooth. Spread mixture evenly over strawberry topping. Cover and freeze 4 hours or until firm. Top with hot fudge and whipped topping just before serving. **Yield: 10 servings (serving size: 1 slice, about 2½ teaspoons hot fudge, and 2 tablespoons whipped topping).**

CALORIES 320; FAT 6.6g (sat 3.7g, mono 2.4g, poly 0.2g); PROTEIN 4.6g; CARB 59.1g; FIBER 0.6g; CHOL 22mg; IRON 1.4mg; SODIUM 182mg; CALC 123mg

kitchen how-to: make frozen pies

Ice cream pies are frosty, easy-to-assemble treats. They're refreshing and simple to serve.

1. Before you begin, let the ice cream stand at room temperature just until it's soft around the edges. Beating the ice cream incorporates ingredients and yields a smooth, even consistency. If the ice cream splatters when you start the mixer, reduce the speed to low and gradually increase to medium.

2. Be careful not to overbeat the ice cream. Ice cream's volume depends in part on air that is incorporated during manufacturing; overbeating may deflate the ice cream. Beat only until smooth. You may need to freeze one layer of filling before adding the next to keep it in place while you spread more ice cream on top. If frozen solid, let the pie stand at room temperature 15 minutes before slicing to bring back its creamy texture.

Frozen Peanut Butter Pie

Lightly coat hands with cooking spray to press the slightly sticky crust into the pie plate. The filling may be thin after mixing but will harden in the freezer.

    1⅔ cups chocolate graham cracker crumbs
         (about 8½ cookie sheets)
      7 tablespoons sugar, divided
      2 large egg whites, lightly beaten
    Cooking spray
    1¼ cups fat-free milk
     ⅔ cup crunchy peanut butter
     ½ teaspoon vanilla extract
     ½ cup (4 ounces) fat-free cream cheese, softened
      1 (8-ounce) container frozen fat-free whipped
         topping, thawed
      3 tablespoons finely chopped salted, dry-roasted
         peanuts
     ¼ cup shaved milk chocolate (about 1 ounce)

1. Preheat oven to 350°.
2. Combine crumbs, 3 tablespoons sugar, and egg whites; toss with a fork until moist. Press into bottom and up sides of a 9-inch deep-dish pie plate coated with cooking spray. Pierce crust with a fork before baking. Bake at 350° for 10 minutes. Remove from oven; cool on a wire rack.
3. Combine milk and remaining ¼ cup sugar in a heavy saucepan over medium-low heat. Cook 2 minutes or until sugar dissolves, stirring constantly; transfer mixture to a bowl. Add peanut butter and vanilla, stirring with a whisk until combined. Cover and chill 30 minutes.
4. Place cream cheese in a large bowl, and beat with a mixer at medium speed until light and fluffy. Add milk mixture, beating at low speed until combined. Fold in whipped topping; pour mixture into prepared piecrust. Freeze, uncovered, 8 hours or overnight or until hard. Sprinkle with peanuts and chocolate. Transfer pie to refrigerator 30 minutes before slicing. **Yield: 10 servings (serving size: 1 slice).**

CALORIES 282; FAT 12.2g (sat 2.4g, mono 5.1g, poly 3g); PROTEIN 9.3g; CARB 34.1g; FIBER 2.1g; CHOL 3mg; IRON 1.1mg; SODIUM 298mg; CALC 152mg

Crunchy Peanut Butter
What it adds: Crunchy peanut butter adds texture and peanutty flavor to this pie. You can substitute creamy peanut butter if you have it on hand.

Chocolate Crust
What it adds: This simple homemade crust provides a delicious chocolate flavor and contributes less saturated fat and fewer calories than a store-bought crust.

Cream Cheese & Whipped Topping
What they add: Combining softened fat-free cream cheese with fat-free whipped topping creates a fluffy, creamy texture with less saturated fat and calories than traditional peanut butter pies.

tarts

These single-layer desserts with pastry at the base show up in all sizes and in both sweet and savory flavors.

kitchen how-to: prepare a tart crust

Removable-bottom tart pans allow you to create a beautiful edge on your tart, and then easily remove it from the pan to a serving plate.

1. Unwrap and place chilled dough on plastic wrap, and cover dough with 2 additional sheets of overlapping plastic wrap, which helps prevent the rolling pin from sticking and tearing the dough. Roll dough, still covered, into a 10-inch circle. Place dough in the freezer for 5 minutes or until the plastic wrap can be easily removed. **2.** Remove top sheet of plastic wrap; fit dough, plastic wrap side up, into a 9-inch round removable-bottom tart pan coated with cooking spray. Remove remaining plastic wrap. Fold the edges under and flute. Cover and refrigerate until you're ready to add the filling, or prebake as instructed by the recipe.

all about satsumas

Prized for their sweet, tender, and juicy flesh, satsuma oranges hit grocery store shelves in early winter; they're best from October to December. Look for satsumas with firm, tight peels with no hollow-feeling or dented spots. Heavier ones are generally juicier. Fresh-looking, bright green twigs and leaves that are still attached signal careful picking (each stem must be clipped by hand), meticulous handling, and freshness—all indicators of high quality. Store at room temperature or, if you prefer, in the refrigerator (refrigeration may prolong storage but can dry them out). Fresh satsumas are most enjoyable, so use within 4 or 5 days.

Satsuma Cloud Tart

Crust:

6.75	ounces all-purpose flour (about 1½ cups)
1½	tablespoons sugar
⅛	teaspoon salt
6	tablespoons chilled butter, cut into small pieces
5	tablespoons ice water

Filling:

½	cup sugar
3	large egg yolks
1.1	ounces all-purpose flour (about ¼ cup)
2	tablespoons grated satsuma orange rind
6	tablespoons satsuma orange juice
2	tablespoons lemon juice
1	tablespoon butter, melted

Meringue:

3	large egg whites
½	cup sugar
½	teaspoon vanilla extract

1. To prepare crust, weigh or lightly spoon 6.75 ounces flour (about 1½ cups) into dry measuring cups; level with a knife. Place 6.75 ounces flour, 1½ tablespoons sugar, and salt in a food processor; process until blended. Add 6 tablespoons butter, and pulse until mixture resembles coarse meal. With processor on, slowly pour 5 tablespoons ice water through food chute; process until dough forms a ball. Shape dough into a 6-inch circle. Wrap in plastic wrap; chill 30 minutes.

2. Preheat oven to 400°.

3. Roll dough into a 10-inch circle on a lightly floured surface. Fit dough into a 9-inch round removable-bottom tart pan. Fold edges under; press dough against sides of pan. Line bottom of dough with a piece of foil; arrange pie weights or dried beans on foil. Bake at 400° for 10 minutes or until edge is lightly browned. Remove pie weights and foil; reduce oven temperature to 375°. Bake an additional 15 minutes or until crust is golden. Cool 10 minutes.

4. To prepare filling, combine ½ cup sugar and egg yolks in a large bowl; beat with a mixer at medium-high speed for 3 minutes or until thick. Weigh or lightly spoon 1.1 ounces flour (about ¼ cup) into a dry measuring cup; level with a knife.

Add flour, rind, and next 3 ingredients to sugar mixture; stir just until combined. Pour mixture into cooled crust. Bake at 375° for 20 minutes or until filling is set. Remove from oven; cool completely. Reduce oven temperature to 325°.

5. To prepare meringue, beat egg whites with a mixer at high speed until soft peaks form using clean, dry beaters. Gradually add ½ cup sugar, 1 tablespoon at a time, beating until stiff peaks form. Gently fold in vanilla. Spread meringue evenly over filling, sealing to edge of crust. Bake at 325° for 25 minutes; cool 1 hour on a wire rack. **Yield: 10 servings (serving size: 1 slice).**

CALORIES 262; FAT 9.5g (sat 5.6g, mono 2.7g, poly 0.6g); PROTEIN 4.3g; CARB 40.4g; FIBER 0.8g; CHOL 83mg; IRON 1.2mg; SODIUM 106mg; CALC 17mg

Meyer Lemon Curd Tart

Crust:
- ⅓ cup macadamia nuts
- ¼ cup flaked sweetened coconut
- 2 tablespoons brown sugar
- ⅛ teaspoon salt
- 36 vanilla wafers
- 3 tablespoons butter, melted

Filling:
- ½ cup granulated sugar
- 2½ teaspoons cornstarch
- Dash of salt
- ½ cup fresh Meyer lemon juice (about 5 lemons)
- 3 large egg yolks
- 2 tablespoons butter
- ½ teaspoon grated Meyer lemon rind

Meringue:
- 3 large egg whites
- ⅛ teaspoon salt
- ¼ cup granulated sugar
- ¼ cup water

1. Preheat oven to 400°.

2. To prepare crust, place first 5 ingredients in a food processor; process until finely ground. With processor on, drizzle 3 tablespoons melted butter through food chute, and process until blended. Press crumb mixture into bottom and up sides of a 9-inch metal tart pan. Bake at 400° for 10 minutes or until toasted. Cool on a wire rack.

3. To prepare filling, combine ½ cup granulated sugar, cornstarch, and dash of salt in a medium heavy saucepan, stirring with a whisk. Stir in lemon juice and egg yolks; bring to a boil over medium heat, stirring constantly with a whisk. Reduce heat, and simmer 1 minute or until slightly thick, stirring constantly. Remove from heat; add 2 tablespoons butter and rind, stirring gently until butter melts. Spoon mixture into a medium bowl; cool slightly. Place plastic wrap directly over surface of lemon curd, and chill at least 4 hours or overnight (mixture will thicken as it cools).

4. Preheat broiler.

5. Spoon curd evenly into prepared crust.

6. To prepare meringue, place egg whites and ⅛ teaspoon salt in a large bowl, and beat with a mixer at high speed until soft peaks form. Combine ¼ cup granulated sugar and ¼ cup water in a saucepan; bring to a boil. Cook, without stirring, until candy thermometer registers 238°. Pour hot sugar syrup in a thin stream over egg whites, beating until stiff peaks form. Spread meringue over tart. Broil 30 seconds or until lightly browned. **Yield: 10 servings (serving size: 1 slice).**

CALORIES 246; FAT 13.2g (sat 5.6g, mono 5.3g, poly 0.5g); PROTEIN 2.8g; CARB 31.6g; FIBER 1.1g; CHOL 80mg; IRON 0.8mg; SODIUM 183mg; CALC 24mg

all about Meyer lemons

Meyer lemons are relatively rare and not always in the best condition when you do find them. Often, you'll find lemons that are too soft, or dry and shriveled. Avoid these. What you want are plump, shiny-skinned fruits that are firm but not hard and seemingly heavy for their size, a good sign—as with any citrus fruit—that they're full of juice. You can store Meyer lemons in a plastic bag in the refrigerator for up to 2 weeks; when they start to feel squishy, they've passed their prime. If you can't find Meyer lemons, you can use other citrus fruits. Although the tart will still be tasty, the flavor won't be as complex. For every ¼ cup Meyer lemon juice, try 3 tablespoons lemon juice plus 1 tablespoon orange juice and ½ teaspoon sugar. For rind, just substitute regular lemon rind in the same quantity.

Meringue-Topped Cranberry Curd Tart

Making perfect pastry depends mostly on how well you coat flour proteins with fat, which is more difficult in a light recipe. You want to leave small clumps of fat in the dough (here, from vegetable shortening) so they'll melt while baking and give off steam, creating luscious layers. We also melted the butter so it would coat the flour more than it would if it were in solid form.

Crust:
- 5 ounces all-purpose flour (about 1¼ cups)
- 1 tablespoon sugar
- ¼ teaspoon salt
- ¼ teaspoon baking powder
- ¼ cup vegetable shortening
- ¼ cup boiling water
- 4 teaspoons butter, melted
- Cooking spray

Filling:
- 1 (12-ounce) package fresh cranberries
- 1 cup sugar, divided
- ¾ cup water, divided
- ⅛ teaspoon salt
- ¼ cup cornstarch
- 2 large egg yolks
- 2 tablespoons butter, softened

Meringue:
- 3 large egg whites
- ⅛ teaspoon salt
- ½ cup sugar
- ¼ cup water

1. To prepare crust, weigh or lightly spoon flour into dry measuring cups; level with a knife. Combine flour and next 3 ingredients in a bowl; cut in shortening with a pastry blender or 2 knives until mixture resembles coarse meal. Make a well in center of flour mixture. Combine ¼ cup boiling water and melted butter in a bowl. Pour butter mixture into center of well. Gently draw flour mixture into butter mixture until moist clumps form. Press dough into a 4-inch circle; cover. Chill 30 minutes.

2. Preheat oven to 400°.

3. Uncover dough; place between 2 sheets of plastic wrap. Roll dough into an 11-inch circle. Remove top sheet of plastic wrap. Fit dough, plastic wrap side up, into a 9-inch round tart pan coated with cooking spray. Remove plastic wrap. Press dough into bottom and up sides of pan; fold excess dough back in and press against sides of pan. Pierce bottom and sides of dough lightly with a fork; freeze 10 minutes. Line bottom of dough with a piece of foil; arrange pie weights or dried beans on foil. Bake at 400° for 18 minutes. Remove pie weights and foil. Bake an additional 15 minutes or until lightly browned. Cool on a wire rack.

4. To prepare filling, combine cranberries, ½ cup sugar, ¼ cup water, and ⅛ teaspoon salt in a medium saucepan. Cook over medium-high heat 10 minutes or until cranberries pop. Combine ½ cup sugar, ½ cup water, cornstarch, and egg yolks in a small bowl; stir with a whisk until smooth. Gradually add 1 cup hot cranberry mixture to egg mixture, stirring constantly. Return egg mixture to pan. Cook until candy thermometer registers 160°, stirring constantly.

5. Place a food mill or fine sieve over a large bowl. Pour cranberry mixture into food mill, and press through. Discard solids. Add 2 tablespoons butter; stir. Spoon into cooled crust. Cover and chill.

6. Preheat broiler.

7. To prepare meringue, place egg whites and ⅛ teaspoon salt in a large bowl; beat with a mixer at high speed until soft peaks form. Combine ½ cup sugar and ¼ cup water in a small saucepan; bring to a boil. Cook, without stirring, until candy thermometer registers 238°. Gradually pour hot sugar syrup into egg white mixture, beating until stiff peaks form. Spread meringue over cranberry curd.

8. Broil meringue 30 seconds or until lightly browned.

Yield: 12 servings (serving size: 1 slice).

CALORIES 245; FAT 8.1g (sat 3.8g, mono 2.3g, poly 1.5g); PROTEIN 2.7g; CARB 41.1g; FIBER 1.7g; CHOL 43mg; IRON 0.7mg; SODIUM 147mg; CALC 15mg

kitchen how-to: make Italian meringue

Italian meringue is a fluffy, stable mixture made by adding boiling sugar syrup—instead of granulated sugar—to whipped egg whites. This heats the egg to a safe temperature. The mixture is a creamy, lighter replacement for a topping made with whipped cream.

1. Before using the mixer, make sure both the bowl and the egg whites are at room temperature. Chilled egg whites take longer to reach full volume.

2. The sugar syrup is ready when the candy thermometer registers 238°.

3. With the mixer running, carefully and slowly pour the syrup in a thin, steady stream into the egg whites, whipping constantly.

4. Continue whipping until the meringue is smooth, satiny, and completely cooled, and stiff peaks have formed. Spread immediately on the pie.

Strawberry-Almond Cream Tart

Nestled in a creamy filling and crumbly graham cracker crust, strawberries—with one of spring's sweetest, brightest flavors—shine in this delectable tart.

Crust:
- 36 honey-flavored graham crackers (9 cookie sheets)
- 2 tablespoons sugar
- 2 tablespoons butter, melted
- 4 teaspoons water
- Cooking spray

Filling:
- ⅔ cup (about 5 ounces) ⅓-less-fat cream cheese, softened
- ¼ cup sugar
- ½ teaspoon vanilla extract
- ¼ teaspoon almond extract

Topping:
- 6 cups small strawberries, hulled and divided
- ⅔ cup sugar
- 1 tablespoon cornstarch
- 1 tablespoon fresh lemon juice
- 2 tablespoons sliced almonds, toasted

1. Preheat oven to 350°.

2. To prepare crust, place crackers in a food processor; process until crumbly. Add 2 tablespoons sugar, butter, and 4 teaspoons water; pulse just until moist. Place cracker mixture in a 9-inch round removable-bottom tart pan lightly coated with cooking spray, pressing into bottom and up sides of pan to ¾ inch. Bake at 350° for 10 minutes or until lightly browned. Cool completely on a wire rack.

3. To prepare filling, combine cream cheese, ¼ cup sugar, and extracts in a medium bowl; stir until smooth. Spread cream cheese mixture evenly over bottom of cooled crust.

4. To prepare topping, place 2 cups strawberries in food processor, and process until smooth. Combine strawberry puree, ⅔ cup sugar, and cornstarch in a small saucepan over medium heat; stir with a whisk. Bring to a boil, stirring constantly. Reduce heat to low; cook 1 minute. Remove glaze from heat. Cool to room temperature, stirring occasionally.

5. Combine remaining 4 cups strawberries and juice; toss to coat. Arrange berries, bottoms up, in a circular pattern over filling. Spoon half of glaze evenly over berries (reserve remaining glaze for another use). Sprinkle nuts around edge. Cover and chill 3 hours.

Yield: 10 servings (serving size: 1 slice).

CALORIES 235; FAT 7.8g (sat 2.9g, mono 1.2g, poly 0.4g); PROTEIN 4.1g; CARB 38.6g; FIBER 2.4g; CHOL 14mg; IRON 0.6mg; SODIUM 176mg; CALC 33mg

kitchen how-to: freeze fresh berries

1 **2** **3**

4

Stocking up on and freezing fresh berries, such as strawberries, blueberries, and cranberries, is an easy way to enjoy their flavors well beyond their season.

1. Trim away any green leaves or stems. Gently rinse the berries in a colander in cool water until clean.

2. Spread berries on a dish towel, and allow them to air-dry completely.

3. Spread the berries evenly on a jelly-roll pan, and freeze for about an hour or until the berries are slightly frozen.

4. Remove from the freezer, and transfer the berries to a zip-top plastic freezer bag. Store in the freezer for up to 6 months.

Upside-Down Fudge-Almond Tart

Cooking spray
1 cup coarsely chopped almonds, toasted
4 ounces bittersweet chocolate, coarsely chopped
6 tablespoons unsalted butter
2.25 ounces all-purpose flour (about ½ cup)
3 tablespoons sifted Dutch process cocoa
¼ teaspoon salt
2 large eggs
6 tablespoons sugar
2 tablespoons golden cane syrup
¾ teaspoon vanilla extract

1. Position oven rack in lowest third of oven. Preheat oven to 350°.
2. Coat a 9-inch round removable-bottom tart pan with cooking spray. Sprinkle almonds in pan.
3. Combine chocolate and butter in the top of a double boiler. Cook over simmering water until chocolate melts, stirring occasionally. Remove from heat; set aside.
4. Weigh or lightly spoon flour into a dry measuring cup; level with a knife. Combine flour, Dutch process cocoa, and salt in a medium bowl, stirring with a whisk.
5. Place eggs in a large bowl; beat with a mixer at medium speed for 2 minutes or until thick and pale. Gradually add sugar, 1 tablespoon at a time, beating at medium speed for 2 minutes or until sugar dissolves. Add golden cane syrup and vanilla; beat at low speed for 1 minute or until blended. Add chocolate mixture; beat for 1 minute or until blended. Add flour mixture, and beat at low speed just until combined.
6. Pour batter over nuts in prepared pan, spreading evenly. Bake in lowest third of oven at 350° for 20 minutes or until a wooden pick inserted in center comes out with a few moist crumbs. Cool in pan 20 minutes on a wire rack. Invert tart onto a serving platter. **Yield: 10 servings (serving size: 1 slice).**

CALORIES 281; FAT 19.8g (sat 7.7g, mono 8.1g, poly 2.1g); PROTEIN 5.9g; CARB 24.6g; FIBER 2.7g; CHOL 60mg; IRON 1.6mg; SODIUM 80mg; CALC 45mg

kitchen how-to:
make upside-down fudge-almond tart

The crunch of toasted nuts provides textural contrast to cut the richness of this splurge-worthy tart.

1. To create crunch, sprinkle toasted almonds in the pan. Once the tart is inverted, the nuts will be on top. Be sure to coarsely chop the nuts; if you chop them finely, they won't have as much dramatic presence.
2. Melt chocolate and butter over simmering water in a double boiler. Be sure your water isn't up to a full boil—the temperature may be too intense and scorch the chocolate.
3. Be sure not to overbake the tart. When you test for doneness, the wooden pick shouldn't come out completely clean. If you know your oven runs hot, check about 5 minutes before the end of the stated bake time.

Plum Galette with Armagnac Cream

Galette:

- 6 ounces all-purpose flour (about 1⅓ cups)
- 3 tablespoons whole-wheat pastry flour
- 2 teaspoons granulated sugar
- ¼ teaspoon salt
- 8 tablespoons chilled butter, cut into small pieces
- ¼ cup ice water
- 3 pounds ripe plums, quartered
- 9 tablespoons brown sugar, divided
- ¼ cup Armagnac or cognac
- 1 vanilla bean, split lengthwise
- 1 (1-ounce) slice whole-wheat bread
- 2 tablespoons butter, melted

Cream:

- 1 cup fat-free sour cream
- ⅓ cup powdered sugar
- 2 tablespoons whole milk
- 2 tablespoons Armagnac or cognac
- 1 teaspoon vanilla extract

1. To prepare galette, weigh or lightly spoon flours into dry measuring cups; level with a knife. Combine flours, granulated sugar, and salt in a medium bowl; cut in butter with a pastry blender or 2 knives until mixture resembles coarse meal. Add ¼ cup ice water; stir just until moist. Pat dough into a 7-inch circle on plastic wrap; cover. Chill 15 minutes.

2. Combine plums, ½ cup brown sugar, ¼ cup Armagnac, and vanilla bean in a large skillet over medium heat; cook 10 minutes or until plums are tender, stirring occasionally. Cool to room temperature.

3. Preheat oven to 300°.

4. Tear bread into 1-inch pieces. Place on a baking sheet; bake at 300° for 30 minutes or until dry and golden. Place bread in a food processor; process until coarse crumbs measure ¼ cup.

5. Increase oven temperature to 425°.

6. Unwrap and place dough on a baking sheet. Roll dough into a 15-inch circle; sprinkle dough with breadcrumbs, leaving a 2-inch border. Arrange plum mixture over crumbs. Fold edges of dough over plum mixture (dough will only partially cover plum mixture). Brush dough edges and top of fruit with melted butter; sprinkle with remaining 1 tablespoon brown sugar. Bake at 425° for 15 minutes. Reduce oven temperature to 375° (do not remove galette from oven); bake an additional 20 minutes or until bubbly and edges are golden. Cool 5 minutes on pan; loosen galette from pan. Cool an additional 30 minutes on pan.

7. To prepare cream, combine sour cream and remaining ingredients in a small bowl, stirring with a whisk. Serve over galette slices. **Yield: 14 servings (serving size: 1 slice and about 1 tablespoon cream).**

CALORIES 245; FAT 9g (sat 5.4g, mono 2.3g, poly 0.4g); PROTEIN 3.4g; CARB 36.8g; FIBER 2.1g; CHOL 24mg; IRON 0.9mg; SODIUM 126mg; CALC 55mg

kitchen how-to: make a galette

These flat, free-form rustic desserts are found in both savory and sweet varieties. They're less intimidating to make than tarts because oddly shaped edges and imperfections are part of their charm.

1. Prepare dough, and pat it into a 7-inch circle on plastic wrap. Cover with another sheet of plastic wrap, and chill 15 minutes.

2. Prepare filling, cooking until tender. Allow the filling to cool to room temperature. You can prepare the filling ahead of time, if you like.

3. Unwrap the dough, and place it in the center of a baking sheet. (Rolling the dough directly on the baking sheet eliminates having to transfer it from a work surface to the baking sheet.) Roll the dough into a 15-inch circle.

4. Spread the filling over the dough, leaving a 2-inch border.

5. Fold the edges of the dough over the filling, working your way around the edge. The dough will only cover the outer portion of the filling, leaving an exposed area of filling in the center. Before baking, you can brush the dough with melted butter or an egg wash to enhance browning, and you can also sprinkle it with sugar for added crunch and a beautiful finish.

Tarte Tatin

6.75 ounces all-purpose flour (about 1½ cups)
  ¼ teaspoon salt
  6 tablespoons butter, softened
  6 tablespoons water, divided
  1 large egg
  1 cup sugar
  2 pounds Golden Delicious apples, peeled, cored, and quartered (about 6 small)
  ¼ teaspoon ground cinnamon
  10 teaspoons crème fraîche

1. Preheat oven to 400°.
2. Weigh or lightly spoon flour into dry measuring cups; level with a knife. Place flour and salt in a medium bowl; cut in butter with a pastry blender or 2 knives until mixture resembles coarse meal. Combine 2 tablespoons water and egg, stirring with a whisk. Add egg mixture to flour mixture, stirring just until moist. Turn dough out onto a large piece of heavy-duty plastic wrap; knead lightly 5 times (dough will be sticky). Pat dough into a disk. Cover with additional plastic wrap; chill 30 minutes.
3. Combine remaining ¼ cup water and sugar in a 9-inch cast-iron skillet over medium-high heat. Cook 10 minutes or until golden, stirring only until sugar dissolves. Remove from heat; gently stir in small circles to evenly distribute cooked sugar. Let stand 5 minutes.
4. Arrange apple quarters tightly in a circular pattern over sugar in pan, beginning at the outside edge. Cut 2 apple quarters in half, and arrange, points up, in center of pan. Place pan over medium heat; cook 20 minutes (do not stir), pressing apples slightly to release juices. Remove from heat; let stand 10 minutes. Sprinkle cinnamon over apples.
5. Remove plastic wrap covering dough. Turn dough out onto a lightly floured surface; roll dough into an 11-inch circle. Place over apple mixture, fitting dough between apples and skillet. Bake at 400° for 20 minutes or until lightly browned. Cool 10 minutes. Invert tart onto a plate. Serve with crème fraîche. **Yield: 10 servings (serving size: 1 slice and 1 teaspoon crème fraîche).**

CALORIES 275; FAT 9.3g (sat 5.6g, mono 2g, poly 0.4g); PROTEIN 3.1g; CARB 46.3g; FIBER 1.7g; CHOL 44mg; IRON 1.1mg; SODIUM 115mg; CALC 13mg

kitchen how-to: make tarte tatin

This classic French upside-down tart gets much of its flavor—and its beautiful finish—from the caramelized fruit layer (usually apples) that becomes the top once inverted.

1. When creating tarte tatin, the first step is caramelizing the sugar. Caramelizing is cooking the sugar until it browns, which adds buttery, nutty, and acidic flavors. Combine the sugar with water, and cook over medium-high heat until the water evaporates and the melted sugar is golden. Mixing the sugar with water (instead of just cooking the sugar by itself) helps prevent the sugar from burning.

2. Remove from heat, and stir gently in small circles to evenly distribute the cooked sugar.

3. Arrange the apple quarters tightly in a circular pattern over the sugar in the pan, beginning at the outside edge. Place the pan over medium heat; cook 20 minutes (do not stir).

4. Roll dough into a circle 2 inches wider than the size of your pan. Place the dough over the apple mixture, fitting it between the apples and skillet. Bake until lightly browned, and cool 10 minutes. Invert the tart onto a serving plate.

cobblers & crisps

These rustic desserts are an ideal way to use seasonal fruits. They're so simple and require only a baking dish, some fruit, and a few other ingredients to create delicious desserts.

kitchen how-to: make cobblers

1

2

3

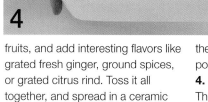
4

Cobblers are deliciously simple and easily adjustable to feature a variety of fruit. The level of natural sugar in most fruits is set when they are harvested, so sample the fruit before making your cobbler. If the fruit is underripe and tastes tart, you can add an extra couple of tablespoons of sugar to the filling.

1. Pick or buy just-ripe fruit. Select fruit that ripened on the vine (or tree). It shouldn't be overripe, especially in the case of stone fruit like peaches or plums. Fruit that's too soft won't hold up to the heat needed to fully cook the topping.
2. Make the filling. The fruit filling can be as simple as you like, or you can get creative. Combine two or more fruits, and add interesting flavors like grated fresh ginger, ground spices, or grated citrus rind. Toss it all together, and spread in a ceramic or glass baking dish.
3. Prepare the topping. There are many interpretations of toppings, ranging from tender biscuit-style to pastry dough, and you can customize them to your tastes. Then sprinkle or pour the topping over the fruit mixture.
4. Bake until bubbly and browned. The key to success is timing: Bake the fruit until it's tender but not mushy and the topping is fully cooked. The best visual cues for doneness are browned topping and pockets of fruit bubbling up to the top.

Lattice-Topped Blackberry Cobbler

1 cup granulated sugar, divided
6 tablespoons butter, softened
1 large egg yolk
½ teaspoon vanilla extract
¾ cup whole almonds, toasted
6 ounces all-purpose flour (about 1⅓ cups)
¼ teaspoon baking powder
¼ teaspoon salt
3 tablespoons ice water
10 cups fresh blackberries (about 5 [12-ounce] packages)
3 tablespoons cornstarch
1 tablespoon fresh lemon juice
Cooking spray
2 tablespoons turbinado sugar or granulated sugar

1. Place ⅓ cup granulated sugar and butter in a large bowl; beat with a mixer until combined (about 1 minute). Add egg yolk, beating well. Stir in vanilla.

2. Place almonds in a food processor; pulse 10 times or until finely ground. Weigh or lightly spoon flour into dry measuring cups; level with a knife. Combine nuts, flour, baking powder, and salt, stirring well with a whisk. Gradually add nut mixture to butter mixture, beating at low speed just until a soft dough forms, adding 3 tablespoons ice water as needed. Turn dough out onto a lightly floured surface; knead lightly 6 times or until smooth. Divide dough into 2 equal portions; wrap each portion in plastic wrap. Chill 1 hour or until firm.

3. Preheat oven to 375°.

4. Combine remaining ⅔ cup granulated sugar, blackberries, cornstarch, and lemon juice; toss gently. Arrange berry mixture in a 13 x 9–inch glass or ceramic baking dish coated with cooking spray.

5. Unwrap dough. Roll each dough portion into a 13 x 9–inch rectangle on a lightly floured surface. Cut 1 rectangle, crosswise, into (1-inch-wide) strips. Cut remaining rectangle, lengthwise, into (1-inch-wide) strips. Arrange strips in a lattice pattern over fruit mixture; sprinkle dough with turbinado sugar. Bake at 375° for 50 minutes or until golden. Let stand 10 minutes. **Yield: 12 servings (serving size: about ⅔ cup).**

CALORIES 301; FAT 11.5g (sat 4.1g, mono 4.6g, poly 1.8g); PROTEIN 5.7g; CARB 47g; FIBER 8.6g; CHOL 32mg; IRON 2mg; SODIUM 103mg; CALC 75mg

Berry-Peach Cobbler with Sugared Almonds

A delicious combination of blueberries, blackberries, and peaches yields a sweet, juicy dessert that's the culinary epitome of summer.

Filling:
- 3 (6-ounce) packages fresh blueberries
- 3 (5.6-ounce) packages fresh blackberries
- 3 medium peaches, peeled and sliced
- Cooking spray
- ⅔ cup granulated sugar
- 2½ tablespoons cornstarch
- 3 tablespoons fresh lemon juice
- ⅛ teaspoon salt

Topping:
- 4.5 ounces all-purpose flour (about 1 cup)
- ¼ cup granulated sugar
- 2 tablespoons cornstarch
- ½ teaspoon baking powder
- ⅛ teaspoon salt
- 6 tablespoons chilled butter, cut into small pieces
- ½ cup half-and-half
- ⅓ cup sliced almonds
- 3 tablespoons turbinado sugar or granulated sugar
- 1 tablespoon egg white

Remaining Ingredient:
- 4 cups vanilla fat-free ice cream

1. Preheat oven to 350°.
2. To prepare filling, combine blueberries, blackberries, and peaches in a 13 x 9-inch glass or ceramic baking dish lightly coated with cooking spray. Sprinkle ⅔ cup granulated sugar, 2½ tablespoons cornstarch, juice, and ⅛ teaspoon salt over fruit; toss gently to combine.
3. To prepare topping, weigh or lightly spoon flour into a dry measuring cup; level with a knife. Combine flour, ¼ cup granulated sugar, 2 tablespoons cornstarch, baking powder, and ⅛ teaspoon salt, stirring well. Cut butter into flour mixture with a pastry blender or 2 knives

until mixture resembles coarse meal. Add half-and-half; gently knead dough just until moistened. Drop dough by spoonfuls evenly over top of filling. Combine almonds, turbinado sugar, and egg white; sprinkle over top. Bake at 350° for 50 minutes or until topping is browned. Let stand 10 minutes. Serve with ice cream.
Yield: 12 servings (serving size: 1 cup cobbler and ⅓ cup ice cream).

CALORIES 321; FAT 8.9g (sat 4.5g, mono 2.7g, poly 0.8g); PROTEIN 5.3g; CARB 58.9g; FIBER 4.2g; CHOL 19mg; IRON 1.1mg; SODIUM 147mg; CALC 101mg

kitchen how-to:
make sugared almonds

Simply combine the almonds, turbinado sugar, and egg white; sprinkle over the top of the dough; and bake until the topping is browned. This easy topping adds a unique sweet crunch to the mixed-fruit cobbler.

Cast-Iron Apple Cobbler

For a small gathering, halve the recipe and bake in a 12-inch cast-iron skillet.

6.75	ounces all-purpose flour (about 1½ cups), divided
12	cups thinly sliced peeled Fuji apple (about 4 pounds)
⅔	cup sugar, divided
2	tablespoons butter, melted
2	teaspoons vanilla extract
¾	teaspoon salt, divided
½	teaspoon ground cinnamon
¼	teaspoon ground nutmeg
½	cup water
2	teaspoons baking powder
¼	cup chilled butter, cut into small pieces
1	cup low-fat buttermilk

1. Preheat oven to 375°.
2. Weigh or lightly spoon flour into dry measuring cups; level with a knife. Combine 2.25 ounces flour (about ½ cup), apple, ⅓ cup sugar, 2 tablespoons butter, vanilla, ½ teaspoon salt, cinnamon, and nutmeg in a large bowl, tossing well. Spoon into a large cast-iron Dutch oven. Add ½ cup water.
3. Combine remaining 4.5 ounces flour (about 1 cup), remaining ⅓ cup sugar, remaining ¼ teaspoon salt, and baking powder in a medium bowl; cut in ¼ cup butter with a pastry blender or 2 knives until mixture resembles coarse meal. Add buttermilk; stir just until moist. Drop batter by tablespoonfuls over apple mixture. Bake at 375° for 1 hour or until bubbly and browned. Serve warm. **Yield: 10 servings (serving size: about ¾ cup).**

CALORIES 257; FAT 7.4g (sat 4.5g, mono 1.9g, poly 0.4g); PROTEIN 3.2g; CARB 46.1g; FIBER 2.3g; CHOL 19mg; IRON 1.1mg; SODIUM 349mg; CALC 96mg

kitchen how-to: season a cast-iron skillet

Seasoning is the process of oiling and heating cast iron to protect its porous surface from moisture. When the pan is heated, the oil is absorbed, creating a nonstick surface. The more you use it, the more nonstick it becomes. However, if your pan rusts, you'll need to scour the pan to remove the rust, which will also remove or damage the seasoning. You'll need to reseason it to restore the nonstick surface. Here's how:

1. Rinse the skillet in hot sudsy water, scouring away any rusted spots. Dry the skillet well with a towel.
2. Rub the skillet generously with vegetable oil.
3. Leave the skillet on a burner turned to low heat for about an hour, or place it in a 350° oven for 2 hours. Let the skillet cool, and then pour out any leftover oil. Repeat steps 2 and 3 two or three times before using the skillet to completely season it.

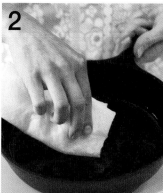

Plum Cobbler

You can also use this recipe to make a large cobbler. Just bake it in a 13 x 9–inch glass or ceramic baking dish for 55 minutes or until golden.

    5   pounds plums, peeled and quartered
    1   tablespoon fresh lemon juice
  1½   teaspoons grated peeled fresh ginger
    ¾   cup granulated sugar, divided
    ¼   teaspoon salt, divided
 6.75   ounces (about 1½ cups) plus 1½ tablespoons
         all-purpose flour, divided
         Cooking spray
    ¾   teaspoon baking powder
    ¼   cup chilled butter, cut into pieces
    1   teaspoon grated lemon rind
    6   ounces chilled ⅓-less-fat cream cheese,
         cut into pieces
    ½   cup buttermilk
    2   tablespoons turbinado sugar or granulated
         sugar

1. Preheat oven to 375°.
2. Combine first 3 ingredients in a bowl. Add ¼ cup granulated sugar, ⅛ teaspoon salt, and 1½ tablespoons flour; toss. Divide mixture evenly among 12 (5-ounce) glass or ceramic ramekins coated with cooking spray.
3. Weigh or lightly spoon 6.75 ounces flour (about 1½ cups) into dry measuring cups; level with a knife. Place 6.75 ounces flour, remaining ½ cup granulated sugar, remaining ⅛ teaspoon salt, and baking powder in a food processor; pulse 3 times. Add butter, rind, and cream cheese; pulse until mixture resembles coarse meal. Add buttermilk; pulse until blended.
4. Drop dough by spoonfuls over plum mixture in ramekins; sprinkle with turbinado sugar. Bake at 375° for 35 minutes or until golden. **Yield: 12 servings (serving size: 1 ramekin).**

CALORIES 293; FAT 8.7g (sat 4.8g, mono 2.7g, poly 0.5g); PROTEIN 5g; CARB 52g; FIBER 3.2g; CHOL 22mg; IRON 1.1mg; SODIUM 169mg; CALC 45mg

kitchen how-to: make individual cobblers

Some people like the homey appeal of a large cobbler baked in a glass or ceramic baking dish. Baking in individual-sized dishes is another option that makes a statement at the table. Cobblers can be baked in any size ramekin or other earthenware, but you'll need to adjust the bake time depending on the size you use.

1. Arrange the fruit filling mixture in ramekins coated with cooking spray.
2. Prepare dough, and drop dough by spoonfuls over the fruit mixture in the ramekins.
3. Sprinkle with turbinado sugar for added sparkle and crunch. Bake until golden.

Cherry Crisp

Filling:
- 6 cups sweet cherries (about 2 pounds), pitted
- ⅓ cup granulated sugar
- ¼ cup cornstarch
- 1 tablespoon fresh lemon juice
- ¼ teaspoon almond extract
- ⅛ teaspoon salt

Cooking spray

Topping:
- 2.25 ounces all-purpose flour (about ½ cup)
- ½ cup old-fashioned rolled oats
- ½ cup packed light brown sugar
- ⅛ teaspoon salt
- 6 tablespoons chilled butter, cut into small pieces
- ⅓ cup sliced almonds

1. Preheat oven to 375°.

2. To prepare filling, combine cherries, granulated sugar, cornstarch, juice, almond extract, and ⅛ teaspoon salt in a large bowl; toss gently. Spoon cherry mixture into an 11 x 7–inch glass or ceramic baking dish coated with cooking spray.

3. To prepare topping, weigh or lightly spoon flour into a dry measuring cup; level with a knife. Combine flour, oats, brown sugar, and ⅛ teaspoon salt in a medium bowl, stirring with a whisk. Cut in chilled butter with a pastry blender or 2 knives until mixture resembles coarse meal. Stir in sliced almonds. Sprinkle oat mixture evenly over cherry mixture. Bake at 375° for 45 minutes or until filling is bubbly and topping is crisp. Let stand 5 minutes; serve warm. **Yield: 8 servings (serving size: ⅛ of crisp).**

CALORIES 311; FAT 11.2g (sat 5.6g, mono 3.5g, poly 0.8g); PROTEIN 4.1g; CARB 51.4g; FIBER 3.4g; CHOL 23mg; IRON 1.1mg; SODIUM 140mg; CALC 43mg

all about crisps & cobblers

These simple desserts offer the comfort of fruit pies but without the work of making a piecrust. Cobblers have a softer biscuit-like topping and texture, while crisps have a crunchy, buttery, streusel-like topping that provides a contrast to the soft fruit in the filling.

Pear Crisp with Oat Streusel Topping

With unpeeled juicy pears, sweet raisins, and old-fashioned rolled oats, one serving of this fall favorite provides one-fourth of your day's fiber.

Crisp:
- 7¾ cups cubed Bartlett or Anjou pears
- 1 cup golden raisins
- 1 tablespoon all-purpose flour
- 1 tablespoon fresh lemon juice
- ½ teaspoon ground cinnamon
- ¼ teaspoon salt
- Cooking spray

Topping:
- 2.25 ounces all-purpose flour (about ½ cup)
- 1 cup old-fashioned rolled oats
- ¼ cup packed brown sugar
- ⅛ teaspoon ground cinnamon
- Dash of salt
- ¼ cup chilled butter, cut into small pieces
- ½ cup frozen fat-free whipped topping, thawed

1. Preheat oven to 375°.
2. To prepare crisp, combine first 6 ingredients in a large bowl; toss to combine. Spoon mixture into an 11 x 7–inch glass or ceramic baking dish coated with cooking spray.
3. To prepare topping, weigh or lightly spoon flour into a dry measuring cup; level with a knife. Combine flour, oats, sugar, ⅛ teaspoon cinnamon, and dash of salt in a small bowl; stir to combine. Cut in butter with a pastry blender or 2 knives until mixture resembles very coarse meal. Sprinkle oat mixture evenly over pear mixture. Bake at 375° for 50 minutes or until browned on top. Serve with whipped topping. **Yield: 8 servings (serving size: about 1 cup crisp and 1 tablespoon whipped topping).**

CALORIES 303; FAT 6.8g (sat 3.8g, mono 1.8g, poly 0.6g); PROTEIN 3.7g; CARB 60g; FIBER 6.9g; CHOL 15mg; IRON 1.7mg; SODIUM 142mg; CALC 40mg

kitchen how-to:
make streusel

This crumbly mixture creates a delicious and beautiful topping.

1. Streusel is typically made from butter, flour, and sugar, but oats, cinnamon, nuts, and brown sugar are common additions. Place the dry ingredients in a bowl, stirring to combine.
2. Cut in butter with a pastry blender or 2 knives until mixture resembles coarse meal.

pastries

These bite-sized baked goods can be sweet or savory, offering rich flavor and texture in small packages.

Cream Puffs with Ice Cream and Caramel

1 cup water
3 tablespoons butter
¼ teaspoon salt
4.75 ounces bread flour (about 1 cup)
3 large egg whites
2 large eggs
2 cups vanilla light ice cream
½ cup fat-free caramel sundae syrup

1. Preheat oven to 425°.
2. Cover a large, heavy baking sheet with parchment paper; set aside.
3. Combine 1 cup water, butter, and salt in a large, heavy saucepan over medium-high heat; bring to a boil, stirring occasionally with a wooden spoon. Weigh or lightly spoon flour into a dry measuring cup; level with a knife. Add flour to pan, stirring well until mixture is smooth and pulls away from sides of pan. Cook 30 seconds, stirring constantly. Remove from heat. Place dough in bowl of a stand mixer. Add egg whites and eggs, 1 at a time, beating at medium speed with a paddle attachment until well combined. Beat at medium speed for 2 minutes.
4. Scoop dough by ¼ cupfuls into 8 mounds 2 inches apart on prepared pan. Bake at 425° for 20 minutes. Reduce oven temperature to 350° (do not remove pan from oven); bake an additional 30 minutes. Remove pan from oven, and turn oven off. Pierce top of each cream puff with a knife; return pan to oven. Cool cream puffs in closed oven 20 minutes. Remove from oven; cool completely on a wire rack.
5. Split cream puffs in half horizontally. Fill each with ¼ cup ice cream; drizzle top with 1 tablespoon syrup.
Yield: 8 servings (serving size: 1 filled cream puff).

CALORIES 229; FAT 6.8g (sat 3.6g, mono 1.6g, poly 0.5g); PROTEIN 7g; CARB 34.6g; FIBER 0.9g; CHOL 67mg; IRON 1mg; SODIUM 213mg; CALC 61mg

1

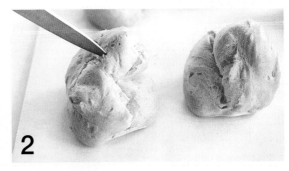

2

kitchen how-to: make cream puffs

Eggs are a critical leavening agent for cream puffs, making the batter rise and expand. Freeze completely cooled cream puffs for up to 1 month.

1. On the stovetop, cook the mixture until it's smooth and pulls away from sides of pan. A stand mixer is crucial for mixing the dough; the batter is too thick to beat with a hand mixer.

2. Scoop the dough into 8 mounds 2 inches apart onto a parchment paper–lined baking sheet, and bake. Remove the pan from the oven, and turn the oven off. Pierce the top of each cream puff with a knife, return the pan to the oven, and let the cream puffs cool in closed oven 20 minutes. Piercing the cooked puffs allows steam to escape so the puffs are almost hollow. Remove from oven; cool completely on a wire rack.

Chocolate, Fig, and Marsala Pastries

⅔ cup water
⅔ cup Marsala wine
½ cup packed brown sugar
1 (8-ounce) bag dried Calimyrna figs, stems removed and chopped
1 teaspoon vanilla extract
¼ teaspoon ground nutmeg
⅓ cup semisweet chocolate chips
1 large egg yolk
12 Sweet Cream Cheese Dough circles (page 313)
1 tablespoon powdered sugar

1. Combine first 4 ingredients in a medium saucepan; bring to a boil. Reduce heat, and simmer 25 minutes or until figs are tender and liquid almost evaporates. Remove from heat. Stir in vanilla and nutmeg. Cover and chill 1 hour. Stir in chocolate and egg yolk.

2. Working with 1 Sweet Cream Cheese Dough circle at a time, remove plastic wrap from dough. Place dough on a lightly floured surface. Spoon about 2 tablespoons fig mixture into center of circle. Fold dough over filling; press edges together with a fork or fingers to seal. Place pie on a large baking sheet covered with parchment paper. Repeat procedure with remaining Sweet Cream Cheese Dough circles and remaining fig mixture. Freeze 30 minutes.

3. Preheat oven to 425°.

4. Remove pies from freezer. Pierce top of each pie once with a fork. Place baking sheet on bottom rack in oven. Bake at 425° for 19 minutes or until edges are lightly browned and filling is bubbly. Cool completely on a wire rack. Sprinkle with powdered sugar. **Yield: 12 servings (serving size: 1 pie).**

CALORIES 270; FAT 7.4g (sat 3.9g, mono 2.1g, poly 0.4g); PROTEIN 4g; CARB 47g; FIBER 2.9g; CHOL 31mg; IRON 1.6mg; SODIUM 88mg; CALC 54mg

kitchen how-to:
make sweet cream cheese dough

Packing the dough into a measuring cup helps it come together without overworking it.

1. Weigh or lightly spoon 9 ounces all-purpose flour (about 2 cups) into dry measuring cups; level with a knife. Place flour, ¼ cup sugar, ¼ teaspoon baking powder, and ⅛ teaspoon salt in a food processor; pulse 3 times or until combined. Add ¼ cup chilled butter, cut into small pieces, ¼ cup (2 ounces) chilled ⅓-less-fat cream cheese, cut into small pieces, and 1 tablespoon cider vinegar; pulse 4 times. Add 4 to 5 tablespoons ice water through food chute, 1 tablespoon at a time, pulsing just until combined (do not form a ball). (Mixture may appear crumbly but will stick together when pressed between fingers.)

2. Place half of dough in a 1-cup dry measuring cup, pressing to compact. Remove dough from cup; form into a ball. Divide ball into 6 equal portions. Repeat procedure with remaining dough. Cover and chill 15 minutes.

3. Place each dough portion between 2 sheets of plastic wrap. Roll each dough portion, still covered, into a 5-inch circle; chill until ready to use. **Yield: 12 servings (serving size: 1 dough circle).**

CALORIES 138; FAT 5.1g (sat 2.6g, mono 1.9g, poly 0.3g); PROTEIN 2.7g; CARB 20.3g; FIBER 0.6g; CHOL 14mg; IRON 1mg; SODIUM 81mg; CALC 14mg

Cherry-Apricot Turnovers

Layers of phyllo are brushed with a mixture of melted butter and oil, and then sprinkled with graham cracker crumbs and brown sugar. The crumbs help keep the phyllo, which envelops the moist filling, dry and crisp.

1 cup apricot nectar
½ cup chopped dried apricots
⅓ cup packed brown sugar
¼ teaspoon grated lemon rind
2 tablespoons fresh lemon juice
3 (3-ounce) bags dried sweet cherries
2 tablespoons chopped almonds
½ teaspoon vanilla extract
2 tablespoons butter, melted
2 tablespoons canola oil
6 (18 x 14–inch) sheets frozen phyllo dough, thawed
¼ cup graham cracker crumbs, divided
2 tablespoons brown sugar, divided
Cooking spray

1. Combine first 6 ingredients in a saucepan; bring to a boil. Reduce heat; simmer 20 minutes or until liquid is absorbed, stirring occasionally. Stir in almonds and vanilla. Cool completely.

2. Preheat oven to 375°.
3. Combine butter and oil. Place 1 phyllo sheet on a large cutting board or work surface (cover remaining dough to keep from drying). Lightly brush phyllo sheet with 1 tablespoon butter mixture. Sprinkle with 1 tablespoon crumbs and 1½ teaspoons brown sugar. Repeat layers once. Top with 1 phyllo sheet. Gently press layers together. Lightly coat top phyllo sheet with cooking spray. Cut stack lengthwise into 4 (3½-inch-wide) strips. Cut each strip in half crosswise. Spoon 2 tablespoons of cherry mixture onto 1 short end of each rectangle, leaving a 1-inch border. Fold 1 corner of edge with 1-inch border over mixture, forming a triangle; continue folding back and forth into a triangle to end of rectangle. Tuck edges under triangle. Place triangles, seam sides down, on a large baking sheet coated with cooking spray; lightly coat triangles with cooking spray. Repeat procedure with remaining phyllo, butter mixture, crumbs, brown sugar, cherry mixture, and cooking spray.
4. Bake at 375° for 15 minutes or until golden brown. Remove from baking sheet, and cool on a wire rack.
Yield: 16 servings (serving size: 1 turnover).

CALORIES 155; FAT 4.3g (sat 1.2g, mono 2.1g, poly 0.8g); PROTEIN 1.9g; CARB 27g; FIBER 1.9g; CHOL 3.8mg; IRON 0.8mg; SODIUM 62mg; CALC 21mg

kitchen how-to: make turnovers

Before beginning, thaw frozen phyllo dough in the refrigerator overnight. Wrap unused dough in plastic wrap, and store in the refrigerator for up to 1 week.

1. Carefully remove 1 sheet of phyllo at a time. Layer a few sheets, one atop the other, for a sturdy pastry. Coat phyllo with cooking spray to prevent tearing.
2. Use a pizza cutter to cut dough into lengthwise strips. Use cooking spray to bond any tearing that occurs while working with the dough.
3. Working with 1 phyllo section at a time, spoon filling onto 1 short end of each rectangle, leaving a 1-inch border around the filling to allow room for folding.
4. Gently fold pastry into a triangle: Start at the filling end, folding the dough over the filling. Continue folding as you would a flag. Avoid wrapping too tightly, which can cause the filling to leak out during baking.

Sautéed Grape Napoleons with Port Reduction

Use a fine mesh strainer to sift 2 tablespoons powdered sugar judiciously over the phyllo as you make the layers. Just a bit of sugar along with the cooking spray helps them adhere to one another. Don't worry if they're loosely stacked; the crisp texture provides a nice contrast to the sautéed grapes and creamy cheese.

9 (14 x 9–inch) sheets frozen phyllo dough, thawed
Cooking spray
2 tablespoons plus 2 teaspoons powdered sugar, divided
¾ cup tawny port or other sweet red wine
1 tablespoon honey
¼ teaspoon salt, divided
2 teaspoons butter
2 cups seedless green grapes
1 cup seedless red grapes
2 teaspoons granulated sugar
2 teaspoons fresh lemon juice
1 ounce goat cheese, softened
1 (3-ounce) package ⅓-less-fat cream cheese, softened
2 tablespoons chopped walnuts, toasted

1. Preheat oven to 350°.
2. Place 1 phyllo sheet on a large cutting board or work surface (cover remaining dough to keep from drying). Lightly coat dough with cooking spray. Place 2 tablespoons powdered sugar in a small sieve; dust phyllo lightly with powdered sugar. Repeat procedure with 2 phyllo sheets, cooking spray, and powdered sugar, ending with powdered sugar; press layers

gently to adhere. Cut phyllo stack lengthwise into 3 (14 x 3–inch) rectangles. Cut each rectangle crosswise into 4 (3½ x 3–inch) rectangles to form 12 rectangles. Carefully stack 1 rectangle on top of another to form 6 stacks; press layers gently. Place stacks on a baking sheet lined with parchment paper. Repeat procedure with remaining phyllo, cooking spray, and powdered sugar to form 18 stacks.
3. Cover phyllo stacks with parchment paper; place another baking sheet on parchment paper. Bake at 350° for 10 minutes or until stacks are golden and crisp. Carefully remove top baking sheet and parchment paper. Cool phyllo stacks completely on baking sheet.
4. Bring port to a boil in a small saucepan over medium-high heat. Cook 10 minutes or until reduced to 1½ tablespoons. Remove from heat; stir in honey and ⅛ teaspoon salt.
5. Melt butter in a nonstick skillet over medium-high heat. Add remaining ⅛ teaspoon salt, grapes, granulated sugar, and juice. Sauté 10 minutes or until grapes are tender, stirring occasionally. Remove from heat, and cool to room temperature.
6. Combine cheeses in a small bowl, stirring well.
7. Place 1 phyllo stack on each of 6 plates, and top with 1 teaspoon cheese mixture and 1 tablespoon grape mixture. Repeat layers once, ending with phyllo stack. Drizzle 1 teaspoon port mixture onto each plate. Sprinkle each serving with 1 teaspoon walnuts, and dust evenly with remaining 2 teaspoons powdered sugar. **Yield: 6 servings (serving size: 1 napoleon).**

CALORIES 297; FAT 8.6g (sat 4.1g, mono 1.7g, poly 1.5g); PROTEIN 4.9g; CARB 43g; FIBER 1.4g; CHOL 16mg; IRON 1.2mg; SODIUM 339mg; CALC 39mg

all about grapes

When it comes to grape selection, the most flavorful ones often have seeds. Muscat grapes deliver sweet, musky flavor. Thompson seedless, found in many grocery stores, are best when allowed to ripen until they're yellow-green. You can use red and green seedless grapes interchangeably in recipes. You may find other varieties, such as Champagne, Flame, or Crimson, at farmers' markets. Look for grapes that are plump, richly colored, and fully attached to their stems. Grapes will keep unwashed in a plastic bag in the refrigerator for up to a week, but they're best eaten sooner. Be sure to rinse grapes thoroughly before eating or using them in a recipe, as dust may cling to the clusters.

Chocolate Chip Cannoli

This lightened version of a classic pastry cut the calories in half and the saturated fat by two-thirds. You can make the homemade ricotta cheese can be made up to 4 days ahead. If you don't have time to make ricotta from scratch, substitute 4 cups part-skim ricotta, and proceed to step 3.

Ricotta:

- 1 gallon 1% low-fat milk
- 4 cups low-fat buttermilk
- ¼ teaspoon kosher salt
- ⅔ cup granulated sugar
- ½ teaspoon vanilla extract
- 6 ounces fromage blanc

Shells:

- ⅓ cup granulated sugar
- ½ teaspoon ground cinnamon
- 24 (14 x 9–inch) sheets frozen phyllo dough, thawed
- Cooking spray

Remaining Ingredients:

- 2 ounces semisweet chocolate, divided
- 2 tablespoons sifted powdered sugar

1. To prepare ricotta, line a large colander or sieve with 3 layers of dampened cheesecloth, allowing cheesecloth to extend over outside edges of colander, and place colander in a large bowl.

2. Combine milk and buttermilk in a large, heavy stockpot. Cook over medium heat until a candy thermometer registers 170°, gently stirring constantly. As soon as the milk mixture reaches 170°, stop stirring (whey and curds will separate at this point). Continue to cook, without stirring, until thermometer registers 190°. (Be sure not to stir, or curds that have formed will break apart.) Immediately remove pan from heat. (Bottom of pan may be slightly scorched.) Pour milk mixture into

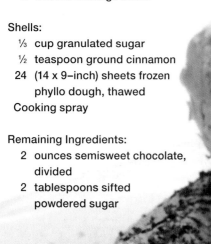

cheesecloth-lined colander. Drain over bowl 5 minutes, and discard liquid (whey). Gather edges of cheesecloth together; tie securely. Hang cheesecloth bundle from kitchen faucet, and drain 12 minutes or just until whey stops dripping. Scrape ricotta into a medium bowl. Sprinkle with salt, and toss gently with a fork to combine. Cool to room temperature.

3. Add ⅔ cup granulated sugar, vanilla, and fromage blanc to ricotta; beat with a mixer at medium speed until combined. Cover mixture, and refrigerate.

4. To prepare shells, preheat oven to 375°.

5. Cut 12 (12 x 4–inch) pieces of parchment paper or foil. Combine ⅓ cup granulated sugar and cinnamon in a small bowl.

6. Place 1 phyllo sheet on a large cutting board or work surface (cover remaining dough to keep from drying); lightly coat with cooking spray. Sprinkle evenly with about ¾ teaspoon sugar mixture. Repeat layers once. Fold phyllo stack lengthwise in half. Using your index finger as a guide, loosely roll up 1 parchment paper piece jelly-roll fashion to form a cylinder with a 1-inch opening. Place cylinder at bottom of 1 phyllo strip; roll up jelly-roll fashion around cylinder. Lightly coat phyllo with cooking spray. Place on a parchment paper–lined baking sheet. Repeat procedure with remaining phyllo, cooking spray, sugar mixture, and parchment paper pieces. Bake at 375° for 12 to 14 minutes or until lightly browned; cool completely on a wire rack. Carefully remove cylinders from phyllo shells by twisting ends of paper in opposite directions and gently pulling paper from shells.

7. Finely chop 1½ ounces chocolate. Combine ricotta mixture and chopped chocolate in a bowl. Transfer mixture to a large zip-top plastic bag; snip off ½ inch of 1 corner of bag. Pipe ricotta mixture evenly into each of 12 prepared shells (about ⅓ cup). Grate remaining ½ ounce chocolate. Dust cannoli evenly with powdered sugar and grated chocolate; serve immediately. **Yield: 12 servings (serving size: 1 cannolo).**

CALORIES 362; FAT 8.7g (sat 7.4g, mono 2.7g, poly 0.4g); PROTEIN 17.9g; CARB 53.7g; FIBER 0.7g; CHOL 20mg; IRON 1mg; SODIUM 396mg; CALC 501mg

kitchen how-to: make light cannoli

Our version of the Sicilian sweet has all the classic crunch and creaminess—crispy, lightly sweetened shells filled with homemade ricotta and chopped chocolate—without the calories and saturated fat. Our lighter version uses easy phyllo-based shells, a simple lower-fat homemade ricotta, and a hint of semisweet chocolate. The best part: You can make the filling and shells ahead.

1. Immerse the tip of a thermometer 2 inches into ricotta liquid to ensure an accurate reading. Be patient—it may take up to 20 minutes to reach 170°.

2. Hang the cheesecloth bag over the sink to allow the whey to drain. The ricotta is ready when whey drips infrequently, yielding a barely moist cheese perfect for blending.

3. Make phyllo molds by rolling heavy-duty foil into cylinders. Lightly coat cylinders with cooking spray before rolling and wrapping dough around molds.

Baklava with Wildflower Honey

Wildflower honey adds a delicate floral scent to this classic dessert, but almond honey would also work well in this recipe. If you can't find unsalted pistachios, use salted and omit the added ⅛ teaspoon salt.

Syrup:
1½ cups wildflower honey
½ cup water
1 tablespoon fresh lemon juice
3 whole cloves
1 (3-inch) cinnamon stick

Filling:
⅔ cup unsalted pistachios, coarsely chopped
½ cup blanched unsalted almonds, coarsely chopped
⅓ cup walnuts, coarsely chopped
¼ cup sugar
¾ teaspoon ground cinnamon
¼ teaspoon ground cardamom
⅛ teaspoon salt

Remaining Ingredients:
Cooking spray
24 (14 x 9–inch) sheets frozen phyllo dough, thawed
1 tablespoon water

1. To prepare syrup, combine honey, ½ cup water, juice, cloves, and cinnamon stick in a medium saucepan over low heat; stir until honey completely dissolves (about 2 minutes). Increase heat to medium; cook, without stirring, until a candy thermometer registers 230° (about 10 minutes). Remove from heat; keep warm. Remove solids with a slotted spoon; discard.

2. Preheat oven to 350°.

3. To prepare filling, combine pistachios and next 6 ingredients.

4. Lightly coat a 13 x 9–inch glass or ceramic baking dish with cooking spray. Working with 1 phyllo sheet at a time (cover remaining dough to keep from drying), place 1 phyllo sheet lengthwise in bottom of prepared pan, allowing end of sheet to extend over edges of dish; lightly coat with cooking spray. Repeat procedure with 5 phyllo sheets and cooking spray for a total of 6 layers. Sprinkle phyllo evenly with one-third of nut mixture (about ⅔ cup). Repeat procedure twice with phyllo, cooking spray, and nut mixture. Top last layer of nut mixture with remaining 6 sheets phyllo, each lightly coated with cooking spray. Lightly coat top phyllo sheet with cooking spray; press baklava gently into pan. Sprinkle surface of baklava with 1 tablespoon water.

5. Make 3 even lengthwise cuts and 7 even crosswise cuts to form 32 portions using a sharp knife. Bake at 350° for 30 minutes or until the phyllo is golden brown. Remove from oven. Drizzle honey mixture evenly over baklava. Cool in pan on a wire rack. Store covered at room temperature. **Yield: 32 servings (serving size: 1 piece).**

CALORIES 117; FAT 3.5g (sat 0.3g, mono 1g, poly 0.9g); PROTEIN 1.9g; CARB 20.7g; FIBER 0.9g; CHOL 0mg; IRON 0.6mg; SODIUM 53mg; CALC 12mg

kitchen how-to: make perfect baklava squares

This rich, sticky pastry is made of layers of phyllo filled with chopped nuts and sweetened with syrup or honey. Cutting the squares before pouring on the sticky honey mixture is the key to creating nicely cut squares.

1. Using a sharp knife, make 3 even lengthwise cuts in baklava.
2. Make 7 even crosswise cuts to form 32 portions. Bake until phyllo is golden brown.
3. Remove from oven, and drizzle honey mixture evenly over baklava. Cool baklava in pan on a wire rack.

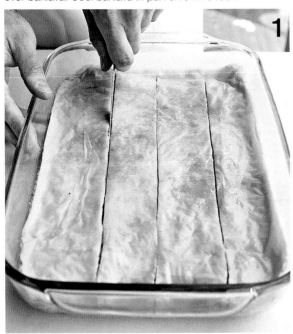

Chocolate Baklava

¾ **cup honey**
½ **cup water**
1 **(3-inch) cinnamon stick**
1 **cup hazelnut-chocolate**
  spread
½ **cup toasted hazelnuts,**
  coarsely chopped
½ **cup roasted pistachios,**
  coarsely chopped
⅓ **cup blanched toasted**
  almonds, coarsely chopped
⅓ **cup toasted walnuts, coarsely**
  chopped
½ **teaspoon ground cinnamon**
⅛ **teaspoon salt**
  Cooking spray
24 **(14 x 9–inch) sheets frozen**
  phyllo dough, thawed
½ **cup butter, melted**

1. Combine first 3 ingredients in a medium saucepan over low heat; stir until honey dissolves. Increase heat to medium; cook, without stirring, until a candy thermometer registers 230° (about 10 minutes). Remove from heat; keep warm. Discard cinnamon stick.
2. Preheat oven to 350°.
3. Place hazelnut-chocolate spread in a microwave-safe bowl; microwave at HIGH 30 seconds or until melted. Combine hazelnuts and next 5 ingredients. Lightly coat a 13 x 9-inch glass or ceramic baking dish with cooking spray. Working with 1 phyllo sheet at a time (cover remaining dough to keep from drying), place 1 phyllo sheet lengthwise in bottom of prepared pan, allowing ends of sheet to extend over edges of dish; lightly brush with butter. Repeat procedure with 5 phyllo sheets and butter. Drizzle about ⅓ cup melted hazelnut-chocolate spread over phyllo. Sprinkle evenly with one-third of nut mixture (about ½ cup). Repeat procedure twice with phyllo, butter, hazelnut-chocolate spread, and nut mixture. Top last layer of nut mixture with remaining 6 sheets phyllo, each lightly brushed with butter. Press gently into pan.
4. Make 3 lengthwise cuts and 5 crosswise cuts to form 24 portions using a sharp knife. Bake at 350° for 35 minutes or until phyllo is golden. Remove from oven. Drizzle honey mixture over baklava. Cool in pan on a wire rack. Cover; store at room temperature. **Yield: 24 servings (serving size: 1 piece).**

CALORIES 238; FAT 13.4g (sat 4.3g, mono 5.6g, poly 2g); PROTEIN 4g; CARB 27.8g; FIBER 1.6g; CHOL 10mg; IRON 1.3mg; SODIUM 148mg; CALC 29mg

Hazelnut-Chocolate Spread
What it adds: This creamy spread adds the chocolate-hazelnut flavor that helps form the base of this classic Middle Eastern pastry.

Mix of Nuts
What they add: Using a variety of nuts adds nuanced flavor and texture. You can use any combination of nuts you like.

way to bake

custards, puddings & soufflés

custards, puddings & soufflés

This collection of desserts is not hard to make, but the recipes do require that you adhere to specific techniques to ensure you get the results you crave.

Custards & Puddings: Tips of the Trade

The base of these desserts is either milk or a combination of milk (or cream) and egg. They can be steamed, cooked on the stovetop, or in the oven, usually in a water bath. Regardless of the method you use to cook them, the key to their success is cooking them slowly to prevent curdling and to create a luscious, creamy dessert. Here are some of the common methods you'll find in these recipes.

• **Tempering:** This is the process of slowly combining a hot liquid with a cold one. In the case of custards, tempering ensures that the hot liquid doesn't scramble the eggs. To temper, slowly add the hot liquid to the eggs while whisking constantly.

• **Ice Bath:** It's important that some stovetop puddings or custards stop cooking as soon as they become thick. In those cases, an ice bath is necessary. Spoon the hot custard into a bowl, and then place the bowl into a larger ice-filled bowl.

• **Stirring:** Never stop stirring a recipe that calls for constant stirring. Failure to stir as needed can cause a delicate dessert to overheat and curdle. Some cooks insist on stirring in a figure eight pattern to maintain the heat, others suggest a zigzag motion, and some claim a simple circular motion is best. Whatever your preference, keep the mixture moving away from the bottom of the pan.

• **Water Bath:** A water bath (a shallow pan of warm water in which containers of food are cooked) insulates and protects the mixture from the heat of the oven so it cooks slowly and evenly. The depth of the water should be half the height of the container (a ramekin, cake pan, etc.). If you're baking multiple custards, the pan must be large enough so that containers don't touch one another.

Soufflés

These baked cakes get their light texture and puffed appearance from the beaten egg whites that are folded in. The base of the dessert can be made from a variety of ingredients—citrus fruit, berries, and chocolate for sweet variations and cheese, vegetables, and meat for savory options. Soufflés can be made in containers of all sizes and shapes, but the most common is a larger soufflé dish or smaller ramekins with straight sides. Soufflés should be served shortly after emerging from the oven, since their striking puffed tops will fall after 5 or 10 minutes.

custards & puddings

Homemade custards and puddings deliver a wonderful blend of richness and creaminess. We'll show you how to prepare them in a delicious array of flavors.

Cardamom-Coconut Crème Caramel

Cooking spray
1 cup sugar, divided
3 tablespoons water
2 cups whole milk
2 cups flaked sweetened coconut
3 green cardamom pods
1 cup half-and-half
¼ teaspoon salt
4 large eggs, lightly beaten

1. Lightly coat 8 (6-ounce) custard cups or ramekins with cooking spray. Combine ½ cup sugar and 3 tablespoons water in a small saucepan over medium-high heat; cook 2 minutes or until sugar dissolves, stirring gently as needed to dissolve sugar evenly. Cook 4 minutes or until golden (do not stir). Immediately pour into prepared custard cups, tipping quickly to coat bottoms of cups.

2. Preheat oven to 300°.

3. Heat milk, coconut, and cardamom over medium-high heat in a medium, heavy saucepan to 180° or until tiny bubbles form around edge (do not boil). Remove from heat; cover and let stand 15 minutes. Strain milk mixture through a cheesecloth-lined sieve into a medium bowl. Gather edges of cheesecloth together; squeeze over bowl to release moisture. Discard solids.

4. Combine remaining ½ cup sugar, half-and-half, salt, and eggs in a large bowl; gradually add milk mixture, stirring constantly with a whisk. Divide mixture evenly among prepared custard cups. Place in a roasting pan; add hot water to pan to a depth of 1 inch. Bake at 300° for 25 minutes or until center barely moves when custard cup is touched. Cool completely in water. Place plastic wrap on surface of custards; chill at least 6 hours. Loosen edges of custards with a knife or rubber spatula. Invert custard cups onto plates. Drizzle any remaining caramelized syrup over custards. **Yield: 8 servings (serving size: 1 custard).**

CALORIES 213; FAT 8.2g (sat 4.3g, mono 1.5g, poly 0.5g); PROTEIN 6g; CARB 29.7g; FIBER 0.1g; CHOL 123mg; IRON 0.5mg; SODIUM 133mg; CALC 114mg

kitchen how-to: make crème caramel

The custard in a crème caramel can be flavored in a variety of ways, but the process for making it remains the same.

1. Combine sugar and water in a heavy saucepan; cook over medium-high heat until the sugar dissolves, stirring frequently.

2. Continue to cook without stirring. The mixture will start to caramelize, turning light brown. Continue to cook the mixture until it's a deep golden brown.

3. Immediately pour just enough of the caramel into each ramekin or custard cup coated with cooking spray to cover the bottom of the cup.

4. Tilt the cup so the bottom is completely covered with caramel.

5. Pour the custard mixture (made of eggs, milk, and flavorings) evenly over the caramelized sugar. Place the cups in a roasting pan; add hot water to the pan to a depth of 1 inch, and bake until the center of the custard barely moves when the ramekin is touched. Keep custards in the pan of water until they're cooled completely.

6. Place plastic wrap on the surface of the custards; chill at least 6 hours. After the custards are chilled, loosen the edges by running a thin knife around the edges.

7. Place a dessert plate upside down on top of each cup. Invert the cup and the plate. Lift the cup; the custard should easily slip out.

Crema Catalana

2   **cups whole milk**
3   **(3 x 1–inch) lemon rind strips**
1   **(2-inch) cinnamon stick**
7   **tablespoons sugar, divided**
2   **tablespoons cornstarch**
⅛ **teaspoon salt**
3   **large egg yolks**

1. Heat milk over medium-high heat in a small, heavy saucepan to 180° or until tiny bubbles form around edge (do not boil). Remove from heat. Add rind and cinnamon stick; cover and let stand 30 minutes. Discard rind and cinnamon stick.
2. Combine ¼ cup sugar, cornstarch, and salt in a small bowl, stirring well with a whisk. Add ¼ cup milk mixture to sugar mixture, stirring until smooth. Return milk mixture to pan; cook over medium-low heat 7 minutes or until almost thick, stirring constantly with a whisk. Place egg yolks in a small bowl. Gradually pour one-third of hot milk mixture into yolks, stirring constantly with a whisk. Carefully return yolk mixture to pan. Cook over low heat to 180° (about 4 minutes), stirring constantly with a whisk. Divide custard evenly among 6 (4-ounce) custard cups; place plastic wrap on surface of custards. Chill at least 4 hours.
3. Remove plastic wrap; discard. Sprinkle remaining 3 tablespoons sugar evenly over custards. Holding a kitchen blowtorch about 2 inches from top of each custard, heat sugar, moving the torch back and forth, until sugar completely melts and is caramelized (about 1 minute). Serve immediately or within 1 hour. **Yield: 6 servings (serving size: 1 custard).**

CALORIES 142; FAT 4.9g (sat 2.3g, mono 1.6g, poly 0.5g); PROTEIN 3.9g; CARB 21g; FIBER 0g; CHOL 111mg; IRON 0.3mg; SODIUM 86mg; CALC 103mg

kitchen how-to: use a kitchen blowtorch

You can find a kitchen blowtorch at most cookware stores. Use it to brown meringues, toast marshmallows, and blister peppers. If you don't have a kitchen blowtorch, cook the sugar in a small saucepan or skillet over medium heat until golden (5 to 8 minutes). Working quickly, evenly drizzle the caramel over the cold custards. Using a rubber spatula coated with cooking spray, spread the caramel evenly to form a thin layer.

1. After the custards are chilled, sprinkle sugar over each custard.
2. Holding a kitchen blowtorch about 2 inches from the top of each custard, heat the sugar, moving the blowtorch back and forth until the sugar is completely melted and caramelized, which will take about 1 minute. Serve immediately or within an hour of caramelizing the sugar topping, or the hard sugar shells will become soft as they start to dissolve into the custards.

Sweet Potato–Buttered Rum Flan

½ teaspoon canola oil
½ cup granulated sugar
1 tablespoon water
1 cup mashed cooked sweet potatoes
½ cup packed brown sugar
2 tablespoons white rum
2 tablespoons butter, melted
¼ teaspoon ground cinnamon
⅛ teaspoon salt
⅛ teaspoon grated whole nutmeg
3 large eggs
1½ cups 1% low-fat milk

1. Preheat oven to 325°.
2. Coat an 8-inch metal cake pan with tall sides with canola oil, tipping to fully coat.
3. Combine granulated sugar and 1 tablespoon water in a small, heavy saucepan over medium-high heat; cook 5 minutes or until golden. Immediately pour into prepared pan, tipping quickly until caramelized sugar coats bottom of pan.
4. Place sweet potatoes and next 7 ingredients in a blender; process until smooth. Add milk; process just until blended. Pour mixture over caramel in pan. Place pan in a 13 x 9–inch glass or ceramic baking dish; add hot water to dish to a depth of 1 inch.
5. Bake at 325° for 1 hour or until a knife inserted in center comes out clean. Remove pan from water. Cool completely on a wire rack. Cover and chill 8 hours or overnight. Invert flan onto a platter, and cut into 8 wedges. Drizzle any remaining caramel syrup over flan. **Yield: 8 servings (serving size: 1 wedge).**

CALORIES 230; FAT 6.6g (sat 3.5g, mono 2.1g, poly 0.6g); PROTEIN 4.6g; CARB 36.1g; FIBER 0.6g; CHOL 81mg; IRON 1.1mg; SODIUM 219mg; CALC 90mg

Whole Nutmeg

What it adds: Grating whole nutmeg yourself adds a fresher, more intense nutmeg flavor to this custard. Use ground nutmeg in place of grated whole nutmeg, if you prefer.

White Rum

What it adds: This light-bodied rum has a very subtle, clean flavor that's slightly sweet.

Chocolate Pudding

Use a good-quality bittersweet or semisweet chocolate bar. Garnish with a dollop of whipped cream, grated chocolate, and a mint sprig.

- 2½ **cups fat-free milk, divided**
- ⅓ **cup sugar**
- 3 **tablespoons cornstarch**
- ¼ **teaspoon salt**
- 2 **large egg yolks**
- 2 **teaspoons butter**
- 1 **teaspoon vanilla extract**
- 5 **ounces semisweet chocolate, chopped**

1. Place 2 cups milk in a medium, heavy saucepan; bring to a boil. Combine sugar, cornstarch, and salt in a large bowl, stirring well with a whisk. Combine remaining ½ cup milk and egg yolks, stirring well with a whisk. Add egg yolk mixture to sugar mixture, stirring well. Gradually add half of hot milk to egg yolk mixture, stirring constantly with a whisk. Return milk mixture to pan; bring to a boil. Reduce heat, and simmer 1 minute or until thick, stirring constantly. Remove from heat. Add butter, vanilla, and chocolate, stirring until butter and chocolate melt.

2. Spoon pudding into a bowl. Place bowl in a large ice-filled bowl for 15 minutes or until pudding cools, stirring occasionally. Cover surface of pudding with plastic wrap; chill. **Yield: 6 servings (serving size: about ½ cup).**

CALORIES 246; FAT 9.6g (sat 5.6g, mono 3.5g, poly 0.5g); PROTEIN 6.4g; CARB 35.8g; FIBER 0g; CHOL 74mg; IRON 0.8mg; SODIUM 157mg; CALC 150mg

kitchen how-to: make great pudding

Preparing stovetop pudding requires little more than a heavy saucepan, whisk, rubber spatula, and plastic wrap.

1. Most stovetop custard recipes combine dry ingredients, such as sugar and starch. This prevents the starch from clumping when it's added to the hot milk. Separately combine eggs with a bit of milk or cream.

2. Tempering is a process that combines a hot liquid with a cool one, protecting the delicate eggs from coagulating too quickly.

3. The pudding is thick enough when it coats the back of a spoon.

4. Butter enriches the flavor and texture of pudding. Add it and other ingredients that may suffer from exposure to heat, such as flavor extracts, after the custard cooks.

5. Place plastic wrap directly on the surface of the pudding to prevent a thin, rubbery skin from developing on the top.

Vanilla Bean Pudding

You can substitute vanilla paste or 1 teaspoon real vanilla extract in place of the vanilla bean, if necessary. Stir in extract with the butter.

2½ cups 2% reduced-fat milk
1 vanilla bean, split lengthwise
¾ cup sugar
3 tablespoons cornstarch
⅛ teaspoon salt
¼ cup half-and-half
2 large egg yolks
4 teaspoons butter

1. Place milk in a medium, heavy saucepan. Scrape seeds from vanilla bean; add seeds and bean to milk. Bring to a boil.
2. Combine sugar, cornstarch, and salt in a large bowl, stirring well. Combine half-and-half and egg yolks, stirring well. Stir egg yolk mixture into sugar mixture. Gradually add half of hot milk mixture to sugar mixture, stirring constantly with a whisk. Return hot milk mixture to pan; bring to a boil. Cook 1 minute, stirring constantly with a whisk. Remove from heat. Add butter, stirring until butter melts. Remove vanilla bean; discard.

3. Spoon pudding into a bowl. Place bowl in a large ice-filled bowl for 15 minutes or until pudding cools, stirring occasionally. Cover surface of pudding with plastic wrap; chill. **Yield: 6 servings (serving size: ½ cup).**

CALORIES 216; FAT 7.1g (sat 4.1g, mono 2.2g, poly 0.4g); PROTEIN 4.6g; CARB 34.2g; FIBER 0g; CHOL 86mg; IRON 0.2mg; SODIUM 125mg; CALC 142mg

Peanut Butter Pudding variation: Omit vanilla bean, salt, and butter; stir in ¼ cup reduced-fat creamy peanut butter after pudding is cooked. **Yield: 6 servings (serving size: about ½ cup).**

CALORIES 257; FAT 8.6g (sat 3.3g, mono 3.6g, poly 1.6g); PROTEIN 6.9g; CARB 39.2g; FIBER 0.7g; CHOL 80mg; IRON 0.5mg; SODIUM 170mg; CALC 142mg

Coconut Pudding variation: Omit vanilla bean. Replace ¾ cup of the milk with ¾ cup light unsweetened coconut milk. Omit butter; stir in ½ cup toasted flaked sweetened coconut after pudding is cooked. **Yield: 6 servings (serving size: about ½ cup).**

CALORIES 224; FAT 7.5g (sat 5.3g, mono 1.5g, poly 0.4g); PROTEIN 4.1g; CARB 36.8g; FIBER 0.3g; CHOL 77mg; IRON 0.5mg; SODIUM 115mg; CALC 105mg

kitchen how-to: cut a vanilla bean

Vanilla beans can be expensive, but their superior flavor is worth the investment.

1. When buying vanilla beans, look for shiny black beans. White crystals on the beans are also a good sign.

2. Revive a dry vanilla bean by wrapping it in a damp paper towel and microwaving it at HIGH 5 to 8 seconds. The bean is easier to cut and more seeds can be scraped out when it's moist, so scrape the seeds after steeping the bean in liquid.

Double Mango Pudding

Prepare and chill pudding the night before. Whip the cream just before serving, and allow guests to dollop some on their own desserts.

    3 **mangoes, peeled and divided**
  2¼ **cups water, divided**
    ½ **cup sugar**
    1 **tablespoon unflavored gelatin**
    ¼ **cup whipping cream**

1. Coarsely chop 2 mangoes. Dice remaining mango.
2. Combine coarsely chopped mangoes and ¼ cup water in a blender; process until smooth. Press puree through a fine sieve over a bowl; discard solids.

3. Bring ¾ cup water to a boil in a medium saucepan. Add sugar to pan, stirring until sugar dissolves. Remove from heat. Stir in remaining 1¼ cups water. Sprinkle unflavored gelatin over water in saucepan; let stand 1 minute. Add mango puree, stirring with a whisk. Divide mixture evenly among 8 (6-ounce) ramekins or custard cups. Cover and chill overnight or until set. Top evenly with diced mango.
4. Place cream in a medium bowl; beat with a mixer at high speed until stiff peaks form. Serve with pudding. **Yield: 8 servings (serving size: 1 ramekin and 1 tablespoon whipped cream).**

CALORIES 127; FAT 3g (sat 1.8g, mono 0.9g, poly 0.1g); PROTEIN 1.3g; CARB 25.9g; FIBER 1.4g; CHOL 10mg; IRON 0.1mg; SODIUM 8mg; CALC 15mg

kitchen how-to: peel & cut mango

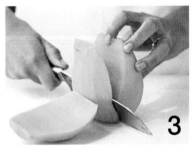

The flavor of mangoes has been compared to a cross between a pineapple and a peach.

1. Use a sharp knife to trim ½ inch from the top and bottom of mango to create a sturdy surface for cutting.
2. Use a vegetable peeler to easily remove the skin from the flesh.
3. Cut the flesh from around the pit with two curved cuts down the plumpest sides; trim the remaining sides.
4. Cut the fruit's flesh according to your needs—diced, chopped, or sliced.

Tiramisu

Espresso Drizzle:
- ½ **cup water**
- 2 **tablespoons granulated sugar**
- 2 **tablespoons instant espresso granules**
- 2 **tablespoons Kahlúa (coffee-flavored liqueur)**

Filling:
- 1 **(8-ounce) block fat-free cream cheese, softened**
- 1 **(3.5-ounce) carton mascarpone cheese**
- ⅓ **cup granulated sugar**
- ¼ **cup packed brown sugar**
- 2 **tablespoons Kahlúa**

Remaining Ingredients:
- 24 **cakelike ladyfingers (2 [3-ounce] packages)**
- 1½ **teaspoons unsweetened cocoa**
- ½ **ounce bittersweet chocolate, grated**

1. To prepare espresso drizzle, combine first 3 ingredients in a small saucepan over medium-high heat; bring to a boil. Cook 1 minute, stirring occasionally. Remove from heat; stir in 2 tablespoons liqueur. Cool completely.

2. To prepare filling, combine cheeses in a large bowl, and beat with a mixer at medium speed until smooth. Add ⅓ cup granulated sugar, brown sugar, and 2 tablespoons liqueur; beat at medium speed until well blended.

3. Split ladyfingers in half lengthwise. Arrange 24 ladyfinger halves, cut sides up, in bottom of an 8-inch square glass or ceramic baking dish. Drizzle half of espresso drizzle over ladyfinger halves. Spread half of filling over ladyfinger halves; repeat procedure with remaining ladyfinger halves, espresso drizzle, and filling. Combine cocoa and chocolate; sprinkle evenly over top of filling. Cover and chill 2 hours.

Yield: 8 servings (serving size: ⅛ of tiramisu).

Note: Place wooden picks in center and in each corner of dish to prevent plastic wrap from sticking to tiramisu as it chills.

CALORIES 260; FAT 8g (sat 4.1g, mono 2.2g, poly 0.5g); PROTEIN 7.1g; CARB 38.4g; FIBER 0.5g; CHOL 55mg; IRON 0.8mg; SODIUM 317mg; CALC 104mg

all about ladyfingers

One of the signature ingredients of a classic tiramisu is the oblong sponge cakes that form liqueur-soaked layers and often a decorative border along the dessert's exterior. Find ladyfingers in the bakery section of your supermarket. Most come already split in half lengthwise, but you can split them yourself with a serrated knife, if needed. Substitute sponge cake or angel food cake if ladyfingers aren't available.

Mascarpone Cheese
What it adds: This recipe uses less of this rich cheese than the traditional version, but a little goes a long way in maintaining the luscious mouthfeel of this Italian favorite.

Instant Espresso Granules
What they add: The granules add rich coffee flavor, a key component of this dessert's signature taste.

Rice Pudding

Rice pudding is a favorite around the world, and there are many variations. Feel free to experiment with this basic recipe.

- 2 **cups cooked Arborio rice or other medium-grain rice**
- 3½ **cups fat-free milk**
- ⅓ **cup sugar**
- ¼ **cup nonfat dry milk**
- ¼ **teaspoon salt**
- 2 **large eggs, beaten**
- ¼ **cup golden raisins**
- 1 **teaspoon vanilla extract**
- 1 **teaspoon ground cinnamon**

1. Combine rice, fat-free milk, sugar, nonfat dry milk, and salt in a large saucepan over medium heat; bring to a simmer. Simmer 30 minutes, stirring occasionally.

2. Place eggs in a medium bowl. Gradually add half of rice mixture to eggs, stirring constantly with a whisk. Return egg mixture to pan over medium-low heat; cook 2 minutes, stirring constantly. Remove from heat; stir in raisins and vanilla. Spoon ½ cup pudding into each of 8 bowls. Sprinkle ⅛ teaspoon cinnamon over each serving.
Yield: 8 servings.

CALORIES 176; FAT 1.4g (sat 0.4g, mono 0.5g, poly 0.2g); PROTEIN 7.6g; CARB 33g; FIBER 0.8g; CHOL 54mg; IRON 1.1mg; SODIUM 160mg; CALC 151mg

kitchen how-to: make rice pudding

Medium-grain, starchy white rice, such as Arborio, provides silky texture and creamy consistency for this satisfying stovetop pudding with universal appeal.

1. Combine rice, milk, sugar, and salt in a large saucepan, and bring to a simmer; simmer 30 minutes, stirring occasionally.
2. Some rice puddings call for eggs, which give the dessert a more custardy consistency. Omit them for a creamier consistency. Beat eggs in a medium bowl; gradually add warm rice mixture to the eggs, stirring constantly with a whisk.
3. Return egg mixture to pan, and cook 2 minutes over medium-low heat, stirring constantly.
4. Stir in additional flavorings, such as raisins (or any other dried fruit), vanilla, nutmeg, cinnamon, and any other ingredients you'd like.

Cinnamon-Apple Raisin Bread Pudding

For an alcohol-free version, substitute apple cider or apple juice for the brandy.

½   cup raisins
½   cup chopped dried apple
2   tablespoons Calvados (apple brandy)
3½ cups 2% reduced-fat milk
¾   cup sugar
1   tablespoon grated lemon rind
1   tablespoon butter, melted
½   teaspoon salt
½   teaspoon ground cinnamon
⅛   teaspoon grated whole nutmeg
4   large eggs
5   cups (1½-inch) cubed cinnamon-raisin
    bread (about 12 ounces)
Cooking spray

1. Preheat oven to 325°.
2. Combine raisins, dried apple, and apple brandy in a microwave-safe bowl. Microwave at HIGH 1 minute; cool. Combine milk, sugar, lemon rind, butter, salt, cinnamon, nutmeg, and eggs in a large bowl, stirring well with a whisk. Stir in bread cubes and raisin mixture. Let stand at room temperature 15 minutes.
3. Pour bread mixture into an 8-inch square metal baking pan coated with cooking spray. Bake at 325° for 50 minutes or until set. Serve warm. **Yield: 10 servings (serving size: ¹⁄₁₀ of pudding).**

CALORIES 285; FAT 8g (sat 3g, mono 1.8g, poly 1.6g); PROTEIN 9.3g; CARB 45g; FIBER 3.4g; CHOL 94mg; IRON 1.6mg; SODIUM 341mg; CALC 120mg

kitchen how-to: make bread pudding

Bread puddings are among the most flexible of recipes. Assemble and bake them immediately, or cover and refrigerate them overnight before baking.

1. Making bread pudding doesn't require special equipment. You'll need a mixing bowl, a wooden spoon, and a baking dish in the appropriate size.
2. With bread puddings, you simply mix together all the ingredients, stir, and bake at a low temperature. For the best texture, use day-old, very dry bread; very fresh bread will yield a slightly spongy texture. Leave the crusts on the bread for more texture. Whole-grain breads give these puddings a nutty taste and a slightly drier texture, and they can be strong in flavor, which might overpower the delicate taste of other ingredients. Be sure to taste the bread before using it for bread pudding.

Steamed Pudding with Lemon Sauce

Golden raisins or dried cherries may be used instead of raisins. If available, you can use blackstrap molasses, a surprising source of iron, to add rich color and flavor.

Pudding:
Cooking spray
⅓ cup applesauce
3 tablespoons butter, softened
11.25 ounces all-purpose flour (about 2½ cups)
½ teaspoon baking soda
Dash of salt
1¼ cups 2% reduced-fat milk
½ cup plus 1 tablespoon molasses
1 cup raisins

Sauce:
¾ cup sugar
4 large egg whites
⅓ cup 2% reduced-fat milk
¼ cup fresh lemon juice
1 tablespoon butter
1 large egg yolk
Dash of salt
½ teaspoon grated lemon rind
¼ teaspoon vanilla extract

1. Preheat oven to 350°.
2. To prepare pudding, lightly coat a 2½-quart ovenproof bowl with cooking spray; line with plastic wrap. Lightly coat surface of plastic wrap with cooking spray. Set aside.
3. Spoon applesauce onto several layers of heavy-duty paper towels; spread to ½-inch thickness. Cover with additional paper towels; let stand 5 minutes. Scrape into a small bowl using a rubber spatula.
4. Place 3 tablespoons butter in a large bowl; beat with a mixer at medium speed for 2 minutes or until fluffy. Weigh or lightly spoon flour into dry measuring cups; level with a knife. Combine flour, baking soda, and salt. Add flour mixture, 1¼ cups milk, and molasses to butter, beating until blended. Stir in applesauce and raisins. Spoon mixture into prepared bowl; cover bowl with plastic wrap.
5. Place bowl in a deep roasting pan. Add hot water to pan until water is one-third of the way up sides of bowl. Tightly cover bowl and pan with foil. Bake at 350° for 2 hours or until a wooden pick inserted in center comes out clean. Remove bowl from pan. Carefully invert bowl onto a serving plate; remove and discard plastic wrap.
6. To prepare sauce, combine sugar and next 6 ingredients in a medium saucepan over medium heat, stirring constantly with a whisk until smooth. Cook 4 minutes or until thickened, stirring frequently. Remove from heat. Stir in rind and vanilla. Let stand at least 5 minutes before serving. **Yield: 12 servings (serving size: 1 slice pudding and about 2 tablespoons sauce).**

CALORIES 293; FAT 5.6g (sat 2.6g, mono 1.8g, poly 0.5g); PROTEIN 5.8g; CARB 55.8g; FIBER 1.5g; CHOL 30mg; IRON 4.5mg; SODIUM 150mg; CALC 185mg

make steamed pudding with lemon sauce

This steamed pudding has a moist texture and a rich lemony sauce.

1. Lightly coat an ovenproof bowl with cooking spray; line with plastic wrap.

2. Lightly coat the surface of the plastic wrap with cooking spray—coating both the dish and the plastic wrap helps you remove the pudding after it's cooked.

3. Once the batter is spooned into the ovenproof bowl, cover the bowl with plastic wrap. Place the bowl in a deep roasting pan. Add hot water to pan until the water is one-third of the way up the sides of the bowl. Tightly cover the bowl and pan with foil, and bake until a wooden pick inserted in the center comes out clean. Remove the bowl from the roasting pan. Carefully invert the bowl onto a serving plate. Remove and discard plastic wrap.

soufflés

Soufflés epitomize the art of French cooking, and mastering them ranks as a top culinary achievement, but they needn't be difficult. With a little practice, you can turn out a delicious soufflé like a pro.

Chocolate Soufflés with Pistachios

Use your favorite chopped nut in place of pistachios, if desired.

Cooking spray
- 7 tablespoons plus 1 teaspoon sugar, divided
- 1 ounce semisweet chocolate
- 4½ teaspoons butter
- 2 tablespoons unsweetened cocoa
- 2 tablespoons all-purpose flour
- ⅛ teaspoon salt
- ½ cup 1% low-fat milk
- 3 large egg whites
- 4 teaspoons chopped pistachios

1. Preheat oven to 375°.

2. Coat 4 (6-ounce) ramekins or custard cups with cooking spray, and sprinkle each ramekin with 1 teaspoon sugar. Place on a baking sheet.

3. Combine chocolate, butter, and 3 tablespoons sugar in a small saucepan. Cook over low heat until chocolate and butter melt. Add cocoa, flour, and salt, stirring with a whisk until blended. Gradually stir in milk; cook over medium heat until mixture thickens (about 3 minutes), stirring constantly. Remove from heat. Cool.

4. Beat egg whites with a mixer at high speed until foamy. Add remaining 3 tablespoons sugar, 1 tablespoon at a time, beating until stiff peaks form. Gently fold one-fourth of egg white mixture into chocolate mixture; gently fold in remaining egg white mixture, one-fourth at a time. Spoon into prepared ramekins; sprinkle each serving with 1 teaspoon nuts. Bake at 375° for 20 minutes. Serve immediately. **Yield: 4 servings (serving size: 1 soufflé).**

CALORIES 221; FAT 9g (sat 4.8g, mono 3.1g, poly 0.6g); PROTEIN 5.7g; CARB 33.1g; FIBER 1.5g; CHOL 13mg; IRON 1.1mg; SODIUM 174mg; CALC 52mg

kitchen how-to:
make soufflés

You need to use a soufflé dish or ramekins with tall, straight sides. A stand mixer with a whisk attachment is an important piece of equipment because it will incorporate the most air into the egg whites. A spatula is also useful when folding the egg whites into the base.

1. Egg whites incorporate more air if they're not completely cold, so separate the eggs first. Leave the whites out on the counter about 20 minutes before whipping—just long enough to take off the chill. Be careful not to get any egg yolk in the whites. Even a small amount of yolk can inhibit the egg whites from reaching their full volume.

2. Lightly coat the soufflé dish or ramekins with cooking spray. Add breadcrumbs (for savory dishes) or sugar (for sweet dishes), and roll the dish around until the interior is completely covered.

3. The base of the soufflé gives this dish its signature flavor. After the base is cooked and cooled, egg yolks and flavorings are added to enrich the dish.

4. Whip egg whites to stiff satiny peaks, but do not overbeat. Egg whites have reached their stiff peak stage when they stand up. Overbeaten egg whites look dry and grainy.

5. Gently fold the egg whites into the base, incorporating as much air as possible. "Cut" down the center and up the sides of the bowl,

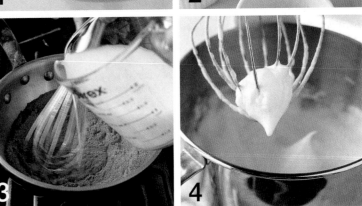

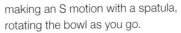

making an S motion with a spatula, rotating the bowl as you go.

6. The soufflé is done when it's puffed and set. To make sure it's

completely cooked, insert a wooden pick or skewer horizontally into the side. If it comes out clean, the soufflé is ready.

kitchen how-to: easily peel peaches

You can remove the skin using a vegetable peeler or a paring knife if the fruit is still firm. But if the fruit is soft or your peeling skills aren't up to par, the easiest way to remove the skin is blanching the fruit.

1. Cut an X in the bottom of each fruit, carefully cutting just through the skin.

2. Bring a large pot of water to a boil, and drop in the fruit. Cook 20 seconds to 1 minute—the riper the peaches are, the less time they need.

3. Remove the peaches from the boiling water with a slotted spoon, and place them in a sink or bowl filled with ice water.

4. Use a paring knife or your fingers to remove the skin, which should come off easily.

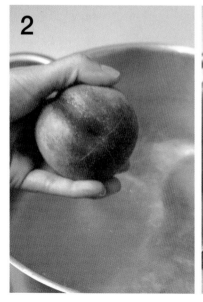

Peach Soufflés

Cooking spray
2 tablespoons granulated sugar
2 cups chopped peeled peaches (about 3 medium)
⅔ cup granulated sugar, divided
2 tablespoons cornstarch
2 tablespoons fresh lemon juice
⅛ teaspoon salt
2 large egg yolks
2 tablespoons butter
1 teaspoon cream of tartar
5 large egg whites
1 teaspoon powdered sugar

1. Place an oven rack in lowest position, and remove middle rack. Preheat oven to 425°.
2. Lightly coat 6 (8-ounce) soufflé dishes with cooking spray. Sprinkle evenly with 2 tablespoons granulated sugar.
3. Place peaches and ⅓ cup granulated sugar in a food processor; process until smooth. Combine peach mixture, cornstarch, juice, salt, and egg yolks in a medium saucepan, stirring well with a whisk; bring to a boil. Cook 1 minute, stirring constantly with whisk. Remove from heat; stir in butter. Cool 5 minutes.
4. Place cream of tartar and egg whites in a large mixing bowl; beat with a mixer at high speed until soft peaks form. Add remaining ⅓ cup granulated sugar, 2 tablespoons at a time, beating until stiff peaks form (do not overbeat). Gently stir one-fourth of egg white mixture into peach mixture; gently fold in remaining egg white mixture. Gently spoon mixture into prepared dishes. Sharply tap dishes 2 or 3 times on counter to level. Place dishes on a baking sheet, and place baking sheet on bottom rack of 425° oven. Immediately reduce oven temperature to 350° (do not remove soufflés from oven). Bake at 350° for 28 minutes or until a wooden pick inserted in side of soufflé comes out clean. Sprinkle evenly with powdered sugar. Serve immediately. **Yield: 6 servings (serving size: 1 soufflé).**

CALORIES 147; FAT 4.1g (sat 2.2g, mono 1.2g, poly 0.3g); PROTEIN 3.2g; CARB 24.8g; FIBER 0.4g; CHOL 59mg; IRON 0.2mg; SODIUM 94mg; CALC 9mg

way to bake

yeast
breads

yeast breads

Yeast breads have a reputation for being complicated, but really, anyone can make them once they've learned the basics.

kitchen how-to: make yeast bread

Glass bowls and wooden spoons are preferable to metal ones, which can react with the dough and affect the bread's flavor.

1. Dissolve dry yeast in water warmed to 100° to 110°—this step is also called proofing. It's always a good idea to use a thermometer to measure the temperature of the water until you feel comfortable recognizing the target temperature. You can also test the warmth of the liquid on your wrist—it should feel no warmer than a hot shower. About 5 minutes after mixing the yeast with the warm water, the mixture will start to bubble. If it doesn't bubble, the water was either too hot, which killed the yeast, or too cold, which inhibited its growth.

2. The remaining ingredients are added to the yeast mixture to create a dough. Turn the dough out onto a smooth, lightly floured surface, and lightly flour your hands. Using the heels of your hands, push the dough away from you.

3. Lift the edge farthest away from you, and fold it toward you. Give the dough a quarter turn. Repeat steps 2 and 3 until the dough feels smooth and elastic; this usually takes about 8 minutes. Using a timer is a good way to ensure proper kneading.

4. After kneading the dough, place it in a bowl coated with cooking spray; turn the dough so all the sides are

Types of Yeast

Yeast is a living organism that produces carbon dioxide bubbles, which cause bread to rise. It's available in several forms, but for our recipes we've used active dry yeast. Always remember to check the expiration date on the package of yeast to make sure it's fresh.

coated. Cover the bowl with plastic wrap or a clean towel, and place it in a warm place (85°), free from drafts. You can create this environment by placing the dough in a cool closed oven above a pan of boiling water.

5. The dough needs to rise until it's doubled in size, which can take anywhere from 30 minutes to 2 hours. To check the dough, gently press 2 fingers about an inch into the dough. If the dough springs back immediately, it hasn't risen enough. If the indentation remains, the dough is ready.

6. Punch the dough down by pressing into the center with a closed fist. Let the dough rest for 5 minutes (this rest period makes the dough easier to handle), and then shape it into the desired form (rolls, loaves, etc.) for the final rise. Place the shaped dough on a baking sheet or in a pan. Coat the dough lightly with cooking spray, and cover it (just as you did for the first rise). The rising procedure and checking for doneness are the same as for the first rise. Then bake the bread according to the recipe's directions.

No-Knead Overnight Parmesan and Thyme Rolls

½ teaspoon dry yeast
2 tablespoons warm water (100° to 110°)
2 tablespoons extra-virgin olive oil, divided
1 teaspoon dried thyme
⅓ cup 2% reduced-fat milk
½ cup (2 ounces) grated Parmigiano-Reggiano cheese, divided
1 tablespoon sugar
½ teaspoon kosher salt
1 large egg, lightly beaten
1.1 ounces whole-wheat white flour (about ¼ cup)
5.6 ounces all-purpose flour (about 1¼ cups), divided
   Cooking spray
½ teaspoon cracked black pepper

1. Dissolve yeast in 2 tablespoons warm water in a large bowl; let stand 5 minutes or until bubbly.
2. Heat 1 tablespoon oil in a small saucepan over medium heat. Add thyme to pan; cook 1 minute or until bubbly and fragrant. Add thyme mixture and milk to yeast mixture, stirring with a whisk; add ¼ cup cheese, sugar, salt, and egg, stirring well.
3. Weigh or lightly spoon whole-wheat white flour into a dry measuring cup; level with a knife. Using a wooden spoon, stir whole-wheat white flour into yeast mixture. Weigh or lightly spoon 4.5 ounces (about 1 cup) all-purpose flour into a dry measuring cup; level with a knife. Add all-purpose flour to yeast mixture, stirring well. Add enough of remaining all-purpose flour, 1 tablespoon at a time, to form a smooth but very sticky dough. Place dough in a large bowl coated with cooking spray, turning to coat top. Cover and refrigerate overnight. (Dough will not double in size.)
4. Remove dough from refrigerator, and uncover. Do not punch dough down. Turn dough out onto a floured surface; sprinkle dough lightly with flour. Roll dough into a 12 x 7–inch rectangle. Brush dough with remaining 1 tablespoon oil. Sprinkle remaining ¼ cup cheese evenly over dough; sprinkle with pepper. Beginning with a long side, roll up dough jelly-roll fashion. Pinch seam to seal (do not seal ends of roll). Cut roll into 8 (1½-inch) slices. Place slices, cut sides up, on a baking sheet lined with parchment paper. Cover and let rise in a warm place (85°), free from drafts, 1 hour or until rolls have risen slightly.
5. Preheat oven to 400°.
6. Uncover rolls. Place pan in oven, and immediately reduce heat to 375°. Bake rolls at 375° for 12 minutes or until golden brown. Serve warm. **Yield: 8 servings (serving size: 1 roll).**

CALORIES 161; FAT 6.3g (sat 2g, mono 3.3g, poly 0.6g); PROTEIN 6.3g; CARB 19.7g; FIBER 1.3g; CHOL 32mg; IRON 1.4mg; SODIUM 246mg; CALC 112mg

kitchen how-to:
make no-knead rolls

Stir the dough together quickly the day before shaping and baking—no kneading necessary. The dough is more like a thick batter; don't add additional flour, or the rolls will turn out dry.

1. Think of these rolls as savory cinnamon rolls. Just like those sweet treats, these have flavorful ingredients (olive oil and Parmigiano-Reggiano cheese) sprinkled over the dough.

2. Roll up the dough so that the filling gets distributed throughout in a spiral pattern. You don't need to roll it too tightly; the dough will rise again and fill in any gaps.

3. Slice the dough using dental floss or a thin, sharp knife. If using floss, wrap the string around the roll, cross the ends, and pull in opposite directions. Cover and let rise for an hour before baking.

Orange-Buttermilk Dinner Rolls

1¼ cups warm buttermilk (100° to 110°)
2 tablespoons sugar
1 tablespoon honey
1 package dry yeast (about 2¼ teaspoons)
3 tablespoons butter, melted and divided
4 teaspoons grated orange rind
1 teaspoon kosher salt
14 ounces all-purpose flour (about 3 cups)
Cooking spray

1. Combine first 3 ingredients in the bowl of a stand mixer fitted with paddle attachment. Sprinkle yeast over buttermilk mixture; let stand 5 minutes or until bubbly. Stir in 2 tablespoons butter, rind, and salt. Remove paddle attachment; insert dough hook. Weigh or lightly spoon flour into dry measuring cups; level with a knife. Add flour to yeast mixture; mix at low speed until a soft, elastic dough forms, about 5 minutes (dough will feel sticky). Place dough in a large bowl coated with cooking spray, turning to coat top. Cover and let rise in a warm place (85°), free from drafts, 1 hour or until doubled in size.

2. Punch dough down; turn out onto a lightly floured surface. Cut dough into 13 equal portions. Working with 1 portion at a time, roll dough into a ball by cupping your hand and pushing against dough and surface while rolling. Arrange dough balls 2 inches apart on a baking sheet coated with cooking spray. Brush lightly with remaining 1 tablespoon butter. Cover; let rise 1 hour or until doubled in size.

3. Preheat oven to 375°.

4. Uncover rolls. Bake at 375° for 20 minutes or until rolls are golden. Remove rolls from pan; cool slightly on a wire rack. **Yield: 13 rolls (serving size: 1 roll).**

CALORIES 163; FAT 3.7g (sat 2.2g, mono 0.7g, poly 0.2g); PROTEIN 4.2g; CARB 28.1g; FIBER 1g; CHOL 10mg; IRON 1.5mg; SODIUM 192mg; CALC 7mg

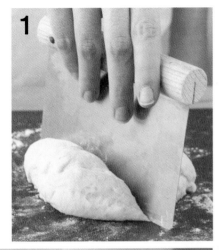

kitchen how-to:
make dinner rolls

These simply shaped rolls bake quickly, yielding delicious golden-brown results.

1. Once dough has doubled in size, punch it down, and turn it out onto a lightly floured surface. Cut into 13 equal portions.

2. Working with 1 portion at a time, roll dough into a ball by cupping your hand and pushing against the dough and surface while rolling.

3. Arrange dough balls 2 inches apart on a baking sheet coated with cooking spray.

4. For added flavor and a beautiful top, brush the dough balls lightly with 1 tablespoon melted butter. Cover and let rise until doubled in size, and then bake until golden.

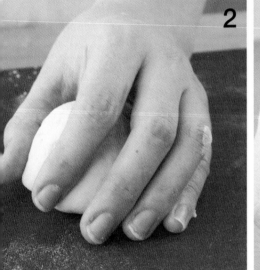

Oatmeal Knots

1	cup old-fashioned rolled oats
½	cup honey
2	tablespoons butter
1½	teaspoons salt
2	cups boiling water
1	package dry yeast (about 2¼ teaspoons)
⅓	cup warm water (100° to 110°)
¼	cup flaxseed meal
14.25	ounces whole-wheat flour (about 3 cups)
6.75	ounces all-purpose flour (about 1½ cups), divided
	Cooking spray
1	teaspoon water
1	large egg
1	tablespoon old-fashioned rolled oats
1	tablespoon sesame seeds
1	tablespoon poppy seeds

1. Combine first 4 ingredients in a large bowl, and add 2 cups boiling water, stirring until well blended. Cool to room temperature.

2. Dissolve yeast in ⅓ cup warm water in a small bowl; let stand 5 minutes. Add yeast mixture to oats mixture; stir well. Stir in flaxseed meal.

3. Weigh or lightly spoon flours into dry measuring cups; level with a knife. Gradually add 14.25 ounces whole-wheat flour (about 3 cups) and 4.5 ounces all-purpose flour (about 1 cup) to oats mixture; stir until a soft dough forms. Turn dough out onto a lightly floured surface. Knead until smooth and elastic (about 8 minutes); add enough of remaining 2.25 ounces all-purpose flour, 1 tablespoon at a time, to prevent dough from sticking to hands (dough will feel sticky).

4. Place dough in a large bowl coated with cooking spray, turning to coat top. Cover and let rise in a warm place (85°), free from drafts, 1 hour or until doubled in size. (Gently press 2 fingers into dough. If indentation remains, dough has risen enough.) Punch dough down, and let rest 5 minutes.

5. Divide dough in half; cut each half into 12 equal portions. Working with 1 portion at a time (cover remaining dough to prevent from drying), shape each portion into an 8-inch rope. Tie each rope into a single knot; tuck top end of rope under bottom edge of roll. Place each roll on a baking sheet coated with cooking spray. Cover with plastic wrap coated with cooking spray; let rise 30 minutes or until doubled in size.

6. Preheat oven to 400°.

7. Uncover rolls. Combine 1 teaspoon water and egg in a small bowl; brush egg mixture over rolls. Combine 1 tablespoon oats, sesame seeds, and poppy seeds; sprinkle evenly over rolls. Bake at 400° for 15 minutes or until golden. Cool on wire racks. **Yield: 24 servings (serving size: 1 roll).**

CALORIES 138; FAT 2.7g (sat 0.9g, mono 0.7g, poly 0.9g); PROTEIN 4.3g; CARB 25.6g; FIBER 2.9g; CHOL 13mg; IRON 1.4mg; SODIUM 160mg; CALC 22mg

kitchen how-to: shape knots

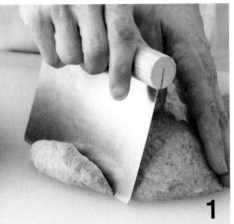

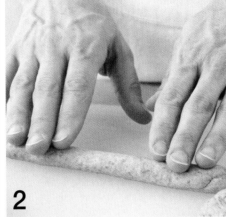

This simple variation on shape is an easy way to upgrade a regular dinner roll.

1. Divide dough in half, and cut each half into 12 equal portions.
2. Working with 1 portion at a time, shape each portion into an 8-inch rope.
3. Tie each rope into a single knot.
4. Tuck top end of rope under bottom edge of roll, and place each roll on a baking sheet coated with cooking spray.

Brioche Rolls

1 package dry yeast (about 2¼ teaspoons)
⅓ cup warm 1% low-fat milk (100° to 110°)
15.75 ounces all-purpose flour (about 3½ cups)
⅓ cup sugar
½ teaspoon salt
4 large eggs, lightly beaten
6½ tablespoons unsalted butter, softened
Cooking spray
1 tablespoon water
1 large egg white
2 tablespoons butter

1. Dissolve yeast in warm milk in the bowl of a stand mixer fitted with paddle attachment; let stand 5 minutes. Weigh or lightly spoon flour into dry measuring cups; level with a knife. Add flour, sugar, salt, and eggs to yeast mixture; beat at low speed until smooth, scraping down sides of bowl with spatula as needed. Remove paddle attachment; insert dough hook. Mix dough at low speed 5 minutes or until soft and elastic and dough just begins to pull away from sides of bowl. Cut 6½ tablespoons butter into large cubes; add half of butter to dough, mixing at medium speed to blend. Add remaining half of butter to dough; mix at medium speed until incorporated. Mix dough at medium speed 4 minutes or until smooth and elastic. Place dough in a large bowl coated with cooking spray, turning to coat top. Cover and let rise in a warm place (85°), free from drafts, 1 hour or until doubled in size. (Gently press 2 fingers into dough. If indentation remains, dough has risen enough.) Punch dough down; form into a ball. Return dough to bowl; cover with plastic wrap, and refrigerate 8 hours or overnight.

2. Uncover dough; let stand 1½ hours or until dough is at room temperature. Divide dough into 4 equal portions. Working with 1 portion at a time (cover remaining dough to prevent drying), cut dough into 6 equal pieces. Roll each piece into a 1½-inch ball. Repeat procedure with remaining 3 dough portions to make 24 rolls total. Place rolls in muffin cups coated with cooking spray. Cover and let rise 45 minutes or until almost doubled in size.

3. Preheat oven to 350°.

4. Uncover rolls. Combine 1 tablespoon water and egg white; stir with a whisk. Gently brush rolls with egg mixture. Bake at 350° for 14 minutes or until golden. Place pans on wire racks. Place 2 tablespoons butter in a microwave-safe bowl; microwave at HIGH 20 seconds or until butter melts. Brush butter onto rolls. **Yield: 24 servings (serving size: 1 roll).**

CALORIES 128; FAT 4.9g (sat 2.8g, mono 1.4g, poly 0.4g); PROTEIN 3.4g; CARB 17.2g; FIBER 0.6g; CHOL 41mg; IRON 1.1mg; SODIUM 94mg; CALC 13mg

kitchen how-to: make brioche rolls

A stand mixer streamlines the prep, and muffin tins keep portions in check. Start a day ahead, as the overnight rise helps the rolls develop texture and is essential for the bakery-fresh flavor.

1. The butter is sufficiently incorporated when the dough forms a rough mass and rides with the dough hook, pulling away from the sides of the bowl.

2. Once risen, the dough should be satiny and smooth. Gently press 2 fingers into the dough; if the indentation remains, the dough is ready.

3. Roll the dough pieces into 1½-inch balls, and place in muffin cups coated with cooking spray.

4. Gently brush the dough with egg wash to create a golden, flaky crust. Once brioche is baked, a final brush of butter ensures rich flavor in each roll.

Baked Soufganiyot

Israelis enjoy jam-filled doughnuts, called soufgani-yot (soof-GHAHN-ee-yote), during Hanukkah. The doughnuts traditionally are fried, but we bake them to trim calories. Store at room temperature for up to 2 days.

1½ teaspoons dry yeast
¾ cup warm 1% low-fat milk (100° to 110°), divided
6 tablespoons granulated sugar
1 tablespoon butter, softened
1 teaspoon grated orange rind
½ teaspoon kosher salt
½ teaspoon vanilla extract
1 large egg
14.5 ounces all-purpose flour (about 3¼ cups), divided
Cooking spray
¾ cup strawberry jam
1 tablespoon powdered sugar

1. Dissolve yeast in ½ cup warm milk in a large bowl; let stand 5 minutes or until foamy. Add remaining ¼ cup warm milk, granulated sugar, and next 5 ingredients; beat with a mixer at medium speed until blended (butter will not melt completely). Weigh or lightly spoon flour into dry measuring cups; level with a knife. Add 9 ounces (about 2 cups) flour to yeast mixture; beat at medium speed until smooth. Stir in 4.5 ounces flour (about 1 cup) to form a soft dough. Turn dough out onto a floured surface. Knead dough until smooth and elastic (about 8 minutes); add enough of remaining 1 ounce flour (about ¼ cup), 1 tablespoon at a time, to prevent dough from sticking to hands (dough will feel sticky).
2. Place dough in a large bowl coated with cooking spray, turning to coat top. Cover and let rise in a warm place (85°), free from drafts, 1 hour or until doubled in size. (Gently press 2 fingers into dough. If indentation remains, dough has risen enough.) Punch dough down; cover and let rest 5 minutes. Divide dough into 16 portions, rolling each portion into a ball.

3. Place dough balls on a large baking sheet lined with parchment paper. Cover and let rise 45 minutes or until dough is doubled in size.
4. Preheat oven to 375°.
5. Uncover dough balls. Bake at 375° for 14 minutes or until browned. Remove from pan; cool completely on a wire rack.
6. Make a pocket in each roll using handle of a wooden spoon, pushing to but not through opposite end. Fill with about 2 teaspoons jam, using a plastic condiment bottle or a piping bag. Sprinkle rolls with powdered sugar. **Yield: 16 servings (serving size: 1 roll).**

CALORIES 158; FAT 1.3g (sat 0.7g, mono 0.4g, poly 0.1g); PROTEIN 3.4g; CARB 33g; FIBER 0.7g; CHOL 1mg; IRON 1.3mg; SODIUM 74mg; CALC 17mg

kitchen how-to:
fill soufganiyot

We found that using a plastic condiment bottle (available at supermarkets and kitchen supply stores) is the easiest way to fill the doughnuts with jam.

1. Once the rolls have baked and cooled completely, make a pocket in each using the handle of a wooden spoon, pushing to but not through the opposite end.
2. Fill each roll with about 2 teaspoons jam, using a plastic condiment bottle or piping bag. Sprinkle rolls with powdered sugar.

Maple-Glazed Sour Cream Doughnut Holes

The happy truth about fried foods is that they can fit into a healthy diet if you fry in the right oil and follow our guidelines carefully.

6 tablespoons warm water (100° to 110°)
¼ cup granulated sugar
1⅛ teaspoons dry yeast
6.75 ounces all-purpose flour (about 1½ cups), divided
⅛ teaspoon salt
3 tablespoons sour cream
1 large egg, lightly beaten
Cooking spray
6 cups peanut oil
1½ cups powdered sugar
2 tablespoons maple syrup
2 tablespoons water

1. Combine first 3 ingredients in a large bowl. Let stand 5 minutes or until bubbly. Weigh or lightly spoon 5.62 ounces flour (about 1¼ cups) into dry measuring cups; level with a knife. Combine 5.62 ounces flour and salt. Add sour cream and egg to yeast mixture; stir until smooth. Add flour mixture; stir until a moist dough forms.
2. Turn dough out onto a lightly floured surface. Knead until smooth and elastic (about 3 minutes); add enough of remaining 1.13 ounces flour, 1 tablespoon at a time, to prevent dough from sticking to hands (dough will feel slightly sticky). Place dough in a clean bowl coated with cooking spray. Cover dough with plastic wrap. Let rise in a warm place (85°),

free from drafts, 1 hour or until almost doubled in size.
3. Punch dough down. Divide dough into 36 equal portions; roll each portion into a ball. Cover dough with plastic wrap coated with cooking spray; let stand 30 minutes.
4. Clip a candy thermometer onto the side of a Dutch oven; add oil to pan. Heat oil to 375°. Combine powdered sugar, syrup, and 2 tablespoons water; stir until smooth. Place 9 dough balls in hot oil; fry 2 minutes or until golden and done,

turning as needed. Make sure oil temperature remains at 375°. Remove doughnut holes from pan; drain. Dip doughnut holes into syrup mixture; remove with a slotted spoon. Drain on a wire rack over a baking sheet. Repeat procedure 3 times with remaining dough balls and syrup mixture.
Yield: 12 servings (serving size: 3 doughnut holes).

CALORIES 178; FAT 5.9g (sat 1.4g, mono 2.5g, poly 1.6g); PROTEIN 2.4g; CARB 29.3g; FIBER 0.5g; CHOL 19mg; IRON 0.9mg; SODIUM 33mg; CALC 11mg

kitchen how-to: make doughnut holes

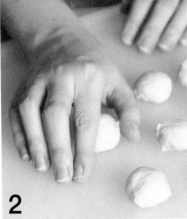

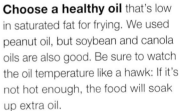

Choose a healthy oil that's low in saturated fat for frying. We used peanut oil, but soybean and canola oils are also good. Be sure to watch the oil temperature like a hawk: If it's not hot enough, the food will soak up extra oil.

1. Divide dough into 36 equal portions.
2. Roll each portion into a ball.
3. Clip a candy thermometer onto the side of a Dutch oven; add oil to pan.
4. Heat oil to 375°. Place 9 dough balls in hot oil; fry 2 minutes or until golden and done. Make sure temperature of oil remains at 375°.
5. Remove doughnut holes from oil; drain.
6. Dip doughnut holes into syrup mixture made of powdered sugar, maple syrup, and water. Remove from syrup mixture with a slotted spoon.

Bagels

1 (12-ounce) can brown beer, divided
5 cups water, divided
1 package dry yeast (about 2¼ teaspoons)
1 large egg white, lightly beaten
21.5 ounces bread flour (about 4½ cups), divided
1½ teaspoons salt
Cooking spray
1 teaspoon brown sugar
1 teaspoon stone-ground yellow cornmeal
1 teaspoon water
1 large egg yolk
1 teaspoon sesame seeds
1 teaspoon poppy seeds

1. Place ½ cup beer and 1 cup water in a small, heavy saucepan over low heat; heat mixture to between 100° and 110°. Combine beer mixture and yeast in a large bowl, stirring until yeast dissolves. Let stand 5 minutes. Stir in egg white.

2. Weigh or lightly spoon flour into dry measuring cups; level with a knife. Add 20.3 ounces flour (about 4¼ cups) and salt to beer mixture; stir until a soft dough forms. Turn dough out onto a floured surface. Knead until smooth and elastic (about 8 minutes); add enough of remaining 1.2 ounces flour (about ¼ cup), 1 tablespoon at a time, to prevent dough from sticking to hands (dough will feel sticky).

3. Place dough in a large bowl coated with cooking spray, turning to coat top. Cover and let rise in a warm place (85°), free from drafts, 1 hour and 15 minutes or until doubled in size. (Gently press 2 fingers into dough; if indentation remains, dough has risen enough.) Punch dough down; cover and let rest 5 minutes.

4. Turn dough out onto a lightly floured surface. Divide dough into 10 equal portions. Working with 1 portion at a time (cover remaining dough to prevent drying), shape each portion into a ball. Make a hole in the center of each ball using your index finger. Using fingers of both hands, gently pull dough away from center to make a 1½-inch hole. Place bagels on a baking sheet coated with cooking spray.

5. Lightly coat bagels with cooking spray; cover with plastic wrap. Let rise 10 minutes (bagels will rise only slightly).

6. Preheat oven to 400°.

7. Combine remaining beer, remaining 4 cups water, and sugar in a Dutch oven. Bring to a boil; reduce heat, and simmer. Gently lower 1 bagel into simmering beer mixture. Cook 30 seconds. Turn bagel with a slotted spoon; cook 30 seconds. Transfer bagel to a wire rack lightly coated with cooking spray. Repeat procedure with remaining bagels.

8. Place bagels on a baking sheet sprinkled with cornmeal. Combine 1 teaspoon water and egg yolk in a small bowl; stir with a fork until blended. Brush bagels with yolk mixture; sprinkle with sesame and poppy seeds.

9. Bake at 400° for 17 minutes or until golden. Transfer to a wire rack to cool. **Yield: 10 servings (serving size: 1 bagel).**

CALORIES 211; FAT 3.2g (sat 0.2g, mono 1.1g, poly 1g); PROTEIN 8.3g; CARB 40.8g; FIBER 1.6g; CHOL 20mg; IRON 2.8mg; SODIUM 357mg; CALC 11mg

kitchen how-to:
shape bagels

Divide the dough into 10 equal portions. Working with 1 portion at a time, shape each portion into a ball. Make a hole in the center of each ball using your index finger. Using fingers of both hands, gently pull the dough away from the center to make a 1½-inch hole.

Soft Pretzels

1 package dry yeast (about 2¼ teaspoons)
1½ teaspoons sugar
1 cup warm water (100° to 110°)
14.5 ounces all-purpose flour (about 3¼ cups), divided
¾ teaspoon salt
Cooking spray
6 cups water
2 tablespoons baking soda
1 teaspoon cornmeal
1 teaspoon water
1 large egg
1 teaspoon kosher salt

1. Dissolve yeast and sugar in 1 cup warm water in a large bowl; let stand 5 minutes.

2. Weigh or lightly spoon flour into dry measuring cups; level with a knife. Add 13.5 ounces flour (about 3 cups) and ¾ teaspoon salt to yeast mixture; stir until a soft dough forms. Turn dough out onto a lightly floured surface; knead until smooth and elastic (about 8 minutes). Add enough of remaining flour, 1 tablespoon at a time, to prevent dough from sticking to hands (dough will feel slightly sticky).

3. Place dough in a large bowl coated with cooking spray, turning to coat top. Cover and let rise in a warm place (85°), free from drafts, 40 minutes or until doubled in size. (Gently press 2 fingers into dough. If indentation remains, dough has risen enough.) Punch dough down; cover and let rest 5 minutes.

4. Preheat oven to 425°.

5. Divide dough into 12 equal portions. Working with 1 portion at a time (cover remaining dough to prevent drying), roll each portion into an 18-inch-long rope with tapered ends. Cross one end of rope over the other to form a circle, leaving about 4 inches at each end. Twist rope at base of circle. Fold ends over circle and into a traditional pretzel shape, pinching gently to seal. Place pretzels on a baking sheet lightly coated with cooking spray. Cover and let rise 10 minutes (pretzels will rise only slightly).

6. Combine 6 cups water and baking soda in a nonaluminum Dutch oven. Bring to a boil; reduce heat, and simmer. Gently lower 1 pretzel into simmering water mixture; cook 15 seconds. Turn pretzel with a slotted spatula; cook 15 seconds. Transfer pretzel to a wire rack coated with cooking spray. Repeat procedure with remaining pretzels.

7. Place pretzels on a baking sheet sprinkled with cornmeal. Combine 1 teaspoon water and egg in a small bowl, stirring with a fork until smooth. Brush a thin layer of egg mixture over pretzels; sprinkle with kosher salt. Bake at 425° for 12 minutes or until pretzels are deep golden brown. Transfer to a wire rack to cool. **Yield: 12 servings (serving size: 1 pretzel).**

CALORIES 140; FAT 1.5g (sat 0.2g, mono 0.5g, poly 0.5g); PROTEIN 4.3g; CARB 27.1g; FIBER 1.1g; CHOL 18mg; IRON 1.8mg; SODIUM 365mg; CALC 8mg

kitchen how-to:
shape & cook pretzels

Professional bakers dip pretzels in a lye bath to produce a chewy exterior and caramel color. For the home cook, dunking pretzels in a mixture of simmering water and baking soda yields similar toothsome results. Be sure to cover the pretzels while they rise to prevent them from deflating. For a lower-sodium option, top the pretzels with 2 teaspoons of sesame seeds instead of kosher salt.

1. Divide dough into 12 equal portions. Working with 1 portion at a time, roll each into an 18-inch-long rope with tapered ends. Cross 1 end of rope over the other to form a circle, leaving about 4 inches at each end. Twist the rope at the base of the circle.

2. Fold the ends over the circle and into a traditional pretzel shape, pinching gently to seal. Place pretzels on a baking sheet lightly coated with cooking spray. Cover and let rise 10 minutes—they'll rise only slightly.

3. Combine water and baking soda in a nonaluminum Dutch oven. Bring to a boil, reduce heat, and simmer. Gently lower 1 pretzel into the simmering water mixture; cook 15 seconds. Turn the pretzel with a slotted spoon or spatula, and cook 15 seconds. Transfer the pretzel to a wire cooling rack coated with cooking spray, and repeat the process with the remaining pretzels.

Sesame–Sea Salt Breadsticks

Fleur de sel is a popular sea salt; substitute any other type of sea salt, if you prefer. Pressed into the exterior of the breadsticks, the coarse grains add savory texture.

    ½ teaspoon sugar
    1 package dry yeast (about 2¼ teaspoons)
    1 cup warm water (100° to 110°)
  1¼ teaspoons fleur de sel, divided
 11.8 ounces all-purpose flour (about 2½ cups plus
       2 tablespoons), divided
    3 tablespoons sesame seeds, toasted
  Cooking spray
    1 tablespoon yellow cornmeal

1. Dissolve sugar and yeast in 1 cup warm water in a large bowl; let stand 5 minutes. Stir in ¼ teaspoon salt. Weigh or lightly spoon flour into dry measuring cups and spoons; level with a knife. Add 9.55 ounces flour (about 2 cups plus 2 tablespoons) and sesame seeds to yeast mixture; stir to form a soft dough. Turn dough out onto a floured surface. Knead until smooth and elastic (about 8 minutes); add enough of remaining 2.25 ounces flour (about ½ cup), 1 tablespoon at a time, to prevent dough from sticking to hands (dough will feel sticky).

2. Place dough in a large bowl coated with cooking spray, turning to coat top. Cover and let rise in a warm place (85°), free from drafts, 45 minutes or until doubled in size. (Gently press 2 fingers into dough. If indentation remains, dough has risen enough.) Punch dough down; cover and let rest 5 minutes.

3. Preheat oven to 375°.

4. Divide dough into 4 equal portions. Working with 1 portion at a time (cover remaining dough to prevent drying), roll portion into a 10 x 5–inch rectangle on a floured surface. Sprinkle with ¼ teaspoon salt; gently roll salt into dough with a rolling pin. Cut dough into 8 (10-inch-long) strips. Gently pick up both ends of each strip; gently twist dough. Place dough twists 1 inch apart on baking sheets coated with cooking spray and sprinkled with cornmeal. Repeat procedure 3 times with remaining dough and remaining ¾ teaspoon salt.

5. Bake at 375° for 12 minutes or until lightly browned on bottom. Remove from pan; cool on wire racks. **Yield: 32 breadsticks (serving size: 2 breadsticks).**

CALORIES 88; FAT 1g (sat 0.1g, mono 0.3g, poly 0.4g); PROTEIN 2.6g; CARB 16.9g; FIBER 0.9g; CHOL 0mg; IRON 1.2mg; SODIUM 181mg; CALC 6mg

kitchen how-to:
shape breadsticks

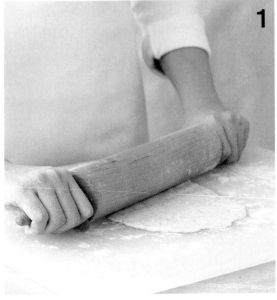

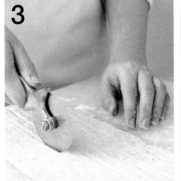

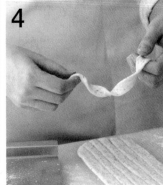

A sprinkling of cornmeal on the baking sheets adds texture to breadsticks.

1. Divide dough into 4 equal portions. Working with 1 portion at a time, roll portion into a 10 x 15–inch rectangle on a floured surface.
2. Sprinkle with ¼ teaspoon salt; gently roll salt into dough with a rolling pin.
3. Cut dough into 8 (10-inch-long) strips.
4. Gently pick up both ends of each strip; gently twist dough.
5. Place dough twists 1 inch apart on baking sheets coated with cooking spray and sprinkled with cornmeal. Repeat procedure 3 times with remaining dough and remaining ¾ teaspoon salt. Bake until lightly browned on the bottom.

kitchen how-to: make cinnamon rolls

Cinnamon rolls are a classic weekend dish. This lightened version uses fat-free milk and less butter in the dough.

1. Combine brown sugar and cinnamon.

2. Place dough on a lightly floured surface; roll dough into an 18 x 11–inch rectangle.

3. Brush melted butter over dough.

4. Sprinkle dough evenly with brown sugar mixture.

5. Beginning with a long side, roll up dough tightly, jelly-roll fashion.

6. Pinch the seam to seal. Do not seal the ends of the roll.

7. Cut roll into 1-inch slices. Arrange slices in glass or ceramic baking dishes coated with cooking spray.

You can also use a metal baking pan. Just decrease the oven temperature by 25°. Cover and let rise until doubled in size, and bake until the rolls are lightly browned.

8. Combine icing ingredients in a bowl, stirring with a whisk until smooth.

9. Spread the icing over the warm rolls, and serve immediately.

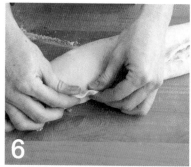

Cinnamon Rolls

Rolls:

1	cup warm fat-free milk (100° to 110°)
6	tablespoons melted butter, divided
⅓	cup granulated sugar, divided
1	package quick-rise yeast (about 2¼ teaspoons)
16.88	ounces all-purpose flour (about 3¾ cups), divided
1	large egg, lightly beaten
¼	teaspoon salt
	Cooking spray
⅔	cup packed brown sugar
1½	tablespoons ground cinnamon

Icing:

3	tablespoons butter, softened
2	tablespoons heavy cream
½	teaspoon vanilla extract
1	cup powdered sugar

1. To prepare rolls, combine milk, 3 tablespoons melted butter, 1 tablespoon granulated sugar, and yeast in a large bowl; let stand 5 minutes. Weigh or lightly spoon flour into dry measuring cups. Add egg and remaining granulated sugar to bowl. Stir in 4.5 ounces flour (1 cup); let stand 10 minutes.

2. Add 11.25 ounces flour (about 2½ cups) and salt to milk mixture; stir until a soft dough forms (dough will feel sticky). Turn out onto a lightly floured surface. Knead until smooth and elastic (about 6 minutes); add enough of remaining 1.13 ounces flour (about ¼ cup), 1 tablespoon at a time, to prevent dough from sticking to hands. Place dough in a large bowl coated with cooking spray, turning to coat top. Cover and let rise in a warm place (85°), free from drafts, 35 minutes or until doubled in size. (Gently press 2 fingers into dough. If indentation remains, dough has risen enough.) Punch dough down; cover and let rise 35 minutes or until doubled in size. Punch dough down; cover and let rest 5 minutes.

3. Combine brown sugar and cinnamon. Turn dough out onto a lightly floured surface; roll dough into an 18 x 11–inch rectangle. Brush remaining 3 tablespoons melted butter over dough; sprinkle evenly with brown sugar mixture. Beginning with a long side, roll up dough tightly, jelly-roll fashion; pinch seam to seal (do not seal ends of roll). Cut roll into 18 (1-inch) slices. Arrange 9 slices, cut sides up, in each of 2 (8-inch) square glass or ceramic baking dishes coated with cooking spray. Cover and let rise 35 minutes or until doubled in size.

4. Preheat oven to 350°.

5. Uncover rolls. Bake at 350° for 22 minutes or until lightly browned. Cool 10 minutes in dishes on a wire rack. Turn rolls out onto wire rack; cool 5 minutes. Turn rolls over.

6. To prepare icing, combine 3 tablespoons softened butter and cream; stir with a whisk. Stir in vanilla. Gradually add powdered sugar; stir until blended. Spread icing over rolls; serve warm. **Yield: 18 servings (serving size: 1 roll).**

CALORIES 234; FAT 6.8g (sat 4.1g, mono 1.8g, poly 0.4g); PROTEIN 3.8g; CARB 39.6g; FIBER 1.1g; CHOL 28mg; IRON 1.7mg; SODIUM 87mg; CALC 40mg

Hawaiian Bubble Bread

1 teaspoon sugar
1 package quick-rise yeast (about 2¼ teaspoons)
1 cup warm water (100° to 110°)
1 cup sliced ripe banana
½ cup pineapple-orange juice concentrate, undiluted
½ cup honey
2 tablespoons butter, melted
23.75 ounces bread flour (about 5 cups), divided
1 teaspoon salt
Cooking spray
¼ cup cream of coconut
2 tablespoons pineapple-orange juice concentrate, undiluted
½ cup sifted powdered sugar

1. Dissolve sugar and yeast in 1 cup warm water; let stand 5 minutes. Combine banana, ½ cup juice concentrate, honey, and butter in a blender; process until smooth, and set aside.

2. Weigh or lightly spoon flour into dry measuring cups; level with a knife. Combine 9.5 ounces flour (about 2 cups) and salt in large bowl, stirring well. Add yeast mixture and banana mixture to flour mixture, stirring until well blended. Add 13.1 ounces flour (about 2¾ cups), stirring to form a soft dough.

3. Turn dough out onto a lightly floured surface; knead until smooth and elastic (about 8 minutes). Add enough of remaining 1.15 ounces flour (about ¼ cup), 1 tablespoon at a time, to prevent dough from sticking to hands.

4. Place dough in a large bowl coated with cooking spray, turning to coat top. Cover and let rise in a warm place (85°), free from drafts, 1½ hours or until doubled in size. Punch dough down. Turn out onto a lightly floured surface; let rest 5 minutes. Form dough into 1½-inch balls (about 30 balls) on a lightly floured surface. Layer balls in a 10-inch tube pan coated with cooking spray; set aside.

5. Combine cream of coconut and 2 tablespoons juice concentrate in a small bowl; stir well. Pour 3 table-spoons juice mixture over dough; set remaining juice mixture aside. Cover dough, and let rise 1½ hours or until doubled in size.

6. Preheat oven to 350°.

7. Uncover dough, and bake at 350° for 30 minutes or until loaf sounds hollow when tapped. Cool in pan 20 minutes. Remove from pan; place on a wire rack. Stir powdered sugar into remaining juice mixture. Drizzle powdered sugar mixture over top of warm bread. **Yield: 18 servings (serving size: 1 slice).**

CALORIES 210; FAT 2.2g (sat 1.1g, mono 0.4g, poly 0.3g); PROTEIN 4.9g; CARB 43g; FIBER 1.3g; CHOL 3mg; IRON 1.8mg; SODIUM 143mg; CALC 8mg

kitchen how-to: make Hawaiian bubble bread

This irresistible sweet yeast bread is a staff favorite. Dough is shaped into balls—"bubbles"— and layered into a tube pan. Cut the bread into slices, or simply let diners pull apart the bubbles.

1. Form the dough into 1½-inch balls (about 30) on a lightly floured surface.

2. Layer the dough balls in a 10-inch tube pan coated with cooking spray.

3. Combine cream of coconut and juice concentrate in a bowl; stir well. Pour 3 tablespoons juice mixture over the dough.

4. Cover the dough, and let rise until doubled in size. Bake for 30 minutes or until the loaf sounds hollow when tapped. Cool in pan 20 minutes. Remove from pan, and place on a wire rack. Stir ½ cup powdered sugar into the remaining juice mixture, and drizzle the mixture over the top of the warm bread.

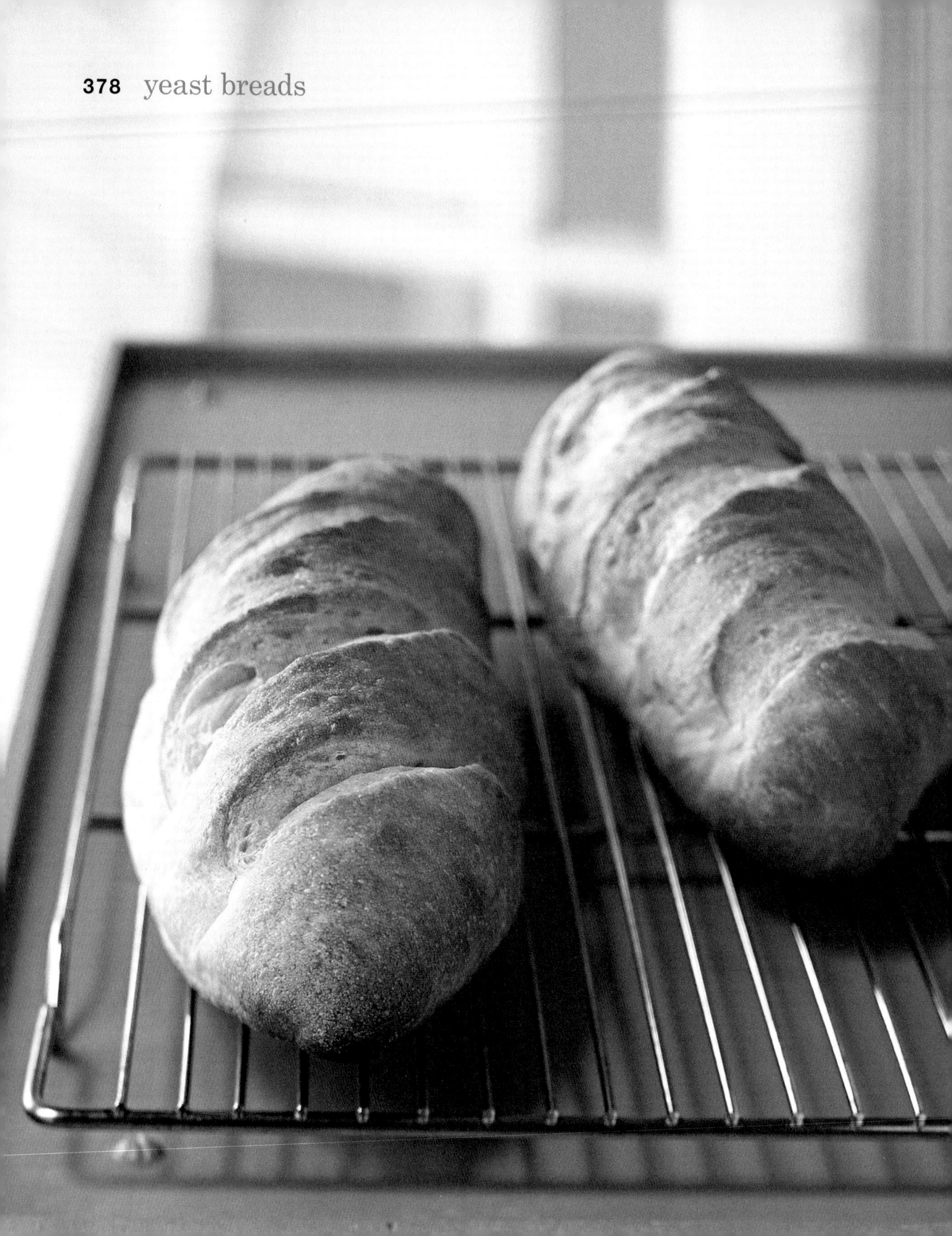

Baguettes

 1   package dry yeast (about 2¼ teaspoons)
 1¼   cups warm water (100° to 110°)
14.25   ounces bread flour (about 3 cups),
     divided
 1   teaspoon salt
Cooking spray
 1   teaspoon cornmeal

1. Dissolve yeast in 1¼ cups warm water in a large bowl; let stand 5 minutes. Weigh or lightly spoon flour into dry measuring cups; level with a knife. Add 13.1 ounces flour (about 2¾ cups) to yeast mixture; stir until a soft dough forms. Cover and let stand 15 minutes. Turn dough out onto a lightly floured surface; sprinkle evenly with salt. Knead until salt is incorporated and dough is smooth and elastic (about 6 minutes); add enough of remaining 1.15 ounces flour (about ¼ cup), 1 tablespoon at a time, to prevent dough from sticking to hands (dough will feel slightly sticky).

2. Place dough in a large bowl coated with cooking spray, turning to coat top. Cover and let rise in a warm place (85°), 40 minutes or until doubled in size. (Gently press 2 fingers into dough. If an indentation remains, dough has risen enough.)

3. Punch dough down; cover and let rest 5 minutes. Divide in half. Working with 1 portion at a time (cover remaining dough to prevent drying), roll each portion into a 12-inch rope, slightly tapered at ends, on a floured surface. Place ropes on a large baking sheet sprinkled with cornmeal. Lightly coat dough with cooking spray; cover and let rise 20 minutes or until doubled in size.

4. Preheat oven to 450°.

5. Uncover dough. Cut 3 (¼-inch-deep) diagonal slits across top of each loaf. Bake at 450° for 20 minutes or until loaves are browned on bottom and sound hollow when tapped. **Yield: 24 servings (serving size: 1 slice).**

CALORIES 53; FAT 0.2g (sat 0g, mono 0.1g, poly 0.1g); PROTEIN 2.1g; CARB 11.2g; FIBER 0.5g; CHOL 0mg; IRON 0.8mg; SODIUM 97mg; CALC 1mg

kitchen how-to: **make baguettes**

A high baking temperature, a high ratio of water to solids, and allowing the mixture of flour, yeast, and water to rest 15 minutes (a process called autolyse) produce the baguette's airy interior and crunchy crust. Autolyse allows the flour to absorb water so the dough is less sticky when you knead it, which helps keep the texture light. Don't add too much flour when kneading and shaping the dough.

1. Divide the dough in half. Roll each on a floured surface into a 12-inch rope with slightly tapered ends.

2. Place the ropes on a large baking sheet sprinkled with cornmeal.

Lightly coat the dough with cooking spray. Cover, and let rise until the dough has doubled in size.

3. Uncover the dough, and cut 3 (¼-inch-deep) diagonal slits across top of each loaf. Bake until loaves are browned on bottom and sound hollow when tapped.

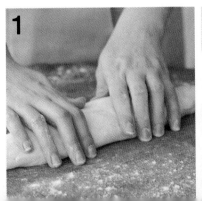

Simple White Bread

Three rises give this basic sandwich-style bread a delicate crumb and a soft texture.

  1 teaspoon sugar
  1 package dry yeast (about 2¼ teaspoons)
1¼ cups warm water (100° to 110°), divided
13.5 ounces all-purpose flour (about 3 cups)
1¼ teaspoons salt
Cooking spray
  1 large egg, lightly beaten

1. Dissolve sugar and yeast in ¼ cup warm water in a large bowl; let stand 5 minutes.
2. Weigh or lightly spoon flour into dry measuring cups; level with a knife. Add remaining 1 cup warm water, flour, and salt to yeast mixture; stir until a soft dough forms. Turn out onto a floured surface. Knead dough until smooth and elastic (about 5 minutes).
3. Place dough in a large bowl coated with cooking spray, turning to coat top. Cover and let rise in a warm place (85°), free from drafts, 45 minutes or until doubled in size. (Gently press 2 fingers into dough. If indentation remains, dough has risen enough.)
4. Uncover dough, and punch dough down. Cover and let rise 30 minutes. Uncover dough; punch dough down. Cover and let rest 10 minutes. Roll into a 14 x 7–inch rectangle on a floured surface. Roll up tightly, starting with a short edge, pressing firmly to eliminate air pockets; pinch seam and ends to seal. Place roll, seam side down, in an 8 x 4–inch loaf pan coated with cooking spray. Cover and let rise 30 minutes or until doubled in size.
5. Preheat oven to 425°.
6. Uncover dough; gently brush with egg. Bake at 425° for 12 minutes. Reduce oven temperature to 350° (do not remove bread from oven); bake an additional 15 minutes or until loaf sounds hollow when tapped. Remove from pan; cool on a wire rack.
Yield: 12 servings (serving size: 1 slice).

CALORIES 123; FAT 0.8g (sat 0.2g, mono 0.2g, poly 0.2g); PROTEIN 4g; CARB 24.5g; FIBER 1g; CHOL 18mg; IRON 1.6mg; SODIUM 253mg; CALC 7mg

kitchen how-to: prepare and use an egg wash

An egg wash creates a glossy top crust on the baked bread.

1. Lightly beat egg in a small bowl.

2. After the dough has risen and right before baking, brush the dough with the beaten egg. Be gentle; brushing the egg on the dough with a heavy hand can deflate the dough.

Whole-Wheat Bread with Caraway and Anise

Aniseed and caraway seeds give this braided bread a licorice flavor. Leave either or both of them out, if you prefer.

    2 tablespoons honey
    1 package dry yeast (about 2¼ teaspoons)
    1 cup warm water (100° to 110°)
    1 teaspoon water
    1 large egg
 10.5 ounces all-purpose flour (about 2⅓ cups), divided
  4.75 ounces whole-wheat flour (about 1 cup)
   1½ teaspoons kosher salt
    1 teaspoon caraway seeds, divided
    ½ teaspoon aniseed
       Cooking spray

1. Dissolve honey and yeast in 1 cup warm water in a large bowl; let stand 5 minutes. Combine 1 teaspoon water and egg, stirring well with a whisk. Place 1 tablespoon egg mixture in a small bowl. Cover and chill. Add remaining egg mixture to yeast mixture.
2. Weigh or lightly spoon flours into dry measuring cups; level with a knife. Add 9 ounces all-purpose flour (about 2 cups), whole-wheat flour, salt, ½ teaspoon caraway seeds, and aniseed to yeast mixture; stir to form a soft dough. Turn dough out onto a floured surface. Knead until smooth and elastic (about 10 minutes); add enough of remaining 1.5 ounces all-purpose flour (about ⅓ cup), 1 tablespoon at a time, to prevent dough from sticking to hands (dough will feel sticky).
3. Place dough in a large bowl coated with cooking spray, turning to coat top. Cover and let rise in a warm place (85°), free from drafts, 45 minutes or until doubled in size. (Gently press 2 fingers into dough. If indentation remains, dough has risen enough.) Punch dough down; cover and let rest 5 minutes. Divide dough in half. Working with 1 portion at a time, roll each portion into a 12-inch rope on a lightly floured surface. Twist ropes together, and pinch ends to seal. Place dough in an 8 x 4–inch loaf pan coated with cooking spray. Cover and let rise 30 minutes or until doubled in size.
4. Preheat oven to 375°.
5. Uncover dough. Brush reserved egg mixture over loaf, and sprinkle with remaining ½ teaspoon caraway seeds. Bake at 375° for 30 minutes or until loaf is browned and sounds hollow when tapped. Remove from pan; cool on a wire rack. **Yield: 12 servings (serving size: 1 slice).**

CALORIES 142; FAT 0.9g (sat 0.2g, mono 0.2g, poly 0.2g); PROTEIN 2.8g; CARB 29.1g; FIBER 2.1g; CHOL 18mg; IRON 1.8mg; SODIUM 243mg; CALC 12mg

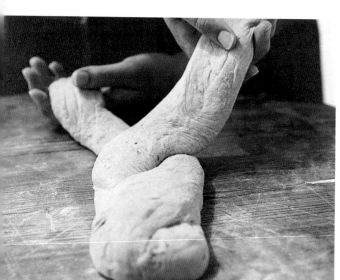

kitchen how-to: shape whole-wheat bread with caraway and anise

Divide dough in half, and roll each portion into a 12-inch rope on a lightly floured surface. Twist ropes together, and pinch ends to seal. Place dough in an 8 x 4–inch loaf pan coated with cooking spray.

Monday Morning Potato Bread and Rolls

1 cup mashed cooked peeled baking potatoes
(about 8 ounces)
1 cup fat-free milk
3 tablespoons honey
2 tablespoons butter
21.35 ounces bread flour (about 4¾ cups), divided
2½ teaspoons dry yeast
1½ teaspoons sea salt
2 large eggs
1 teaspoon olive oil
Cooking spray

1. Combine first 4 ingredients in a microwave-safe bowl.
Microwave at HIGH 2 minutes or until mixture is 110°.
Stir with a whisk until smooth.
2. Weigh or lightly spoon flour into dry measuring cups;
level with a knife. Combine 6.75 ounces flour (about
1½ cups), yeast, and salt in a large mixing bowl. Add
potato mixture to flour mixture, stirring with a fork until
combined. Add eggs; stir until combined.
3. Add 10.1 ounces flour (about 2¼ cups) to potato
mixture; stir until a soft dough forms. Turn dough out
onto a floured surface. Knead until smooth and elastic
(about 10 minutes); add enough of remaining 4.5 ounces
flour (about 1 cup), 1 tablespoon at a time, to prevent
dough from sticking to hands (dough will feel sticky).
4. Place dough in a large bowl coated with olive oil,
turning to coat top. Cover and let rise in a warm place
(85°), free from drafts, 1 hour or until doubled in size.
(Gently press 2 fingers into dough. If indentation
remains, dough has risen enough.) Punch dough down;
cover and let rest 5 minutes.
5. Divide dough in half. Working with 1 portion at a time
(cover remaining dough to prevent drying), roll each
portion into a 14 x 7–inch rectangle on a floured surface.
Roll up rectangle tightly, starting with a short edge,
pressing firmly to eliminate air pockets; pinch seam
and ends to seal. Place loaf, seam side down, in an
8 x 4–inch loaf pan coated with cooking spray.
6. Shape remaining portion into 9 portions, and shape
each into a ball. Place balls in an 8-inch square glass

or ceramic baking dish coated with cooking spray.
Coat top of loaf and rolls with cooking spray. Cover
and let rise 30 minutes or until doubled in size.
7. Preheat oven to 350°.
8. Bake at 350° for 30 minutes or until tops of rolls
are browned and loaf sounds hollow when tapped on
the bottom. Remove from pans; cool on wire racks.
Yield: 18 servings (serving size: 1 roll or ⅑ of loaf).

CALORIES 168; FAT 2.8g (sat 1.1g, mono 0.8g, poly 0.4g); PROTEIN 5.7g; CARB 30.1g;
FIBER 1.1g; CHOL 28mg; IRON 1.8mg; SODIUM 207mg; CALC 24mg

kitchen how-to:
easily measure honey
When measuring honey, molasses, or syrup,
lightly spray the inside of the measuring cups or spoons
with cooking spray to prevent sticking.

Chocolate Babka

Dough:
- 1 teaspoon granulated sugar
- 1 package dry yeast (about 2¼ teaspoons)
- ¾ cup warm 1% low-fat milk (105° to 110°)
- 6 tablespoons granulated sugar
- ½ teaspoon vanilla extract
- ¼ teaspoon salt
- 1 large egg yolk, lightly beaten
- 7.5 ounces all-purpose flour (about 1⅔ cups), divided
- 5.58 ounces bread flour (about 1¼ cups)
- 5 tablespoons butter, cut into pieces and softened
- Cooking spray

Filling:
- ½ cup granulated sugar
- 3 tablespoons unsweetened cocoa
- ½ teaspoon ground cinnamon
- ¼ teaspoon salt
- 4 ounces semisweet chocolate, finely chopped

Streusel:
- 2 tablespoons powdered sugar
- 1 tablespoon all-purpose flour
- 1 tablespoon butter, softened

1. To prepare dough, dissolve 1 teaspoon granulated sugar and yeast in warm milk in the bowl of a stand mixer with dough hook attached; let stand 5 minutes. Stir in 6 tablespoons granulated sugar, vanilla, ¼ teaspoon salt, and egg yolk. Weigh or lightly spoon flours into dry measuring cups; level with a knife. Add 6 ounces (about 1⅓ cups) all-purpose flour and bread flour to milk mixture; mix at medium speed until well blended (about 2 minutes). Add 5 tablespoons butter, beating until well blended. Scrape dough out onto a floured surface (dough will be very sticky). Knead until smooth and elastic (about 10 minutes); add remaining 1.5 ounces all-purpose flour (about ⅓ cup), 1 tablespoon at a time, to prevent dough from sticking to hands (dough will be very soft).

2. Place dough in a large bowl coated with cooking spray, turning to coat top. Cover and let rise in a warm place (85°), free from drafts, 1½ hours or until doubled in size. (Gently press 2 fingers into dough. If indentation remains, dough has risen enough.) Punch dough down; cover and let dough rest 5 minutes.

3. Line bottom of a 9 x 5–inch loaf pan with parchment paper; coat sides of pan with cooking spray.

4. To prepare filling, combine ½ cup granulated sugar, cocoa, cinnamon, ¼ teaspoon salt, and chocolate in a medium bowl; set aside.

5. Place dough on a generously floured surface; roll dough into a 16-inch square. Sprinkle filling over dough, leaving a ¼-inch border around edges. Roll up dough tightly, jelly-roll fashion; pinch seam and ends to seal. Holding dough by ends, twist dough 4 times as if wringing out a towel. Fit dough into prepared pan. Cover and let rise 45 minutes or until doubled in size.

6. Preheat oven to 350°.

7. To prepare streusel, combine powdered sugar, 1 tablespoon all-purpose flour, and 1 tablespoon softened butter, stirring with a fork until mixture is crumbly; sprinkle streusel evenly over dough. Bake at 350° for 40 minutes or until loaf is browned on bottom and sounds hollow when tapped. Cool bread in pan 10 minutes on a wire rack; remove from pan. Cool bread completely on wire rack before slicing.

Yield: 16 servings (serving size: 1 slice).

CALORIES 220; FAT 7.1g (sat 4.3g, mono 2g, poly 0.5g); PROTEIN 4.1g; CARB 36g; FIBER 1.5g; CHOL 25mg; IRON 1.4mg; SODIUM 111mg; CALC 23mg

kitchen how-to: shape beautiful babka

To get a jump-start on baking, roll out the dough, fill, shape, and refrigerate overnight in the pan. It will rise to the top of the pan in the refrigerator, and then the next morning you can let it come to room temperature, top with the streusel, and bake as directed.

1. Roll the dough into a square, and sprinkle with the filling almost to the outside edges. It's OK if some of the filling leaks out as you shape the bread—that'll make it prettier.

2. Twist the dough 4 times as if wringing out a towel, but with a lighter touch. This creates an interior spiral that distributes the chocolate filling in a beautiful pattern.

3. Fit the dough into the prepared pan; it may be a tight squeeze, but rest assured that any lumps or bumps will create interest once baked.

4. Sprinkle the top of the dough with buttery streusel for added texture and flavor.

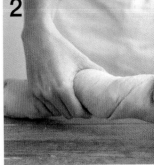

Sweet Challah

Allowing the dough to rise three times gives the yeast more time to develop, resulting in a rich, complex flavor. Although this bread is best eaten the day it's made, you can also bake it 1 day in advance.

    1   package dry yeast (about 2¼ teaspoons)
    1   cup warm water (100° to 110°)
    3   tablespoons honey
Dash of crushed saffron threads
    3   tablespoons butter, melted and cooled
    1   teaspoon salt
    1   large egg
14.25   ounces bread flour (about 3 cups), divided
Cooking spray
    1   teaspoon cornmeal
    1   teaspoon water
    1   large egg yolk, lightly beaten
    ¼   teaspoon poppy seeds

1. Dissolve yeast in 1 cup warm water in a large bowl; stir in honey and saffron threads. Let stand 5 minutes. Add melted butter, salt, and egg; stir well with a whisk.
2. Weigh or lightly spoon flour into dry measuring cups; level with a knife. Add 13.1 ounces flour (about 2¾ cups) to yeast mixture, and stir until a soft dough forms. Cover and let stand 15 minutes.
3. Turn dough out onto a lightly floured surface. Knead until smooth and elastic (about 8 minutes); add enough of remaining 1.15 ounces flour (about ¼ cup), 1 tablespoon at a time, to prevent dough from sticking to hands (dough will be very soft).
4. Place dough in a large bowl coated with cooking spray, turning to coat top. Cover and let rise in a warm place (85°), free from drafts, 40 minutes or until doubled in size. (Gently press 2 fingers into dough. If indentation remains, the dough has risen enough.)
5. Punch dough down. Shape dough into a ball; return to bowl. Cover and let rise 40 minutes or until doubled in size. Punch dough down; cover and let rest 15 minutes.
6. Divide dough into 3 equal portions. Working with 1 portion at a time (cover remaining dough to prevent drying), on a lightly floured surface, roll each portion into a 25-inch rope with slightly tapered ends. Place ropes lengthwise on a large baking sheet sprinkled with cornmeal; pinch ends together at untapered ends to seal. Braid ropes; pinch loose ends to seal. Cover and let rise 20 minutes or until almost doubled in size.
7. Preheat oven to 375°.
8. Combine 1 teaspoon water and egg yolk, stirring with a fork until blended. Uncover dough, and gently brush with egg yolk mixture. Sprinkle evenly with poppy seeds. Bake at 375° for 30 minutes or until loaf sounds hollow when tapped. Cool on a wire rack. **Yield: 12 servings (serving size: 1 slice).**

CALORIES 157; FAT 4.1g (sat 2.1g, mono 1.2g, poly 0.4g); PROTEIN 5g; CARB 26.9g; FIBER 0.9g; CHOL 42mg; IRON 1.7mg; SODIUM 202mg; CALC 7mg

kitchen how-to: shape challah

Divide the dough into 3 equal portions.
Working on a lightly floured surface, roll each portion into a 25-inch rope with slightly tapered ends. Place ropes lengthwise on a large baking sheet sprinkled with cornmeal; pinch ends together at untapered ends to seal. Braid ropes; pinch loose ends to seal. Cover and let rise 20 minutes or until almost doubled in size.

Swedish Saffron Bread

Traditionally served in Sweden on December 13 to commemorate St. Lucia, this light, rich-tasting bread is great anytime and makes a fitting accompaniment for breakfast or brunch.

    1   cup hot water
    ½   cup golden raisins
    ¼   cup dried currants
    ¼   cup sugar, divided
    ½   teaspoon saffron threads, crushed
    1   package dry yeast (about 2¼ teaspoons)
    1   cup warm 2% reduced-fat milk (100° to 110°)
    15 ounces all-purpose flour (about 3⅓ cups),
        divided
    1   teaspoon salt
    ½   teaspoon ground cinnamon
    3   tablespoons butter, melted
    2   large eggs, divided
    Cooking spray

1. Combine 1 cup hot water, raisins, and currants in a bowl. Cover and let stand 10 minutes or until raisins and currants plump. Drain and set aside.
2. Dissolve 1 tablespoon sugar, saffron threads, and yeast in warm milk in a small bowl; let stand 5 minutes. Weigh or lightly spoon flour into dry measuring cups; level with a knife. Combine 13.5 ounces flour (about 3 cups), remaining 3 tablespoons sugar, salt, and cinnamon in a large bowl. Add raisins, currants, yeast mixture, butter, and 1 egg to flour mixture; stir until dough forms.
3. Turn dough out onto a lightly floured surface. Knead until smooth and elastic (about 10 minutes); add enough of remaining 1.5 ounces flour (about ⅓ cup), 1 tablespoon at a time, to prevent dough from sticking to hands.
4. Place dough in a large bowl coated with cooking spray, turning to coat top. Cover and let rise in a warm place (85°), free from drafts, 1 hour or until doubled in size. (Gently press 2 fingers into dough. If indentation remains, dough has risen enough.) Punch dough down. Turn out onto a lightly floured surface; knead 3 times.

5. Divide dough into 3 equal portions, shaping each portion into a 16-inch rope. Place ropes lengthwise on a baking sheet coated with cooking spray (do not stretch); pinch ends together at 1 end to seal. Braid ropes; pinch loose ends to seal. Cover and let rise 1 hour or until doubled in size.
6. Preheat oven to 375°.
7. Lightly beat remaining egg in a small bowl. Gently brush dough with egg. Bake at 375° for 25 minutes or until loaf sounds hollow when tapped. Remove from pan; cool on a wire rack. **Yield: 16 servings (serving size: 1 slice).**

CALORIES 164; FAT 3.4g (sat 1.8g, mono 0.9g, poly 0.3g); PROTEIN 4.4g; CARB 29.3g; FIBER 1.2g; CHOL 33mg; IRON 1.6mg; SODIUM 180mg; CALC 32mg

all about saffron

Saffron has a luminous red-orange color, a delicate bittersweet flavor, and a honeylike fragrance. Saffron is sold as threads or a powder. The powder releases its aroma and flavor immediately when added to a dish, but it may have additives such as the plant's yellow stamen and turmeric. The flavor of powdered saffron diminishes after 3 to 6 months. Saffron threads last longer. When they are soaked in hot water, broth, or milk, or room-temperature alcoholic or acidic liquids, these threads release flavor and aroma for up to 24 hours; they also tinge dishes a characteristic golden hue. Look for saffron packaged in a glass jar or vials or a sealed plastic container. Small quantities should suffice and will not grow stale before they're used. Stored tightly sealed in a cool, dark place, saffron threads retain their flavor for up for 2 years.

Classic Walnut Boule

- 3 tablespoons sugar
- 1 package dry yeast (2¼ teaspoons)
- 1 cup warm water (100° to 110°)
- 1 tablespoon toasted walnut oil
- 10.7 ounces bread flour (about 2¼ cups), divided
- 4.75 ounces whole-wheat flour (about 1 cup)
- 1½ teaspoons salt
- Cooking spray
- ½ cup coarsely chopped walnuts, toasted
- 2 tablespoons yellow cornmeal
- 1 tablespoon fat-free milk
- 1 large egg white

1. Dissolve sugar and yeast in 1 cup warm water in a large bowl; let stand 5 minutes. Stir in oil. Weigh or lightly spoon flours into dry measuring cups; level with a knife. Add 9.5 ounces bread flour (about 2 cups), whole-wheat flour, and salt to yeast mixture; stir until a soft dough forms. Turn dough out onto a lightly floured surface. Knead until dough is smooth and elastic (about 5 minutes); add enough of remaining 1.2 ounces bread flour (about ¼ cup), 1 tablespoon at a time, to prevent dough from sticking to hands (dough will feel sticky).
2. Place dough in a large bowl coated with cooking spray, turning to coat top. Cover and let rise in a warm place (85°), free from drafts, 1 hour or until doubled in size. (Gently press 2 fingers into dough. If indentation remains, dough has risen enough.) Punch dough down; knead in walnuts. Shape dough into a 9-inch round on a lightly floured surface. Place dough on a large baking sheet sprinkled with cornmeal. Cover and let rise 1 hour or until doubled in size.
3. Preheat oven to 350°.
4. Uncover dough. Combine milk and egg white; brush over dough. Score dough by making 2 diagonal slits with a sharp knife; make 2 diagonal slits in the opposite direction to create a crosshatch pattern. Bake at 350° for 30 minutes or until loaf is browned on bottom and sounds hollow when tapped. Cool on a wire rack. **Yield: 16 servings (serving size: 1 slice).**

CALORIES 122; FAT 3.4g (sat 0.3g, mono 0.6g, poly 2.3g); PROTEIN 4.1g; CARB 20.3g; FIBER 1.7g; CHOL 0mg; IRON 1.2mg; SODIUM 226mg; CALC 8mg

kitchen how-to:
shape boule

Boule, the French word for "ball," often refers to round loaves of crusty bread. You can use any leftovers to make sandwiches for lunch, or simply toast a slice, slather it with butter or jam, and enjoy it for breakfast.

1. Shape dough into a 9-inch round on a lightly floured surface.
2. Place dough on a large baking sheet sprinkled with cornmeal. Cover and let rise until doubled in size.
3. Uncover dough. Combine milk and egg white, and brush over dough.
4. Score the dough by making 2 diagonal slits with a sharp knife. Make 2 diagonal slits in the opposite direction to create a crosshatch pattern. The purpose of scoring is to control where and how the bread will expand as it bakes. Intentionally creating a break in the surface of the dough prevents the bread from bursting at any weak spots created while shaping the loaf.

Moroccan Country Bread

1½ packages dry yeast (about 1 tablespoon)
2½ cups warm water (100° to 110°)
31.5 ounces all-purpose flour (about 7 cups) plus 2 teaspoons, divided
2 teaspoons kosher salt
Cooking spray
1 tablespoon extra-virgin olive oil

1. Dissolve yeast in 2½ cups warm water in a large bowl. Weigh or lightly spoon flour into dry measuring cups; level with a knife. Stir salt into yeast mixture. Gradually stir in 31.5 ounces flour (about 7 cups), 1 cup at a time; beat with a mixer at medium speed until dough forms a ball. Turn dough out onto a lightly floured surface; shape dough into a 12-inch log. Divide dough into 3 pieces; shape each piece into a 4-inch dome-shaped loaf. Place loaves on a baking sheet lightly dusted with flour; dust tops lightly with 2 teaspoons flour, and lightly coat with cooking spray. Cover and let rise in a warm place (85°), free from drafts, 1 hour or until doubled in size. (Gently press 2 fingers into dough. If indentation remains, dough has risen enough.)

2. Position oven rack in lower third of oven. Preheat oven to 350°.

3. Uncover loaves, and brush each with 1 teaspoon oil. Bake at 350° for 30 minutes or until loaves sound hollow when tapped (bread doesn't brown). Remove from oven; cool on wire racks. **Yield: 24 servings (serving size: ⅛ of a loaf).**

CALORIES 139; FAT 0.9g (sat 0.1g, mono 0.5g, poly 0.2g); PROTEIN 4g; CARB 28g; FIBER 1.1g; CHOL 0mg; IRON 1.8mg; SODIUM 161mg; CALC 6mg

kitchen how-to: make Moroccan country bread

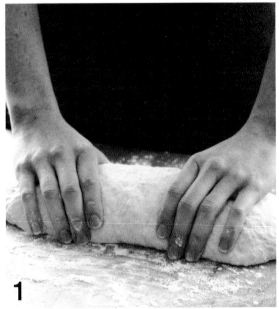

1

2

Many Moroccan home cooks prepare and bake bread every morning to serve at meals throughout the day. These plain, rustic loaves are a good accompaniment to tagines, and a slice makes a tasty scoop for eating a carrot or beet salad. This dough is deliberately not kneaded to help achieve the characteristic coarse texture. Though it's best eaten the day it's made, you can also freeze the bread for up to 1 month; thaw at room temperature, wrap in foil, and reheat at 300° for 15 minutes.

3

4

1. Turn dough out onto a lightly floured surface, and shape into a 12-inch log.
2. Divide dough into 3 pieces.
3. Shape each piece into a 4-inch dome-shaped loaf.
4. Place loaves on a baking sheet lightly dusted with flour; dust tops lightly with 2 teaspoons flour, and lightly coat with cooking spray. Cover and let rise until doubled in size.
5. Uncover loaves, and brush each with 1 teaspoon oil. Bake until the loaves sound hollow when tapped—this bread doesn't brown.

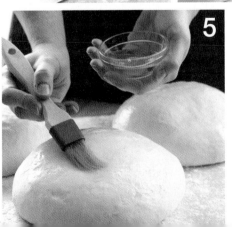

5

Ciabatta

Sponge:

4.75	ounces bread flour (about 1 cup)
½	cup warm fat-free milk (100° to 110°)
¼	cup warm water (100° to 110°)
1	tablespoon honey
1	package dry yeast (about 2¼ teaspoons)

Dough:

16.6	ounces bread flour (about 3½ cups), divided
3.13	ounces semolina flour (about ½ cup)
¾	cup warm water (100° to 110°)
½	cup warm fat-free milk (100° to 110°)
1½	teaspoons salt
1	package dry yeast (about 2¼ teaspoons)
3	tablespoons semolina flour, divided

1. To prepare sponge, weigh or lightly spoon 4.75 ounces bread flour (about 1 cup) into a dry measuring cup; level with a knife. Combine 4.75 ounces flour and next 4 ingredients in a large bowl, stirring well with a whisk. Cover; chill 12 hours.
2. To prepare dough, let sponge stand at room temperature 30 minutes. Weigh or lightly spoon 16.6 ounces bread flour (about 3½ cups) and 3.13 ounces semolina flour (about ½ cup) into dry measuring cups; level with a knife. Add 14.2 ounces bread flour (about 3 cups), 3.13 ounces semolina flour, ¾ cup warm water, ½ cup warm milk, salt, and 1 package yeast to sponge, and stir well to form a soft dough. Turn dough out onto a floured surface. Knead until smooth and elastic (about 8 minutes). Add enough of remaining 2.4 ounces bread flour (about ½ cup), 1 tablespoon at a time, to prevent dough from sticking to hands. Divide dough in half.
3. Working with 1 portion at a time (cover remaining dough to prevent drying), roll each into a 13 x 5–inch oval on a lightly floured surface. Place 3 inches apart on a large baking sheet sprinkled with 2 tablespoons semolina flour. Taper ends of each loaf to form a "slipper." Sprinkle 1 tablespoon semolina flour over dough. Cover and let rise in a warm place (85°), free from drafts, 45 minutes or until doubled in size.

4. Preheat oven to 425°.
5. Uncover dough. Bake at 425° for 18 minutes or until loaves are lightly browned and sound hollow when tapped. Remove from pan, and cool on a wire rack. **Yield: 16 servings (serving size: 1 slice).**

CALORIES 150; FAT 0.1g (sat 0g, mono 0.1g, poly 0g); PROTEIN 6.3g; CARB 32.1g; FIBER 1.3g; CHOL 0mg; IRON 2.1mg; SODIUM 227mg; CALC 21mg

kitchen how-to:
make a sponge

Most yeast breads made without a sponge have two rises—one after they're mixed and another after they're shaped. Yeast breads made with a sponge have a tremendous yeast flavor that is difficult to achieve in breads that have risen only twice.

1. Traditional sponges combine flour, water, and yeast—you can add milk or additional flavorings, such as honey. Combine ingredients in a bowl, stirring well with a whisk.
2. Cover and chill 12 hours. Letting the sponge rest 12 hours adds complex flavor and texture.

Fig and Mascarpone Focaccia

  1 teaspoon honey
  1 package dry yeast (about 2¼ teaspoons)
1¼ cups warm water (100° to 110°), divided
  2 tablespoons olive oil
14.6 ounces all-purpose flour (about 3¼ cups),
    divided
  1 teaspoon kosher salt, divided
Cooking spray
  ¼ cup (2 ounces) mascarpone cheese
  3 dried figs, quartered
  ½ teaspoon olive oil

1. Dissolve honey and yeast in ½ cup warm water in a large bowl; let stand 10 minutes. Add remaining ¾ cup warm water and 2 tablespoons oil; stir until blended. Weigh or lightly spoon flour into dry measuring cups; level with a knife. Add 12.35 ounces flour (about 2¾ cups) and ½ teaspoon salt to yeast mixture; stir until blended. Turn dough out onto a floured surface. Knead until smooth and elastic (about 10 minutes); add enough of remaining 2.25 ounces flour (about ½ cup), 1 table-spoon at a time, to prevent dough from sticking to hands (dough will feel sticky).

2. Place dough in a large bowl coated with cooking spray, turning to coat top. Cover and let rise in a warm place (85°), free from drafts, 1 hour or until doubled in size. (Gently press 2 fingers into dough. If indentation remains, dough has risen enough.)

3. Punch dough down. Place dough in a 13 x 9–inch metal baking pan coated with cooking spray. Pat dough to fit pan. Cover and let rise 30 minutes. Uncover dough. Make indentations in top of dough using the handle of a wooden spoon or fingertips. Cover and let rise 45 minutes or until doubled in size.

4. Preheat oven to 400°.

5. Uncover dough. Spoon small dollops of cheese over dough. Gently spread cheese over dough. Sprinkle fig quarters evenly over cheese. Drizzle ½ teaspoon oil over dough. Sprinkle with ¼ teaspoon salt. Bake at 400° for 23 minutes or until loaf is browned on bottom and sounds hollow when tapped. Sprinkle with remaining ¼ teaspoon salt. Serve warm or at room temperature.

Yield: 14 servings (serving size: 1 piece).

CALORIES 155; FAT 4.3g (sat 1.4g, mono 2.2g, poly 0.3g); PROTEIN 3.6g; CARB 25.5g; FIBER 1.4g; CHOL 5mg; IRON 1.5mg; SODIUM 138mg; CALC 15mg

kitchen how-to:
make focaccia

Focaccia is dimpled after its first rise, giving it its characteristic appearance. This dimpling is done to relieve bubbling on the surface of the bread and to catch olive oil that's drizzled or brushed on before baking. After the dough has risen once, use the handle of a wooden spoon or your fingertips to make indentations across the surface of the dough.

kitchen how-to:
make naan

Naan, one of the daily breads of India, is dense and chewy, almost like focaccia but thinner. If you don't have a pizza peel, use the back of a baking sheet to transfer the dough to a hot pizza stone. You can also bake naan on a heavy baking sheet lined with parchment paper.

1. After mixing the dough and letting the dough rise for the first time, the batter will be bubbly, lacy, and weblike.
2. Stir in salt and oil, and add the bread flour, ½ cup at a time.
3. Stir with a wooden spoon. The dough will become very difficult to stir. Turn dough out onto a lightly floured surface; knead until smooth and elastic (about 10 minutes); add bread flour, 1 tablespoon at a time, to prevent the dough from sticking to your hands (the dough will feel sticky).
4. Place dough in a bowl coated with cooking spray. Cover and let rise until doubled in size. Punch the dough down, and turn out onto a lightly floured surface. Cover and let rest 5 minutes. Divide dough into 8 equal portions. Working with 1 portion at a time (cover remaining dough to keep from drying), stretch each portion into a 6-inch oval. Cover and let rest 5 minutes.
5. Make indentations in the top of each dough portion using the handle of a wooden spoon or your fingertips; cover and let rise 20 minutes. Bake until lightly browned.

Naan

    1   teaspoon dry yeast
    ¾   cup warm water (100° to 110°)
    ½   cup plain low-fat yogurt
10.75   ounces bread flour (about 2¼ cups), divided
 4.75   ounces whole-wheat flour (about 1 cup)
    1¼   teaspoons sea salt
    1   tablespoon olive oil
Cooking spray
    ¼   cup cornmeal, divided

1. Dissolve yeast in ¾ cup warm water in a large bowl; let stand 5 minutes. Stir in yogurt. Weigh or lightly spoon flours into dry measuring cups; level with a knife. Add 2.4 ounces bread flour (about ½ cup) and whole-wheat flour to yeast mixture; stir with a whisk until smooth. Cover and let rise in a warm place (85°), free from drafts, 2 hours (batter will be bubbly, lacy, and weblike).
2. Stir in salt and oil. Add 7.1 ounces bread flour (about 1½ cups), ½ cup at a time; stir with a wooden spoon (dough will become very difficult to stir).
3. Turn dough out onto a lightly floured surface. Knead until smooth and elastic (about 10 minutes); add enough of remaining 1.25 ounces bread flour (about ¼ cup), 1 tablespoon at a time, to prevent dough from sticking to hands (dough will feel sticky). Place dough in a large bowl coated with cooking spray, turning to coat top. Cover and let rise in a warm place (85°), free from drafts, 2 hours or until doubled in size. (Gently press 2 fingers into dough. If indentation remains, dough has risen enough.)
4. Place pizza stone on bottom rack in oven. Preheat oven to 500°. Punch dough down; turn out onto a lightly floured surface. Cover and let rest 5 minutes.
5. Divide dough into 8 equal portions. Working with 1 portion at a time (cover remaining dough to keep from drying), stretch each portion into a 6-inch oval. Cover and let rest 5 minutes.
6. Make indentations in top of dough portions using the handle of a wooden spoon or your fingertips; cover and let rise 20 minutes.
7. Place 2 dough portions on the back of a pizza peel dusted with 1 tablespoon cornmeal. Slide onto preheated pizza stone or baking sheet lined with parchment paper. Bake at 500° for 6 minutes or until lightly browned. Repeat with remaining dough and cornmeal. Serve immediately. **Yield: 8 servings (serving size: 1 naan).**

CALORIES 216; FAT 2.9g (sat 0.5g, mono 1.4g, poly 0.6g); PROTEIN 7.5g; CARB 40.4g; FIBER 3.1g; CHOL 1mg; IRON 2.4mg; SODIUM 371mg; CALC 39mg

pizza dough

Homemade pizza dough is one of the most satisfying and easiest recipes to cook at home. Plus, there's comfort in knowing that your pizza is impeccably fresh and a lot healthier than delivery.

Pizza Margherita

- 1 cup warm water (100° to 110°), divided
- 10 ounces bread flour (about 2 cups plus 2 tablespoons)
- 1 package dry yeast (about 2¼ teaspoons)
- 4 teaspoons olive oil
- ½ teaspoon kosher salt
- Cooking spray
- 1 tablespoon yellow cornmeal
- ¾ cup Basic Pizza Sauce or prepared pizza sauce
- 1¼ cups (5 ounces) thinly sliced fresh mozzarella cheese
- ⅓ cup small fresh basil leaves

1. Pour ¾ cup warm water into bowl of a stand mixer with dough hook attached. Weigh or lightly spoon flour into dry measuring cups and spoons; level with a knife. Add flour to ¾ cup warm water; mix until combined. Cover and let stand 20 minutes. Combine remaining ¼ cup warm water and yeast in a small bowl; let stand 5 minutes or until bubbly. Add yeast mixture, oil, and ½ teaspoon salt to flour mixture; mix 5 minutes or until a soft dough forms. Place dough in a large bowl coated with cooking spray; cover surface of dough with plastic wrap lightly coated with cooking spray. Refrigerate 24 hours.

2. Remove dough from refrigerator. Let stand, covered, 1 hour or until dough comes to room temperature. Punch dough down. Press dough out to a 12-inch circle on a lightly floured baking sheet without raised sides, sprinkled with cornmeal. Crimp edges to form a ½-inch border. Cover dough loosely with plastic wrap.

3. Position an oven rack in the lowest setting. Place a pizza stone on lowest rack. Preheat oven to 550°. Preheat pizza stone 30 minutes before baking dough.

4. Remove plastic wrap from dough. Spread sauce evenly over dough, leaving a ½-inch border. Arrange cheese evenly over pizza. Slide pizza onto preheated pizza stone, using a spatula as a guide. Bake at 550° for 11 minutes or until crust is golden. Sprinkle evenly with basil. **Yield: 5 servings (serving size: 2 wedges).**

CALORIES 421; FAT 10.9g (sat 4.7g, mono 4.7g, poly 1g); PROTEIN 16.9g; CARB 62.8g; FIBER 6.5g; CHOL 22mg; IRON 4.4mg; SODIUM 658mg; CALC 267mg

Basic Pizza Sauce

- 2 tablespoons extra-virgin olive oil
- 5 garlic cloves, minced
- 1 (28-ounce) can San Marzano tomatoes
- ½ teaspoon kosher salt
- ½ teaspoon dried oregano

1. Heat oil in a medium saucepan over medium heat. Add garlic to pan; cook 1 minute, stirring frequently. Remove tomatoes from can using a slotted spoon, reserving juice. Crush tomatoes. Stir tomatoes, juice, salt, and oregano into garlic mixture; bring to a boil. Reduce heat, and simmer 30 minutes, stirring occasionally. **Yield: 6 servings (serving size: about ⅓ cup).**

CALORIES 66; FAT 4.7g (sat 0.7g, mono 3.3g, poly 0.6g); PROTEIN 1.2g; CARB 6.2g; FIBER 1.4g; CHOL 0mg; IRON 1.4mg; SODIUM 175mg; CALC 48mg

all about **pizza dough**

Pizza crusts come in many forms—cracker thin, medium, and thick crusts. Homemade crusts do slow down the process a little, but you can make them the night before or freeze them so that cooking time can actually be quite quick. If you make the dough ahead, let it rest for 24 hours, and then

freeze it in a zip-top plastic freezer bag. To defrost, put it back in the refrigerator overnight. Once the dough is thawed, proceed with the recipe from the step that calls for removing the dough from the refrigerator to bringing it to room temperature. If you can't make homemade dough, store-bought pizza dough can be a quick substitute, and our toppings will work on those crusts. Refrigerated canned dough and fresh pizza dough are available in the bakery section in many supermarkets. You can also sometimes buy dough from pizzerias— check out the local ones rather than big-name chains.

Pepperoni Deep-Dish Pizza

 1 cup warm water (100° to 110°), divided
12 ounces bread flour (about 2½ cups)
 1 package dry yeast (about 2¼ teaspoons)
 4 teaspoons olive oil
 ½ teaspoon kosher salt
    Cooking spray
1¼ cups (5 ounces) shredded part-skim mozzarella
    cheese, divided
1½ cups Basic Pizza Sauce (page 403) or prepared
    pizza sauce
 2 ounces pepperoni slices
 2 tablespoons grated Parmigiano-Reggiano
    cheese

1. Pour ¾ cup warm water into the bowl of a stand mixer with dough hook attached. Weigh or lightly spoon flour into dry measuring cups; level with a knife. Add flour to ¾ cup warm water; mix until combined. Cover and let stand 20 minutes. Combine remaining ¼ cup water and yeast in a small bowl; let stand 5 minutes or until bubbly. Add yeast mixture, oil, and salt to flour mixture; mix 5 minutes or until a soft dough forms. Place dough in a large bowl coated with cooking spray; cover surface of dough with plastic wrap lightly coated with cooking spray. Refrigerate 24 hours.

2. Remove dough from refrigerator. Let stand, covered, 1 hour or until dough comes to room temperature. Punch dough down. Roll into a 14 x 11–inch rectangle on a lightly floured surface. Press dough into bottom and partially up sides of a 13 x 9–inch metal baking pan coated with cooking spray. Cover dough loosely with plastic wrap.

3. Place a baking sheet on bottom rack in oven. Preheat oven to 450°.

4. Arrange ¾ cup mozzarella evenly over dough, and top with Basic Pizza Sauce, pepperoni, Parmigiano-Reggiano, and remaining ½ cup mozzarella. Place pan on baking sheet in oven; bake at 450° for 25 minutes or until crust is golden. Cut pizza into 6 rectangles. **Yield: 6 servings (serving size: 1 rectangle).**

CALORIES 404; FAT 16.3g (sat 5.9g, mono 7.8g, poly 1.5g); PROTEIN 16.9g; CARB 47.1g; FIBER 2.7g; CHOL 26mg; IRON 3.9mg; SODIUM 607mg; CALC 244mg

all about Chicago-style pizza

Chicago-style pizza has a thick, bready, chewy crust, meaty toppings, and loads of tomato sauce—it's a knife, fork, and two napkins kind of pie. You need more dough, so use more flour. Roll it into shape with a rolling pin, creating a denser crust texture. This style pizza is defined by a layer of cheese on top of the dough, then meat and veggie toppings, and then tomato sauce. This has a practical advantage: Because the dough cooks longer and at a lower temperature than other styles of pizza, separating the dough from the sauce with a layer of cheese helps keep the crust from becoming soggy. For eye appeal, we also layered some pepperoni and extra cheese on top. Cook it in a baking pan set atop a preheated baking sheet, which helps the bottom of the crust to crisp.

calzones

Calzones are extremely versatile. You can use whatever fillings you like—shredded chicken, ground turkey or beef, and an assortment of vegetables and cheeses. The combinations are virtually limitless.

Chicken and Basil Calzones

Ground chicken breast is a lean alternative to beef. Substitute ground sirloin, if you prefer.

Cooking spray
2 garlic cloves, minced
1 pound ground chicken breast
¾ cup lower-sodium prepared pizza sauce
¼ teaspoon crushed red pepper
¼ cup chopped fresh basil
1 (13.8-ounce) can refrigerated pizza crust dough
½ cup (2 ounces) shredded part-skim mozzarella cheese

1. Preheat oven to 425°.
2. Heat a large nonstick skillet over medium-high heat. Coat pan with cooking spray. Add garlic and chicken to pan; sauté 5 minutes or until chicken is no longer pink, stirring to crumble. Stir in pizza sauce and pepper. Reduce heat, and simmer 5 minutes, stirring occasionally. Remove from heat; stir in basil. Let stand 10 minutes.
3. Roll out dough on a lightly floured surface; cut dough into quarters. Pat each portion into an 8 x 6–inch rectangle. Divide chicken mixture evenly among rectangles; top each serving with 2 tablespoons cheese. Working with 1 rectangle at a time, fold dough in half over filling, pinching edges to seal. Repeat procedure with remaining rectangles. Transfer calzones to a baking sheet coated with cooking spray. Bake at 425° for 12 minutes or until golden. **Yield: 4 servings (serving size: 1 calzone).**

CALORIES 446; FAT 12.1g (sat 3.4g, mono 4g, poly 1.6g); PROTEIN 36.3g; CARB 49.5g; FIBER 2.1g; CHOL 73mg; IRON 2.9mg; SODIUM 778mg; CALC 116mg

kitchen how-to: assemble a calzone

Since the bake time for calzones is relatively short and only cooks the crust and melts the cheese inside, be sure to cook the filling ingredients before baking.

1. Place the dough on a lightly floured surface, and roll out.

2. Apply the spreadable fillings first, and then sprinkle the vegetables, meats, and cheese on half of the dough. Leave a ½-inch border around the edges. Fold the dough in half over the filling, and pinch the edges to seal. Transfer the calzones to a baking sheet coated with cooking spray.

Baking Substitution Guide

If you're right in the middle of cooking and realize you don't have
a particular ingredient, refer to the substitutions in this list.

Ingredient	Substitution
Baking Products	
Baking powder, 1 teaspoon	½ teaspoon cream of tartar and ¼ teaspoon baking soda
Chocolate	
Semisweet, 1 ounce	1 ounce unsweetened chocolate and 1 tablespoon sugar
Unsweetened, 1 ounce	3 tablespoons cocoa and 1 tablespoon butter or margarine
Cocoa, ¼ cup	1 ounce unsweetened chocolate (decrease fat in recipe by ½ tablespoon)
Coconut, fresh, grated, 1½ tablespoons	1 tablespoon flaked coconut
Cornstarch, 1 tablespoon	2 tablespoons all-purpose flour or granular tapioca
Flour	
All-purpose, 1 tablespoon	1½ teaspoons cornstarch, potato starch, or rice starch
Cake, 1 cup sifted	1 cup minus 2 tablespoons all-purpose flour
Self-rising, 1 cup	1 cup all-purpose flour, 1 teaspoon baking powder, and ½ teaspoon salt
Sugar, Powdered, 1 cup	1 cup sugar and 1 tablespoon cornstarch (processed in food processor)
Honey, ½ cup	½ cup molasses or maple syrup
Eggs	
1 large	2 large egg yolks for custards and cream fillings or large 2 egg yolks and 1 tablespoon water for cookies
1 large	¼ cup egg substitute
2 large	3 small eggs
1 egg white (2 tablespoons)	2 tablespoons egg substitute
1 egg yolk (1½ tablespoons)	2 tablespoons sifted dry egg yolk powder and 2 teaspoons water or 1½ tablespoons thawed frozen egg yolk
Fruits and Vegetables	
Lemon, 1 medium	2 to 3 tablespoons juice and 2 teaspoons grated rind
Juice, 1 teaspoon	½ teaspoon vinegar
Peel, dried	2 teaspoons freshly grated lemon rind
Orange, 1 medium	½ cup juice and 2 tablespoons grated rind
Tomatoes, fresh, chopped, 2 cups	1 (16-ounce) can (may need to drain)
Tomato juice, 1 cup	½ cup tomato sauce and ½ cup water
Tomato sauce, 2 cups	¾ cup tomato paste and 1 cup water

Ingredient	Substitution
Dairy Products	
Milk	
Buttermilk, low-fat or nonfat, 1 cup	1 tablespoon lemon juice or vinegar and 1 cup low-fat or fat-free milk (let stand 10 minutes)
Fat-free milk, 1 cup	4 to 5 tablespoons fat-free dry milk powder; enough cold water to make 1 cup
Sour cream, 1 cup	1 cup plain yogurt
Seasonings	
Allspice, ground, 1 teaspoon	½ teaspoon ground cinnamon and ½ teaspoon ground cloves
Apple pie spice, 1 teaspoon	½ teaspoon ground cinnamon, ¼ teaspoon ground nutmeg, and ⅛ teaspoon ground cardamom
Bay leaf, 1 whole	¼ teaspoon crushed bay leaf
Chives, chopped, 1 tablespoon	1 tablespoon chopped green onion tops
Garlic, 1 clove	1 teaspoon bottled minced garlic
Ginger	
Crystallized, 1 tablespoon	⅛ teaspoon ground ginger
Fresh, grated, 1 tablespoon	⅛ teaspoon ground ginger
Herbs, fresh, 1 tablespoon	1 teaspoon dried herbs or ¼ teaspoon ground herbs (except rosemary)
Lemongrass, 1 stalk, chopped	1 teaspoon grated lemon zest
Mint, fresh, chopped, 3 tablespoons	1 tablespoon dried spearmint or peppermint
Mustard, dried, 1 teaspoon	1 tablespoon prepared mustard
Parsley, fresh, chopped, 1 tablespoon	1 teaspoon dried parsley
Vanilla bean, 6-inch bean	1 tablespoon vanilla extract

Nutritional Analysis

How to Use It and Why

Glance at the end of any *Cooking Light* recipe, and you'll see how committed we are to helping you make the best of today's light cooking. With chefs, registered dietitians, home economists, and a computer system that analyzes every ingredient we use, *Cooking Light* gives you authoritative dietary detail like no other magazine. We go to such lengths so you can see how our recipes fit into your healthful eating plan. If you're trying to lose weight, the calorie and fat figures will probably help most. But if you're keeping a close eye on the sodium, cholesterol, and saturated fat in your diet, we provide those numbers, too. And because many women don't get enough iron or calcium, we can also help there, as well. Finally, there's a fiber analysis for those of us who don't get enough roughage.

Here's a helpful guide to put our nutritional analysis numbers into perspective. Remember, one size doesn't fit all, so take your lifestyle, age, and circumstances into consideration when determining your nutrition needs. For example, pregnant or breast-feeding women need more protein, calories, and calcium. And women older than 50 need 1,200mg of calcium daily, 200mg more than the amount recommended for younger women and men.

We Use These Abbreviations in Our Nutritional Analysis

sat	saturated fat	**CHOL**	cholesterol
mono	monounsaturated fat	**CALC**	calcium
poly	polyunsaturated fat	**g**	gram
CARB	carbohydrates	**mg**	milligram

Daily Nutrition Guide

	Women Ages 25 to 50	Women over 50	Men over 24	Men over 50
Calories	2,000	2,000 or less	2,700	2,500
Protein	50g	50g or less	63g	60g
Fat	65g or less	65g or less	88g or less	83g or less
Saturated Fat	20g or less	20g or less	27g or less	25g or less
Carbohydrates	304g	304g	410g	375g
Fiber	25g to 35g	25g to 35g	25g to 35g	25g to 35g
Cholesterol	300mg or less	300mg or less	300mg or less	300mg or less
Iron	18mg	8mg	8mg	8mg
Sodium	2,300mg or less	1,500mg or less	2,300mg or less	1,500mg or less
Calcium	1,000mg	1,200mg	1,000mg	1,000mg

The nutritional values used in our calculations come from either The Food Processor, Version 8.9 (ESHA Research), or are provided by food manufacturers.

Metric Equivalents

The information in the following charts is provided to help cooks outside the United States successfully use the recipes in this book. All equivalents are approximate.

Cooking/Oven Temperatures

	Fahrenheit	Celsius	Gas Mark
Freeze Water	32° F	0° C	
Room Temp.	68° F	20° C	
Boil Water	212° F	100° C	
Bake	325° F	160° C	3
	350° F	180° C	4
	375° F	190° C	5
	400° F	200° C	6
	425° F	220° C	7
	450° F	230° C	8
Broil			Grill

Liquid Ingredients by Volume

¼ tsp	=	1 ml						
½ tsp	=	2 ml						
1 tsp	=	5 ml						
3 tsp	=	1 tbl	=	½ fl oz	=	15 ml		
2 tbls	=	⅛ cup	=	1 fl oz	=	30 ml		
4 tbls	=	¼ cup	=	2 fl oz	=	60 ml		
5⅓ tbls	=	⅓ cup	=	3 fl oz	=	80 ml		
8 tbls	=	½ cup	=	4 fl oz	=	120 ml		
10⅔ tbls	=	⅔ cup	=	5 fl oz	=	160 ml		
12 tbls	=	¾ cup	=	6 fl oz	=	180 ml		
16 tbls	=	1 cup	=	8 fl oz	=	240 ml		
1 pt	=	2 cups	=	16 fl oz	=	480 ml		
1 qt	=	4 cups	=	32 fl oz	=	960 ml		
				33 fl oz	=	1000 ml	=	1 l

Dry Ingredients by Weight

(To convert ounces to grams, multiply the number of ounces by 30.)

1 oz	=	¹⁄₁₆ lb	=	30 g
4 oz	=	¼ lb	=	120 g
8 oz	=	½ lb	=	240 g
12 oz	=	¾ lb	=	360 g
16 oz	=	1 lb	=	480 g

Length

(To convert inches to centimeters, multiply the number of inches by 2.5.)

1 in	=			2.5 cm	
6 in	=	½ ft	=	15 cm	
12 in	=	1 ft	=	30 cm	
36 in	=	3 ft	= 1 yd =	90 cm	
40 in	=		=	100 cm	= 1 m

Equivalents for Different Types of Ingredients

Standard Cup	Fine Powder (ex. flour)	Grain (ex. rice)	Granular (ex. sugar)	Liquid Solids (ex. butter)	Liquid (ex. milk)
1	140 g	150 g	190 g	200 g	240 ml
¾	105 g	113 g	143 g	150 g	180 ml
⅔	93 g	100 g	125 g	133 g	160 ml
½	70 g	75 g	95 g	100 g	120 ml
⅓	47 g	50 g	63 g	67 g	80 ml
¼	35 g	38 g	48 g	50 g	60 ml
⅛	18 g	19 g	24 g	25 g	30 ml

subject index

recipe index

(continued)